Critical Social Studies

Editors: JOCK YOUNG and PAUL WALTON

The contemporary world projects a perplexing picture of political, social and economic upheaval. In these challenging times the conventional wisdoms of orthodox social thought whether it be sociology, economics or cultural studies become inadequate. This series focuses on this intellectual crisis, selecting authors whose work seeks to transcend the limitations of conventional discourse. Its tone is scholarly rather than polemical, in the belief that significant theoretical work is needed to clear the way for a genuine transformation of the existing social order.

Because of this, the series will relate closely to recent developments in social thought, particularly to critical theory – the emerging European tradition. In terms of specific topics, key pivotal areas of debate will be selected – for example, mass culture, inflation, problems of sexuality and the family, the nature of the capitalist state, natural science and ideology. The scope of analysis will be broad: the series will attempt to break the existing arbitrary divisions between the social studies disciplines. Its aim is to provide a platform for critical social thought (at a level quite accessible to students) to enter into the major theoretical controversies of the day.

Critical Social Studies

PUBLISHED

FORTHCOMING

IQ and Mental Testing

An Unnatural Science and its Social History

Brian Evans

and

Bernard Waites

First published 1981 by
THE MACMILLAN PRESS LTD
London and Basingstoke
Associated companies in Delhi Dublin
Hong Kong Johannesburg Lagos Melbourne
New York Singapore and Tokyo

Printed in Hong Kong

British Library Cataloguing in Publication Data

Evans, Brian
  IQ and mental testing. – (Critical
  social studies).
  1. Intelligence tests – Social aspects
  I. Title   II. Waites, Bernard
  III. Series
  153.9′3   BF431

  ISBN 0–333–25648–4
  ISBN 0–333–25649–2 Pbk

Contents

Preface

Interdisciplinary studies are very much in vogue at present in academic institutions, but it is not at all easy to put them into practice successfully. All too frequently the disciplines coming together simply collude in mutual congratulation. Ideally, disciplines should collide with a sense of shock. A special sort of shock can come to both the social historian and the psychologist who cares to dig back into the history of psychology. Social historians are apt to assume that their methods for analysing social phenomena, in terms of certain key areas of social relations, are inapplicable to the growth of knowledge in any discipline having the slightest claim to being a natural science. They have shown only half-hearted interest in the current debates as to how scientific knowledge is produced, tending to assume that there is an easy well-charted passage to a realm of objective knowledge which is no concern of theirs as social historians. An investigation into the history of psychology can quickly disabuse the social historian of this innocent belief.

Psychologists, if they show any interest in the past of their own discipline, are equally likely to display an innocent and disingenuous view. Most histories of psychology have been written by professional psychologists with a strong commitment to the body of belief accepted as achieved knowledge within their profession and also with a strong commitment to the corporate integrity of the profession which produced it. Such histories are not necessarily uncritical, but the critical point of view is very restricted. Past error appears merely as a series of hurdles successfully overcome on the road to current theory. In the particular branch of psychology with which we are dealing, some of the best-known practitioners betray an utterly cavalier attitude to their profession's past. They are prepared to ransack its voluminous literature for any data (or, perhaps more accurately, 'scholarly citations') which will support current theory without, at the very least, acknowledging the gross social prejudices that accompanied its making.

It is not easy to disturb psychologists wedded to an internal and terminal view of their subject, for this view insulates them against an historically critical view of their profession's past. But we hope that they, like we, can still be shocked by some of the more flagrant instances of social prejudice in the history of psychology, and can start wondering what exactly was the status of the psychological knowledge produced by the people who shared and cultivated these prejudices. Consider these quotations from a lecture by Sir Cyril Burt to a group of London social workers in January 1918 on the subject of 'Individual Psychology and Social Work':[1]

> The nature of the mental differences in different individuals, the frequency with which particular differences occur among certain classes, the signs by which they may be recognised, the causes which will produce or remove them – these problems, one and all, may legitimately form the theme of scientific enquiry. To the social worker they are plainly of the greatest interest: indeed it is very largely to the social worker that we must look for their future solution. Solved or unsolved, they constitute a new and growing branch of knowledge – the science of individual psychology . . .

Burt suggested that a key tool in diagnostic social case work would soon become the psychological profile or 'psychogram', but he saw it as having applications far beyond this narrow field:

> Eventually a complete 'psychogram' of every school child might be compiled. Each, as it left school, would be the subject of a special *dossier*, passed on, like the school leaving form, to some juvenile advisory committee. In such a *dossier* innate abilities, both general and specific,

would be noted according to some comparable quantitative scheme.... Everybody might be thus indexed according to their mental powers... mental and moral resources are a far greater asset to a nation than agricultural [or] mineral [and] if we are to make a rapid recovery from our present sacrifice of wealth and men, not only man power but mind power must be registered and organised. Such a census of our psychological resources might easily be undertaken through the schools.

Burt then suggested that such a numbering of abilities would be a basic step towards replacing the traditional system of apprenticeship and labour recruitment, whose deficiencies had been exposed by the needs of the war-time economy:

A method of placing young workers which ignores each individual's aptitudes and disabilities must inevitably issue in vast preventable waste.... The key, then, to social efficiency is vocational fitness – a place for every man, and every man in his place. The place must be suited to the man by a careful study both of the qualifications required by the one and of the qualifications possessed by the other.

At a later point, Burt enlightened his audience as to how social work might be informed by 'abnormal' individual psychology:

In different ranks of society mental conflicts appear to differ somewhat in their origin. Among the so-called lower orders they seem due chiefly to external and material causes; among the so-called higher orders they are more often due to internal and social causes.... The view, common among those of superior intellect, that the poor are by nature a little mad, comes considerably closer to the truth than does the still commoner view that they are more than a little wicked. Indeed, the psychology of madness often helps us to understand their insufficiencies, just as it helps us to understand the inefficiencies of ourselves.

We have come to such programmatic statements – and the more technical papers which gave them scientific credence – from very different directions. One of us (Bernard Waites) began with an interest in the rearticulation of perceptions of social class during that great divide in human society, the First World War. Increasingly, he came to feel that British psychometrics has mediated not simply a view of class, but a view of society, throughout its history, and that this was worth examining in its own right. He also found that this could not be undertaken simply by using statements in which the small world of psychometrics outlined its relationship with the wider world, as Burt did in his lecture. Some attempt had to be made to go beyond a disciplinary competence and grapple with the history of the science. The other (Brian Evans) began with a disciplinary competence in mathematical psychology and an interest in the scientific validity of IQ psychology, but felt that no treatment of this issue would be complete without an historical analysis of how this psychology has functioned as an ideology and as an instrument of social administration and selection.

For help in preparing this book we should like to thank Jo Borill, David Edwards, Donald Gillies, Lesley Goodman, John Leavold, Les Levidov, Peggy Mackay, Bernard Norton, Bill Ristow, Steven Rose, Tim Shallice and the Archivists of the Public Record Office (Kew) and of the Scottish Record Office.

1

Introduction

Measurement, precise objective measurement, has long been an aim of intellectual pursuits aspiring to scientific status. This book is concerned with one of the most controversial types of measurement carried on in technologically advanced societies – mental measurement or psychometrics. We have focused our attention primarily, although not exclusively, on that sphere of mental measurement where psychometricians have been at greatest pains to establish their scientific status, and where this status has been most fiercely contested – the measurement of intelligence.

Psychometrics purports to be the science of individual mental differences. Its foundations were first laid by the Englishman, Francis Galton (1822–1911), but were much more thoroughly developed by the German, William Stern (1871–1938). Stern adopted the title differential psychology for the new discipline, and saw it as an extension of the laboratory-based experimental psychology pioneered by Wundt, Ebbinghaus and others in Germany since 1879. But whereas experimental psychology was concerned with universal lower mental processes, the domain of the new discipline was to be individual differences in higher intellective processes.[1]

Stern was responsible for introducing the concept of an intelligence quotient, or IQ, which was originally reckoned by dividing an individual's 'mental age', as assessed by a standardised mental test, by his or her actual age, and multiplying by 100.[2] The procedure becomes inapplicable after the age of about 16, and alternative numerical procedures were devised for scaling up the 'raw score' (the number of correct answers) so that the average adjusted score for any age group is approximately 100. It would be more accurate nowadays to refer to the adjusted score as an intelligence index, but the original term IQ has remained in our vocabulary as the scientific measure of intelligence of young and old alike.

When Stern published his treatise on differential psychology, parallel movements towards the systematic study of individual differences were already under way in Britain, where Charles Spearman (1863–1945) was elaborating a theory of intelligence as a general factor which enters all cognitive processes, and in France, where Alfred Binet's mental tests were the first standardised measures of intelligence to be used in education; Binet (1857–1911) himself, however, did not subscribe to the conception of intelligence as a unitary mental function.

From its origins just before the First World War, psychometrics quickly came to monopolise the field of differential psychology, and now constitutes the most important way in which psychological science is applied to society. Wherever psychologists are employed outside academia, psychological tests are part of their stock in trade. The tests are administered in schools by educational psychologists, for occupational guidance and personnel selection by occupational psychologists, and to the psychologically disturbed by clinical psychologists. Testing has enabled psychology to establish for itself an important place in the twentieth-century managerial professions.

Much of the controversy surrounding IQ testing has resulted from the great significance which has been attached, both inside and outside the mental testing movement, to the role of heredity in accounting for IQ differences. Hereditary influences have been investigated using quite a variety of psychometric tests, but the amount of research into the heritability of IQ exceeds by far the sum total of heritability research using other types of test. Although various shades of opinion can be discerned among psychometricians, the history of the subject has been dominated by a number of individuals who have argued forcefully for their view that heredity, as opposed to the environment, is of overwhelming potency in producing IQ differences. These individuals have also argued that IQ has great social significance on the grounds that it is the principal determinant of educational and occupational success. This emphasis on heredity as a source of social inequality contrasts sharply with the emphasis which many political thinkers have placed on differences in the circumstances into which children are born and in which they grow up. The issue is in fact considerably older than the mental testing movement. For example, John Stuart Mill wrote in his autobiography, published shortly after his death in 1873:

> In particular, I have long felt that the prevailing tendency to regard all the marked distinctions of human character as innate, and in the main indelible, and to ignore the irresistible proofs that by far the greater part of those differences, whether between individuals, races, or sexes, are such as not only might but naturally would be produced by differences in circumstances, is one of the chief hindrances to the rational treatment of great social questions, and one of the chief stumbling blocks to human improvement.[3]

In this century the mental testing movement has played the principal role in keeping alive the views against which Mill was protesting. The mental testers have placed great emphasis on their finding that the average IQs of the different socio-economic strata correspond closely to the ranking of the strata in the social hierarchy. Although individual IQ differences in the occupational groups vary almost as much as the IQ differences of the population at large, there is still a significant correlation between an individual's IQ and the income or social prestige of his or her occupation. (The statistical techniques of correlation are referred to repeatedly throughout this book. For a brief non-technical explanation, see the Appendix.) In the hereditarian view this results from the gravitation of the innately more able to the better-paid and more prestigious occupations. These people, it is assumed, marry amongst their social and intellective peers, and their children benefit from a superior innate endowment. Since, in this argument, IQ is a precondition of socio-economic success, differences in IQ are held to be an important cause of upward and downward social mobility. Moreover, it has been predicted that, as society equalises its opportunities for social advancement, and mobility corresponds more and more closely to innate endowment, then an hereditary meritocracy will gradually come into being.[4] The thesis, then, is that there are genetic or 'natural' causes of present inequality, and as unnatural causes of inequality are removed, then natural inequality will make itself more and more manifest.

Hereditarian interpretations have also been provided for other population group differences, especially in the USA, where it has been a consistent finding that blacks and some other ethnic minorities have average IQs significantly below the white average (although again the IQ variation within these minorities is almost as great as for the total population). This particular hereditarian view, nowadays at least, commands much less support within the mental testing movement than the hereditarian interpretation of individual and social class differences for the white population. But the huge amount of publicity which has been given to the hereditarian views of A. R. Jensen, ever since he resurrected the subject in 1969,[5] has ensured that this is still a major issue today.

THE ORIGINS OF HEREDITARIAN SCIENCE

The hereditarian IQ tradition is rooted in a much wider intellectual tradition which uses 'natural law' as a rationalisation of social competition, dominance and hierarchy. This tradition pre-dates the Darwinian revolution in biology, but when the full impact of evolutionary theory was felt, and some progress made in understanding the mechanisms of heredity, then the tradition was expanded to encompass biological explanations of nearly all aspects of human behaviour. In 1913, Ronald Fisher (1890–1962) wrote:

From the moment we grasp, firmly and completely, Darwin's theory of evolution, we begin to realise that we have obtained not merely a description of the past, or an explanation of the present, but a veritable key to the future; and this consideration becomes the more forcibly impressed upon us the more thoroughly we apply the doctrine; the more clearly we see that not only the organisation and structure of the body, and the cruder physical impulses, but that the whole constitution of our ethical and aesthetic nature, all the refinements of beauty, all the delicacy of our sense of beauty, our moral instincts of obedience and compassion, pity or indignation, our moments of religious awe, or mystical penetration – all have their biological significance, all – from the biological point of view – exist in virtue of their biological significance . . . .[6]

One might expect this tradition to have inspired a deep pessimism as to the possibility of human improvement through collective will and rationality, and a scepticism as to whether there can be any meaningful systems of human value; for if human behaviour is ultimately determined by natural law, then it can be no more good or bad than the behaviour of inanimate objects acting in obedience to physical law. But for Fisher value was actually inscribed into the evolutionary process, 'Darwinism is not content to reveal the possible, perhaps the necessary destiny of our race; in this case the method is as clear as the ideal; the best are to become better by survival.'[7]

This tradition has blossomed in the last fifty years. By the use of analogies drawn from studies of the social behaviour of animals together with speculative reconstructions of human evolutionary history, sociobiologists, as they nowadays call themselves, have put forward biological explanations for many aspects of human behaviour and cultural institutions which are normally thought of as constituting subject matter for the historian, the anthropologist, and the sociologist. These explanations have encompassed such diverse phenomena as crime and delinquency, wars, the incest taboo, kinship systems, the division of roles in the nuclear family, homosexuality, and even altruism. Sociobiology, like psychometrics, remains the subject of acrimonious debate, but it would be beyond the scope of this book to discuss it here.[8] We shall simply note that there is a close affinity between sociobiology and the preoccupations of the mental testing movement. Consider, for example, a paper by the eminent biologist C. D. Darlington which appeared in the *British Journal of Psychology* in 1963. Darlington states that 'A social class is already imprinted on a newborn child: it is imprinted by heredity and it is therefore a genetic class.'[9] His direct evidence for this claim is some psychometric evidence, now hotly disputed, that there is a disparity between the achieved socio-economic status of adopted children and that of their adoptive parents (which is usually higher than that of their biological parents).[10] His metahistorical explanation of 'genetic social class' might surprise historians. It runs thus: at the early stage of civilisation tribes with different genetic endowments came to cooperate but did not interbreed; conjointly, the tribes evolved into civilised societies composed of:

> classes or castes descended from the tribes and which retained their character because they continued to breed within the class or caste almost as strictly as they had within the tribe .... It happens just the same today .... Cooperation without cohabitation is thus the inevitable process by which all stratified societies, that is to say all advanced societies, have come into being. By it the separate tribes, freely spread like an extended pavement, are now piled up into the towering masses of our social classes .... The differences in intelligence and temperament which adapt each class to its different functions in society have been preserved by constant selection, and above all by selective mobility, up and down in society. The overriding principle which no society can evade, is that the character of each class is maintained by the ability of its members, genetic and psychological, bodily and mental, to make its living by its own kind of work .... If most human beings appear to fit their environments, it is not on account of any active effort.

Most people are living in environments that have been created by or for their own kind of people with their own kind of heredity: people of their own class.[11]

THE RECENT IQ CONTROVERSY

The recent IQ controversy was sparked off by an article which appeared, accompanied by a considerable fanfare of publicity, in the 1969 *Harvard Educational Review*, entitled, 'How much can we boost IQ and scholastic achievement?'[12] In this article the American psychometrician A. R. Jensen argued that the Headstart programmes of compensatory education for (mainly black) ghetto children had failed; and he proceeded to restate the main themes of the hereditarian IQ tradition: IQ tests measure general intelligence, a fundamentally important characteristic in determining educational achievement and subsequent occupational success. IQ is largely genetically fixed so that attempts to boost it are a waste of time and money. Differences in average IQs between social classes and between blacks and whites are also largely genetically determined, so that we cannot reasonably expect to eliminate differences by social and educational reforms.

Jensen concluded that compensatory education schemes should abandon attempts to stimulate sophisticated intellectual processes, and should concentrate instead on drilling the children in basic educational skills using conventional rote learning methods of instruction. He also touched briefly on the subject of dysgenic trends: the decline in the average levels of intelligence which hereditarians believe takes place in populations where low IQ parents have more children than high IQ parents. Jensen suggested that this was in fact happening, especially in the American black population; and the subject was taken up by William Shockley, a Nobel prizewinning physicist who went on to suggest that welfare payments should be made to be contingent upon low IQ parents having eugenical sterilisations.[13]

Although there was nothing very original in what Jensen

wrote, the paper enabled him to achieve instant fame, or notoriety, and he is now the undisputed intellectual leader of an expanding group of 'new wave' hereditarians. The reason for this lies partly in his skill as a self-publicist, aided by popularisations of the hereditarian position which appeared soon afterwards by Richard Herrnstein in the USA,[14] and H. J. Eysenck in Britain,[15] but more especially in the fact that he had raised the subject of genetic black–white differences at a politically sensitive time, when the civil rights movement was attracting much support from academics. Jensen's unfashionable view provoked an extraordinary quantity of critical responses. Some of these responses came from within the ranks of the mental testing movement, from psychometricians who were broadly sympathetic to Jensen's views about the social significance of IQ and the substantial role of heredity, but who argued that the environmental contribution is also substantial, quite sufficient to justify compensatory education programmes and a cultural interpretation of black–white differences.[16] Much further criticism came from outside the mental testing movement, from the representatives of a variety of disciplines in the biological and social sciences. These criticisms went much further than those of Jensen's fellow psychometricians, and came to cover all the basic tenets of the mental testing movement.[17] It was argued that psychometrics has no sound theoretical foundations, that the research which appears to demonstrate the influence of heredity is methodologically flawed and fully compatible with environmental interpretations, and that hereditarians had completely misunderstood some basic principles of human genetics. By the mid–1970s the 'Jensen controversy' had become the 'IQ controversy'.

The most influential critique has been provided by Leon Kamin in his 1974 book, *The Science and Politics of IQ*[18]. In the first part of this book Kamin quotes extensively from the writings of the pioneers of IQ testing in the USA, showing that they held extreme hereditarian views, some of them quite viciously racist, long before any serious research had been carried out into the heritability of IQ. He also shows that these pioneers argued strongly in support of laws which were enacted in a number of states permitting the eugenical sterilisation of the feeble-minded and also for the establishment of immigration quotas favouring the allegedly superior 'nordic races' of Northern Europe. The bulk of the book consists of a re-examination of the original research literature into the heritability of individual IQ differences, long regarded as the strongest point in the hereditarian argument. Kamin shows that there are innumerable methodological flaws in the research and, following extensive statistical re-analysis, he comes to the remarkable conclusion that, 'there exist no data which should lead a prudent man to accept the hypothesis that IQ test scores are in any degree heritable.' He also points out that successive generations of review writers and popularisers of the topic have been highly selective in choosing from among an essentially ambiguous body of research, and grossly biased in their hereditarian interpretations, to a degree which is scientifically indefensible. Thus, he argues, the politics of IQ has held sway over the science of IQ.

The most spectacular feature of Kamin's analysis concerns the heritability studies of Sir Cyril Burt, who was the doyen of British psychometrics until his death in 1972, and whose research findings played a key role in the arguments of Jensen, Eysenck, and other hereditarians. Kamin shows that Burt's reports of his research were seriously defective and that his results contain a number of impossible coincidences. Although Kamin did not make the allegation at the time, his findings strongly suggested that Burt's work was fraudulent, and this allegation was finally made in 1976 by the scientific journalist Oliver Gillie, who provided evidence indicating that the research assistants with whom Burt claimed to have conducted his research probably never existed at all, and certainly had nothing to do with the research which he purported to have carried out.[19] The allegations of fraud were challenged vigorously at first by hereditarians, but they were eventually proved conclusively to be correct following a re-analysis of an important Burt paper by D. D. Dorfman, and following an examination of Burt's personal diary by his official biographer Leslie Hearnshaw.[20]

The Burt scandal, together with the broader critical onslaught against the mental testing movement, has now placed its exponents very much on the defensive. Although they may initially have felt grateful to Jensen for re-invigorating the subject, psychometricians and the companies who produce the tests may now have good cause to regret his appearance on the scene and the ensuing spotlight which has been turned onto the movement. One consequence has been that lawsuits, based on American civil rights legislation have been brought by groups seeking to ban various educational uses of the tests on the grounds that they discriminate against blacks and other minority groups. A crucial test case has recently been decided in California, where IQ tests have long been used to decide which children to place in classes for the 'educable mentally retarded'. Expert testimony for the plaintiffs was provided by Kamin and other critics, while the defence drew on a number of leading representatives of the American psychometrics establishment. Judge Peckham's ruling in October 1979 can only be described as an unmitigated disaster for the testing movement. Finding for the plaintiffs against the Californian educational authorities, the judge states in his summary that:

> defendants have utilised standardised intelligence tests that are racially and culturally biased, have a discriminatory impact against black children, and have not been validated for the purpose of essentially permanent placements of black children into educationally dead-end, isolated, and stigmatising classes for the so-called educable mentally retarded.[21]

In the detailed ruling, the judge begins:

> We must recognise at the outset that the history of the IQ test, and of special education classes built on IQ testing, is not the history of neutral scientific discoveries translated into educational reform. It is, at least in the early years, a history of racial prejudice, of Social Darwinism, and of the use of a scientific 'mystique' to legitimate such prejudices.[22]

After discussing 'the impossibility of measuring intelligence' he points out that no attempt has been made to eliminate cultural bias from the tests, but that 'Rather, the experts have from the beginning been willing to tolerate or even encourage tests that portray minorities, especially blacks, as intellectually inferior'.[23] As regards the genetic argument, he states:

> First, it is not at all clear whether 'intelligence,' whatever that may be, is inherited rather than a product of the environment, or at least whether the environment can substantially overcome any inherited weaknesses. Second, even if intelligence is inherited, it is not to be assumed that black persons are less intelligent as a group than white persons as a group. That conclusion depends upon one's view of the objectiveness of the IQ tests, and, as noted before, at the very least the testing personnel do not claim to have examined systematically whether the tests are as valid for black children as for white children in measuring the capacity to learn.[24]

SCIENCE AND IDEOLOGY

Philosophers are fond of admonishing us to separate facts from values. You cannot, they tell us, derive an 'ought' from an 'is', or an 'is' from an 'ought'. Hereditarians nowadays also like to make this distinction. They tell us, quite correctly, that the mental testing movement, whatever the ideological commitments of its paractitioners may be, has produced a considerable quantity of empirical research; and they assert that this should be the main object of interest. Thus, in a recent article, Jensen states:

> But the IQ controversy, for better or worse, has also come to mean a kind of controversy beyond the realm of normal science. Much of the controversy is not intrinsic to the scientific issues, but is ideological, stemming from differing philosophic ideals, opinions, or sentiments as to which form of social, political, and economic order is

most desirable. In this respect, the present IQ controversy has much in common with other great controversies in the history of science, controversies inflamed by philosophic or religious issues not intrinsic to the scientific questions involved, such as surrounded Galileo's claim of Jupiter's moons, Copernicus's heliocentric theory, and Darwin's theory of evolution. In each case, the extrinsic debate falls away in due time and the intrinsic scientific controversies proceed as normal science, making for advances in our knowledge and its practical uses.[25]

Let us ignore the immodest comparisons between hereditarian science and the work of Galileo, Copernicus, and Darwin, and concentrate on the major thesis of Jensen's paper, that IQ psychology can be appraised according to the accepted standards of scientific rationality, and found to be not wanting. Although there are many critics who would dispute this thesis, it has at least managed to find one supporter among philosophers of science. In a 1974 paper, P. Urbach analyses the IQ controversy using the methodology of Imre Lakatos (which is described in the next section) as a conflict between hereditarian and environmentalist 'research programmes', 'falsely associated in the public mind [with] political positions'.[26] He argues that the hereditarian research programme has been 'progressive' in the sense that it has made many empirical predictions which have turned out to be correct, and even dealt with anomalies in a progressive manner, altering or extending the original theory in such a manner that further predictions could be made. However, an inspection of Urbach's paper reveals something which must by now make the paper quite excruciatingly embarrassing for its author to contemplate. By far the greater part of the evidence cited where hereditarian predictions have been successful turns out to be the fraudulent results of Burt, his fictitious collaborators Conway and Howard, and secondary material from other psychometricians which in fact re-analyses Burt's 'data'. Anyone with a taste for irony will derive some amusement from one of Urbach's footnotes in which he mentions Lakatos's conjecture that 'protagonists of degenerating research programmes tend to succomb to moral degeneration'. It was of course unfortunate for Urbach that his paper should have appeared just as the Burt scandal was about to break, but two further comments are still worth making. Firstly, as we shall show in Chapter 5, Burt's original reports were of such an appallingly low standard, treated simply as scientific reports, that it is difficult to see how anyone, who does not have a heavy prior investment in the matter, should ever have taken them seriously. Secondly, besides Burt's data, there is a good deal of alternative research literature which *is* properly reported; but if hereditarian science really is in the healthy state which Urbach claims it is, why should he, when seeking out examples of successful predictions, have homed in so unerringly on the work of Sir Cyril Burt?

The distinction between facts and values is clearly not evident in Burt's work, nor in the secondary review literature in which, as Kamin shows (see Chapter 5), the original research is selectively and dishonestly presented by hereditarian reviewers. In this field of enquiry, the non-specialists, and indeed most specialists (scientists are usually happy to rely on review articles, especially where the original research dates back over many years), are likely to encounter many facts which are heavily value-laden.

There are other reasons for thinking that it is hereditarians rather than their critics who are unable to make a clear distinction between facts and values. Just as the facts have sometimes been derived from prior values, so have values subsequently been derived from these already value-laden facts. Hereditarians have always been keen to pontificate about social policy. We have already noted that Fisher attempted quite generally to derive value and purpose from the facts of evolutionary theory. The mental testers have also frequently made such logical errors in the field of education. Writing in 1970 in the right wing Black Papers on education, Burt and his former student H. J. Eysenck were maintaining a long tradition in arguing that we ought to adopt elitist educational policies because of the facts of inheritance.[27] They overlook the point that one can argue for or against the virtues of elitist educational policies whether or not there is any genetic contribution to individual intellectual differences.

Critics of IQ psychology, such as Noam Chomsky,[28] have taken the question further by asking what *human and social interests* are served by investigating issues such as the hereditary component in black–white IQ differences. Even if the matter could be settled in favour of the hereditarian position (which Chomsky does not concede), why should this have any bearing on what we consider to be socially just and proper? Hereditarians reply in their own defence that there can be no arbitrary boundaries to the growth of scientific knowledge and that psychometrics is merely concerned with scientific truth and not with its social and political application. This defence might carry more weight with sceptics if psychometricians behaved as scientists detached from the prejudices of their time, but they clearly have not.

The defence appears even less weighty if we bear in mind that psychometrics has never been 'pure' but always 'applied' knowledge. It is, in fact, a form of technology, and it has all the characteristics of what the German social philosopher, Jürgen Habermas,[29] and others have called 'technocratic rationality'. Such rationality always entails, though rarely acknowledges, social and political direction and domination, for it limits the choices which can be made amongst political, social or educational policies, and prescribes the 'correct' strategies to be adopted. It uses its own constructs, 'facts', as limits to political and social action. In the welter of attention it gives to technical detail it removes the total framework of interests in which strategies are chosen or technologies applied from the realm of public discussion. It excludes discussion of long term goals by presenting economic (or educational) development as a series of technical problems. 'Monetarism' in economics, for example, takes the capitalist market economy for granted. The influence of psychometrics on education in Britain, it can be argued, was to produce a consensus view of educability which favoured a selective educational system, and removed from discussion the possibility of comprehensive or multilateral alternatives.

Technocratic rationality also involves a posture of 'doublethink' towards those who oppose it on the basis of alternative political ethics or ideology; although the political and social strategies favoured by technocratic rationality are themselves influenced by prevailing values, it presents them as value-free. Indeed, it tends to suppress ethical considerations in political and social life.

This perhaps explains why psychometricians have remained unmoved by recent documentation of the many unsavoury features of the history of the mental testing movement. There is a tendency to assume that the history of the subject becomes of interest only if it can first be shown that the scientific findings are false. But this is an unreasonable position. Even if the hereditarian IQ position, as outlined for instance by Jensen, is substantially correct, there are still a number of historical questions worth asking. Why did the measurement of individual differences and the assessment of hereditary influences commence when they did? To what extent did they follow on previous scientific developments and to what extent upon changes taking place in society? What is the relationship between social change and scientific developments? Once individual differences were successfully measured and the potency of heredity was established, how was this knowledge incorporated into the fabric of society? In what ways, if at all did society change, and what was the response of various groups in society to the new scientific knowledge and the associated social change? These are surely not trivial questions.

On the other hand, if the hereditarian IQ position is false, all of the above questions can still be asked, although we would now be considering the social circumstances of false scientific knowledge, how it won widespread acceptance, and perhaps also how it came to be rejected finally. A further interesting question concerns the manner in which the false knowledge becomes established among the practitioners themselves. Is it simply the result of intellectual blunders, or can a consideration of socio-political issues provide a stronger interpretation? Without prejudging the results of our appraisal of the scientific issues, we can at least point out that there is one indisputable blemish on the scientific record of psychometrics for which a social historical analysis proves useful. In Chapter 3 we provide what we believe to be a convincing answer to the hitherto unanswered question: why did Burt began to publish his fraudulent results on the heritability of IQ at the time that he did?

Although it is often difficult to separate facts from values when considering the mental testing movement, we believe that the approach is a productive one. Kamin, for example, carefully separates his discussions of the politics and science of IQ, while at the same time intending the former to shed light on the latter. J. M. Blum adopts the same approach in his own broader treatment of the issues (although, like Kamin, he is concerned primarily with the American context).[30] He argues that the subject is a pseudoscience, comparable with the Lysenko period in Soviet genetics when, for political reasons, a collection of crackpot genetic theories were officially sanctioned while the scientifically sound Mendelian genetics was suppressed. The comparison is an amusing one because hereditarians have often compared themselves with the Soviet Mendelians battling against prejudice, not to mention Galileo, Copernicus and Darwin; and their critics with the Lysenkoists. The problem that inevitably arises is, how does one go about appraising the scientific credentials of a discipline which its practitioners believe to be a science? The obvious place to look is among the characterisations of scientific method which have been extensively developed in recent years by philosophers of science.

THE NATURE OF SCIENTIFIC METHOD

Generally, historians and philosophers of science are concerned with the 'internal' production of autonomous scientific knowledge rather than the 'external' relations of scientific activity with political and social belief. The foun-

dations for modern theories of the logic of the growth of
scientific knowledge were laid by Sir Karl Popper in his
Logik der Forschung (1934) published in English as *The Logic
of Scientific Discovery* (1959).[31] Popper had for some time
been seeking a criterion of demarcation between scientific
and non-scientific theories or statements. It had long been
apparent that the Baconian conception of science as general
laws inductively arrived at from observation and verified by
repeated experiments was logically untenable. Instances
cannot prove a theory, they can only refute it. The logical
conclusion that the refutation of the deductive consequences of a theory invalidate the theory itself was turned by
Popper into his famous falsifiability criterion. For a theory
to be scientific, he argued, the scientist must specify in
advance a critical test of the theory which, if failed, would
lead him to abandon it. A classic instance of such a test was
the eclipse predictions made by Einstein in 1917 and
confirmed by the British expedition of 1919. Popper
allowed that falsifiability *tout court* is not operational as a
universal criterion. It demands, first of all, agreement as to
the nature of a critical test and agreement on how to
interpret an empirical result (which might have a different
theoretical meaning for conflicting theories). Moreover,
theories can be legitimately 'immunised' by subordinate
hypotheses, as, for example, when Newtonian theory,
seemingly refuted by the irregular orbit of Uranus, was
'immunised' by the hypothesis of an undiscovered planet.
The subsequent discovery of that planet, Neptune, was a
spectacular triumph for the Newtonian theory. Popper
suggested that, as a methodological rule of thumb, the
acceptance or rejection of an auxiliary hypothesis should
depend on whether the hypothesis adds to the explanatory
content of the original theory. His conception of the growth
of scientific knowledge is that of a Darwinian struggle for
survival involving hypotheses and factual refutation, with
theories constantly being overthrown by others with greater
content and therefore greater testability.

Popper's criterion has generally been incorporated into
notions of scientific method, but his conception of the
growth of knowledge has been an indifferent guide to the

actual history of science. It is based overwhelmingly on the small number of predictive achievements with which one theory has dramatically struck down another. These apart, scientists have often not behaved in the way which this conception would lead us to expect. They have clung stubbornly to theories in the face of conflicting evidence, and sometimes their tenacity has been vindicated. Thomas Kuhn[32] has argued that historically, scientific activity has fallen into a pattern of 'normal' and 'revolutionary' phases. 'Normal science', he suggests, consists of 'puzzle-solving' within a scientific 'paradigm'. No scientific theory can be sufficiently well articulated to specify all of its logical consequences or 'tests', and all theories generate anomalies or 'puzzles' to be investigated. Paradigms in the natural sciences provide a basis for the investigation of these puzzles. They are defined as universally recognised scientific achievements that for a time provide model problems and solutions to a community of practitioners.[33] They set the parameters of theory testing, lay down its procedures, and determine the relevant problems. 'Normal science' is not the critical activity which Popper took it to be since the paradigm is a dogma, a network of hypotheses *shared* by a community of scientists which determines for them what is proper scientific activity in that field.

In Kuhn's view, scientists only act as critical philosophers during 'revolutionary' phases when they are forced to choose between competing paradigms. When a 'paradigm shift' occurs it takes the form of a change in the consensus within the scientific community as to the proper problems of the field, its methodology and so on. The fact that the choice between paradigms is apparently made in 'extra-scientific' terms (for the new paradigm is incompatible with, and therefore 'falsified' by its predecessor) has led many to suppose that Kuhn is advancing a relativist view of scientific activity as ultimately socially determined.

Kuhn has taken pains to eschew this position.[34] He concedes that, during the pre-paradigmatic or immature stages in the development of a new field, social needs and social values are a major determinant of the problems on which its practitioners concentrate. During this period, concepts are extensively conditioned by common sense, by a prevailing philosophical tradition, or by the most prestigious contemporary sciences. But once a field has entered its paradigmatic or mature stage, its practitioners become a special subculture effectively insulated from their wider social and cultural milieu. They share a body of theory and a common training in instrumental, mathematical and verbal techniques, and constitute an exclusive audience for, and judges of, each other's work. Their scientific problems are no longer presented by external society, but by an internal challenge to increase the scope and precision of the fit between existing theory and nature. Although external factors may influence the timing of paradigm shifts, the decisive consideration is the accumulation, within the scientific community, of anomalous empirical findings.

Kuhn presents us with a 'group psychology' of research rather than a 'logic of discovery'; his concerns are historical rather than demarcational. Imre Lakatos attempted to re-unite a normative conception of scientific rationality with a historiographical methodology for reconstructing the 'internal' history of science.[35] His argument is that the descriptive unit of scientific achievements is not an isolated hypothesis but a 'research programme' consisting of a 'hard core' together with a protective belt of subsidiary hypotheses. Scientific progress is achieved by a sophisticated falsificationism in which a succession of theories, and not one given theory, is appraised. Rival research programmes are akin to Kuhn's competing paradigms, and the choice between them is eventually one between a 'degenerating' and a 'progressive' programme. A progressive programme has a positive heuristic with which not only novel facts but also novel theories are anticipated. A degenerating programme makes theoretical changes to accomodate new facts as they become known, but it lives a hand-to-mouth existence, carrying out degenerating 'problem shifts' which serve only to insulate it against refutation. The heuristic power of progressive programmes in the mature sciences ensures the relative autonomy of scientific theory from its social and cultural milieu. Lakatos proposes this typology as a historiographical method for reconstructing the growth of scientific knowledge. Taking it as a guide, the historian will look for rival research programmes in the history of a field; and will exclude the external and 'irrational' in explaining the growth of knowledge, although these considerations would be vital in telling us why certain branches of science flourished or withered in particular socio-cultural *milieux*.

THE APPROACHES ADOPTED IN THIS BOOK

We do not consider that it is possible to draw from the philosophy of science adequate demarcation criteria to evaluate psychometrics as science or pseudoscience. Although the methods discussed above have been used by philosophers of science to have some fun at the expense of Marxist historiographers, psychoanalysts, and astrologers, the methods have their shortcomings. As Paul Feyerabend[36] has shown at length, all characterisations of scientific method are either too rigid, in that they would exclude some undisputed scientific achievements, notably the Copernican revolution, or too loose, in that they would permit the inclusion of many activities which no one would characterise as science. It does not follow, however, that the above methods are worthless. In examining the mental testing movement we shall look for the development, testing, extension, or overthrow, of hypotheses and theories; for theories which have 'stuck their neck out'; for 'normal science puzzle-solving'; and for 'progressive and degenerating research programmes'. We shall argue that, judged according to any or all of these criteria, there has not been *any* significant growth of scientific knowledge. Our thesis is that the movement is in essentially the same state today as it was soon after it was first established, and that it is probably best characterised in Kuhn's terms as a pre-paradigmatic science, or more simply as a scientific blind alley.

We shall argue that there has been no breakthrough to autonomous knowledge, but that psychometric concepts remain conditioned by common sense, by a very one-sided dependence on the mature science of human genetics, and, most important of all, by external factors which lie within the field of the social historian rather than the historian of science. These external factors have governed not only the emergence of the subject, but also the very form which its theories have taken. Insofar as a scientific methodology can be extracted from the research activities of psychometricians, it is the discredited inductivist methodology, rather than the hypothetico-deductive approach which has now won acceptance from nearly all scientists and philosophers of science.

In the next two chapters we shall examine the history of the mental testing movement in Britain. This begins with a group of interrelated social issues and intellectual ideas which were dominant at the turn of the century, and gave rise to the movement; proceeds to an account of the rise of applied psychology, when the mental testers applied their science to industry and education; and concludes with an examination of the influence of the movement on the reshaping of educational policy during and after the Second World War. Our historical investigations include a detailed analysis of two major features of the scientific history of psychometrics, the development of Spearman's theory of the 'general factor of intelligence', and the issue of 'declining national intelligence'.

In Chapters 4 and 5 we provide an analysis of the scientific issues, taking account of their relationship to contemporary theories in a number of relevant scientific disciplines, rather than solely in terms of the methods of psychometrics. The distinction is an important one because most existing accounts can be divided into those which take place within the overall framework which has become established in the psychometric tradition and those concerned with the underlying assumptions which make up this framework. The former are assessments of the extent to which satisfactory answers have been given to the questions which psychometricians have themselves asked, while the latter are assessments of whether the psychometricians have been asking the right questions in the first place.

For the most part, treatments of the subject which accept the overall framework of psychometrics have been provided by psychometricians themselves or by those broadly sympathetic to the approach. (The most notable exception is Kamin's treatment of the heritability literature in which he, so to speak, takes on hereditarians at their own game). Among recent books of this kind there are some which maintain a long tradition of presenting a grotesquely one-sided account and ignoring all serious criticism. One example is H. J. Eysenck's 1979 book, written in conjunction with D. W. Fulker, *The Structure and Measurement of Intelligence*. There are also some relatively fairminded treatments,[37] but none can be described as satisfactory because, in examining psychometric science, it is essential to examine the underlying assumptions. Using as an example one underlying assumption which is commonly made, the philosopher J. P. White makes the point as follows:

> Like the religious and political propositions I have mentioned, the proposition that we all have innately determined upper intellectual limits has become the hub of a new ideological system. Around it, too, have accreted all kinds of other propositions, both descriptive, for instance about the constancy of IQ, normal distributions and so on, and prescriptive, for example about the different kinds of educational provision which ought to be made for children of different 'innate capacities'. As such a system grows in complexity and the more its supporters occupy themselves with discussions about details, about the more peripheral parts of the system, the greater the likelihood that the basic beliefs, presupposed to these peripheral ones, get taken for granted and so made all the harder to relinquish. If two people, for instance, are arguing whether God is one person or three, they are each committed to the belief that God exists. If two others are arguing whether one's IQ is a valid indication of one's intellectual ceiling, they are each committed to the belief that we have such ceilings.[38]

In examining the scientific issues we have drawn from a

variety of major critiques directed at various underlying assumptions of psychometrics,[39] and used them to throw some light on the technical discussions which have dominated the internal history of the subject. The preparation of this book has involved extensive collaboration between us, but the treatment of the scientific issues (Chapters 4 and 5) was prepared by the first author, and that of the historical issues (Chapters 2 and 3) by the second author. For stylistic reasons we have retained the first person plural throughout.

2

Mental Testing and Society – I: the Origins and Ideological Relations of the Mental Testing Movement

By the 1930s the term 'psychological' or 'mental' test was applied in Britain to basically three types of measurement of mental ability: tests of general mental ability (or intelligence), tests of performance in, or aptitude for, more specific abilities (both mental and concrete),[1] and tests of scholastic achievement. These tests had certain features in common: they were devised by professional psychologists, they were so standardised that their results would fall within the normal or Gaussian curve of distribution and they depended on a pre-conceived norm of a mental function (or, in the case of certain aptitude tests, a concrete function). In this book we are primarily concerned with the most controversial branch of mental testing, intelligence or IQ testing, and the conception of intelligence which sustained it. But a judicious historical and social perspective on the mental testing movement requires that we think of it – at least initially – as a whole. The testers themselves did not fragment their interests (the same psychologists were devising tests of all kinds for use in schools, industry and commerce) and their motives and estimation of the social function of testing cannot be grasped without bearing this in mind.

These motives and that estimation will be returned to in greater detail later. For the present we shall simply note that at certain junctures between science and society (such as psychology textbooks used in universities and training colleges, teachers' training manuals, handbooks on testing practice drawn up for local education authorities by psychologists and so on) they appeared in most grandiose forms. The testing movement presented itself as a technocracy vital to a society which was generally becoming more test-conscious and meritocratic. To a long-standing concern for the selection of the racially and biologically 'fit', the movement had added selection of children for the highly competitive system of secondary education which began (for the selected few) at eleven, selection of children for 'streaming' within elementary schools (partly to facilitate selection at eleven), the devising of aptitude tests in order to 'scientifically' guide school leavers into the most 'appropriate' occupations, and of tests to be used by employers to secure the 'scientific' selection of the labour force.

There was remarkable confidence in the diagnostic and prognostic value of the group intelligence test. Prospective teachers could scarcely question its value to pedagogy when they read in a training manual jointly written by a former district inspector of schools and a lecturer in education:

> It is not too much to say that by using a group intelligence test a teacher can obtain in an hour more knowledge of the intelligence of the individuals of his class than he could by ordinary methods during a term.[2]

And once the intelligence of children was known, then the way was clear to assigning them to the occupation appropriate to their innate and (so it was asserted) more or less immutable intellectual endowment. Though not formally encoded, there was an implicit testing programme which, if adopted, opened up great vistas of organic social amelioration. Thouless's much used psychology textbook had, in its discussion of the 'Practical Implications of the Results of Intelligence Testing', laid it down that 'inherited intellectual endowment . . . is the best single indicator of [a child's] educability and of his later success' and that this fact had 'important bearings on the problems of education and of

the efficient fitting of individuals into the economic structure of society . . . . In an *ideal organisation of society*, every
man would be in an employment suited to his intelligence'[3]
[our emphasis]. For the textbook author, one consequence
of the present imperfect correspondence between intelligence and occupation was that there arose 'social misfits
[who] represent a serious loss of efficiency in the social
organism.'[4] The implication here (and in other texts) was
that problems like occupational maladjustment, industrial
discontent, juvenile delinquency and adult criminality
could be substantially ameliorated by the diagnostic
methods of individual psychology. Timely identification
by testing of the educationally sub-normal would decrease
the incidence of juvenile delinquency. Widespread adoption of scientific selection and promotion procedures would
promote industrial harmony, maximise the efficiency and
contentment of the labour force, lessen the frequency of
strikes and so on.

The 'ideal organisation of society' the testers had in mind
was clearly a replica of the one in which they lived, but with
its class and occupational hierarchy validated by psychological science, and its class antagonisms and social problems resolved by testing.

How are we to explain the speciousness of these claims on
behalf of a bundle of simple tests? Doubtless, the pretensions reflect, to some degree, the self-conscious youth of the
movement and the stridency of educational, industrial and
vocational psychology trying to carve out their respective
professional niches. Routine psychological testing, for
example, had had little impact on education before 1930
and, though it spread rapidly after that date, only about
half of local authorities in the English and Welsh education
system had incorporated it into their selection procedure
for secondary schools by 1940.[5] Again, during a period of
labour surplus, only a few entrepreneurs in a rather narrow
sector of industry and commerce were particularly attuned
to the overtures of industrial psychology. But these are
marginal explanations.

Possibly, the textbooks vulgarised the science. We might
infer this from an academic psychologist who later admitted

that 'in many respects the theories given in older textbooks, which are commonly accepted both by teachers and laymen today [the mid-1950s] are inaccurate'.[6] But when examined, the implication of textbook vulgarisation cannot stand. The textbooks represented the theories quite adequately. In fact the specious claims derive directly from the pretensions of the 'pure' scientists who formulated the modern 'scientific' conception of intelligence and devised the tests. The textbooks were often more sober than the scientists. Lewis Terman, whose Stanford–Binet revision became available in Britain in 1919, had urged on his readers the uses of intelligence tests in ringing tones. They were a prophylactic against criminal and moral defect since:

> all feeble-minded are at least potential criminals. That every feeble-minded woman is a potential prostitute would hardly be disputed by any one. Moral judgement, like business judgement, social judgement, or any other kind of higher thought process, is a function of intelligence ... here [the treatment of vice and crime] is one of psychological testing's richest applications.[7]

With respect to the selection of the labour force:

> The time is probably not far distant when intelligence tests will become a recognized and widely used instrument for determining vocational fitness .... When thousands of children who have been tested by the Binet scale have been followed out into the industrial world, and their success in various occupations noted we shall know fairly definitely the vocational significance of any given degree of mental inferiority or superiority. Researches of this kind will ultimately determine the minimum 'intelligence quotient' necessary for success in each leading occupation.[8]

Spearman had envisaged an application of intelligence testing which – had it ever been realised – would have amounted to social control of positively Orwellian dimensions. Together with Bernard Hart, he concluded an article on 'General Ability' in the *British Journal of Psychology* for 1912 with the claim that the possible applications of intelligence testing were so many as to render it difficult to speak freely of them 'without seeming extravagant.' With respect to the nation's children:

> It seems even possible to anticipate the day when there will be yearly official registration of the 'intellective index', as we will call it, of every child throughout the kingdom.
> This registration, controlled and digested by an expert bureau, could scarcely fail to shed a flood of light on many vital problems .... In the course of time, there seems no reason why the intellective index (or system of indices) should not become so well understood, as to enable every child's education to be properly graded according to his or her capacity ...[9]

And once the measured, indexed, controlled children had left school, what then?

> Still wider – though doubtless, dimmer – are the vistas opened up as to the possible consequences in adult life. It seems not altogether chimeric to look forward to the time when citizens, instead of choosing their career at almost blind hazard, will undertake just the professions really suited to their capacities. One can even conceive the establishment of a minimum index to qualify for the parliamentary vote, and, above all for the right to have offspring.

That these sentiments were Spearman's and not simply his co-author's is amply demonstrated by a passage in his *The Abilities of Man* (1927). Here, he returned to the consideration that 'an accurate measurement of every-one's intelligence would seem to herald the feasibility of selecting the better endowed persons for admission into citizenship – and even for the right to have offspring.' Furthermore (and we must recall that Spearman was writing in the aftermath of the General Strike) social selection by the criterion of intelligence would resolve class antagonism by locating every individual in the socio-economic status appropriate to his ability. It is even hinted that such selection would finally dissolve the phenomenon of class itself:

> a suitable selection secures a continual rise in the intellectual status of the people taken in the mass [and] the same power of measuring intelligence should also make possible a proper treatment of each individual: to each can be given an appropriate education, and therefore a fitting place in the state – just that which he or she demonstrably deserves. Class hatred, nourished upon preferences that are believed to be unmerited, would seem at last within reach of eradication; perfect justice is about to combine with maximum efficiency.[10]

There are self-evident preoccupations shared by the scientists who formulated the conception of intelligence and the minions who wrote the textbooks for undergraduates, trainee teachers and the like. To the historian familiar with the wider intellectual currents of late nineteenth and early twentieth century Britain, these preoccupations advertise themselves through a certain vocabulary. Words such as 'stock', 'breed', 'fit', 'unfit', 'degeneracy', 'efficiency' were common currency in Britain between the late 1890s and 1914. They reflected two interconnected concerns: one for the biological or 'racial' qualities of a nation facing sterner competition for empire and the other for the declining competitiveness of British industry and commerce in the face of growing German and American competition. For the sake of brevity, we can say that the late Victorian and Edwardian intelligentsia perceived an inter-related group of problems concerning race and empire on the one hand, and industrial efficiency and human ability on the other. The psychologists' conception of intelligence originated in the 'science' of eugenics which was itself a synthesised response to these problems. Eugenic science, and modes of thought influenced by eugenics, served to 'rationalise' (in the senses of both explain away and deal with) the demographic, social, economic and imperial 'problems' of state and society at a point where British industry and statecraft were experiencing considerable discomfort.

MENTAL TESTING AND RATIONALISATION

The notion of 'rationalisation' is a useful one on which to build a preliminary historical interpretation of the phenomenon of mental testing and the psychologists' conception of intelligence. Rationalisation is a key concept in Marxism and classical sociology; in both intellectual traditions it seeks to define the historical process *and* the mode of thought (or ideology) by which capitalist societies have understood and exploited nature, and by which the capitalist class has understood and exploited human labour. In the sociology of Max Weber, capitalism is depicted as being dependent more or less on formal rationality in all spheres of social life. Capitalism is seen, moreover, as driven by irresistible forces to create conditions which would allow a maximum of productivity and a maximum degree of efficiency. This involves the increasingly sophisticated application of science to industry, the specialisation of processes and the sub-division of labour. The feature of capitalist rationalisation which Weber saw as most specific to his own day (he died in 1920) was bureaucratisation and its accompanying growth and formalisation of professions offering calculable services to industry, commerce and the state. But the entrepreneur's market is, for Weber, the *locus classicus* of the rationality which characterised capitalist civilisation, for the market obliges the capitalist to calculate and predict as a way of life. In particular, the employer is driven to calculate ever more finely the maximum capacity of labour. Of his workers (and prospective workers) he needs to know the optimum of aptitude for the job, the optimum of skill acquired through practice and the optimum of incentive for the work. Weber remarks in his *Economy and Society* that 'Aptitude, regardless of whether it is the product of hereditary or environmental and educational influences, can only be determined by testing'.[11] Although Weber was seeking to theorise capitalist society at a very high level of abstraction he was also demonstrating the inner rationality of a quite concrete phenomenon of his own time, namely the growing links between behavioural science and industry. Aptitude testing by psychologists working for large-scale German enterprises was well established by 1914, the tests devised by Hugo Münsterberg for the Berlin tramway system being the best known. But for Weber, the 'ideal type' of capitalist rationality in this respect was the Taylor system of scientific management introduced in the USA.[12]

Weberian sociology sought to dissect capitalist society as a functioning system, while the Marxist tradition sought to expose those irrational tendencies of capitalism which lay beneath the rationality of its productive technique and its de-mystified outlook on the world. The intellectual ground they share should not be allowed to obscure this critical central divergence. In Georg Lukács's essay collection, *History and Class Consciousness*, the discussion of rationalisation highlights, even to the point of detailed illustration, much of the common ground. Lukács, too, sees the continuous trend towards greater rationalisation in capitalist society most amply illustrated in the operation of the labour market. He sees the process of labour progressively broken down into abstract, rational, specialised operations so that the worker loses contact with the finished product. Like Weber, he recognises that behavioural science was providing the capitalist with the new methods with which to calculate the efficiency of labour and to isolate and 'objectify' specific attributes of the human worker:

> With the modern 'psychological' analysis of the work process [namely, in the Taylor system and subsequent developments of it] this rational mechanisation extends right into the worker's soul: even his psychological attributes are separated from his total personality and placed in opposition to it so as to facilitate their integration into specialised rational systems and their reduction to statistically viable concepts.[13]

His concluding remarks were peculiarly prophetic, since in

the late 1920s and 1930s American psychologists engaged in the increasingly fatuous identification of 'specific' abilities through the analysis of masses of correlation data.

In Lukács's analysis, however, capitalist rationalisation is contextualised within an identification of commodity exchange as the dominating and all-pervasive principle of bourgeois society. Commodity fetishism is the ontological characteristic of capitalism which determines its reduction of labour, ability, intelligence, energy and special attributes to measurable quantities external to the human being. These quantities then become negotiable on the labour market. Additionally, Lukács sought to establish the intrinsic relationship between commodity fetishism and the dominant cognitive method in bourgeois society. For him, the economic calculation is the matrix of logical and scientific thought. The increasingly sophisticated economic accounting of bourgeois society is paralleled by the sophistication of a cognitive method which directs itself to quantifiable 'accounts' of particular phenomena. Moreover, the tendency of behavioural science to fragment the total human personality is, for Lukács, merely a specific instance of the general tendency of bourgeois science to fragment itself into isolated disciplines. He did not deny the formidable achievements of science nor question its ability to arrive at objective truths about the world. But, in seeking to impose meaning and order on the intrinsically meaningless phenomena of the natural world, science developed into a series of discrete and ahistorical explanations of invariants: 'The more highly developed [a modern science] becomes and the more scientfic, the more it will become a formally closed system of partial laws'.[14] When scientific method was reimposed on the phenomena of the social world, its exclusion of history and its failure to account for man as a conscious entity in a dialectical relationship with nature, impaired its explanatory power. For Lukács, scientific method in the bourgeois economic, social and behavioural sciences provided high-level 'rationalisations' (in the pejorative sense of the word) for the contradictions in bourgeois society.

In deploying the notion of rationalisation as a preliminary historical explanation for the mental testing movement, it is not suggested that we have to hand a bludgeon with which to beat all problems of historical causality into submission. Rather, it can be seen as a paradigm within which to interrogate the past; an overarching theory of historical change which will generate hypotheses and direct enquiry. The preceding brief review of the pretensions of the mental testing movement establishes the *a priori* case for discussing mental testing as a species of bourgeois rationalisation.

THE ORIGINS OF PSYCHOMETRIC THEORY

During the age of bourgeois revolution (1780–1848) psychology (though not yet so called) stressed the plasticity of human nature. The mind was conceived of as a *tabula rasa* on which ideas impressed themselves by 'association', a view of cognition inspired by seventeenth century mechanics. The doctrine was individualistic and egalitarian and formed part of the intellectual challenge which bourgeois ideas posed to an *ancien régime* dominated politically by hereditary monarchy and aristocracy. In Britain the growth of bourgeois economic, and later political power, elicited its own intellectual consolidation, chiefly in the fields of economics, Malthusian demography and social evolutionism, all of which were interrelated. From the mid-nineteenth century, a changed view of human nature – a new psychology – became an increasingly important part of this intellectual consolidation. Doctrines of human nature as plastic and of innate human equality gave way to a more structured view of the mind and to concepts of innate human inequality with which to rationalise the economic and political inequalities of bourgeois society.

Clearly, this is grossly over-schematised. We can find pedagogues, such as the influential Maria Edgeworth, who held the *tabula rasa* view of the mind and yet supported the old society of fixed estates, and a successful bourgeois such as Robert Owen, whose experience of the malleability of human nature impelled him to socialism. Yet it is entirely in accord with the schema that Herbert Spencer, the bourgeois ideologue *par excellence*, should have produced a psychological concept which eventually, after a ragged, uneven development, came to take a central position in the bourgeois view of man.

Spencer is generally accredited with re-introducing the term 'intelligence' to psychological theory. By it he understood the fundamental capacity of cognition which enables the human organism to adjust itself more effectively to a complex and ever-changing environment: 'intelligence ... consists in the establishment of correspondences between relations in the organism and relations in the environment...'[15] With individual growth and social evolution, he argued, this capacity differentiated itself into a hierarchy of more special abilities. A near contemporary, Alexander Bain, had a similar conception of intelligence as a unitary function; both, that is, abandoned a more customary division into separate cognitive faculties. In Bain's theory, these were simply different processes of intelligence or 'different forms of an unique law; that to imagine, to deduct, to induct, to perceive, etc., is to combine ideas in a different manner; and that the differences of faculties are only differences of association'.[16] For Bain, the primitive and fundamental attributes of intelligence were consciousness of difference, consciousness of resemblance and retentiveness, which included memory and recollection.

Spencer's psychology had a critical role in his sociology, for he believed that underneath social phenomena lay 'certain vital phenomena'; accordingly the structural and functional complexity of the higher societies related to the innate capacities of their populations:

> We need but to glance, on the one hand, at the varieties of civilized men and the structures of their nations, to see inference verified by fact. And thus recognising, both *a priori* and *a posteriori*, these relations between the phenomena of individual human nature and the phenomena of incorporated human nature, we cannot

fail to see that the phenomena of incorporated human nature form the subject matter of a science.[17]

Spencer's social evolutionism rested on the Lamarckian presumption of the heritability of acquired characteristics; social differentiation reflected the progressive intra-species differentiation brought about through the unfettered competition and struggle of the myriad individuals within the social organism.

Spencer's conception of intelligence did not displace the orthodox psychological doctrine of faculties and the term is rarely found in turn of the century dictionaries of psychology and philosophy. The orthodoxy up to the turn of the century usually envisaged mental activity as the resolution of the activities of Intellect, Perception, Memory and Imagination. Certain ready-made faculties, such as memory, were presumed to come into play at an earlier stage in the individual mind, while higher faculties made their appearance later. Once the faculties had appeared, the difference between the child's and the adult's mind was regarded as quantitative rather than qualititative. Faculty psychology lent, then, some support to contemporary pedagogy which made the logically arranged principles and facts which are the subject matter of adult thought the natural 'studies' of the child. So little did intelligence theory figure as a problematic in psychology that Spearman could still (in 1923) write that 'a large number of the best accredited books on psychology do not so much as mention "intelligence" from cover to cover'.[18] In his old age, Burt was to assert that intelligence did not figure much in everyday usage either; he recalled the word as rarely used in his own boyhood and claimed that he had never heard either teachers or parents talk of a child's 'intelligence' or describe him as 'intelligent'.[19] This greatly distorts the case. Intelligence was a common enough expression in everyday parlance.

Neither Spencer's psychology nor his sociology proved seminal in the sense of creating 'schools' in the infant British social sciences; though recognised as a great synthesising intellect, he was a figure whom people reacted against, rather than the source of ideas which were developed by a later generation. The case of Francis Galton – a far less systematising figure – is entirely different. Though he wrote no single treatise expounding his psychology in the fashion of Spencer, he is universally acknowledged as the father of individual psychology and mental measurement in Britain. Spearman recognised him as 'that master mind' and during Burt's childhood Galton was held up to the young Cyril as 'a supreme example of the Ideal Man'.[20] Throughout his adult life, Burt returned again and again to the suggestiveness and fertility of Galton's ideas, claiming that all the basic concepts, statistical devices and procedures of mental measurement derived from, or had been adumbrated, in them. After his appointment to the Chair of Psychology at University College, London, Burt was to look upon Galton's work as constituting a programme of research which he believed it was the special duty of psychology at University College to continue.[21] A summary of Galton's contributions confirms the claim. Pre-eminent were the statistical: he was amongst the first to apply the normal curve of frequency to mental phenomena; his calculus for arriving at the correlation coefficients of heterogenous data was indispensable to the analysis of test responses and the mathematical 'proof' of a central factor, governing test performance; he also devised the system of percentile ranking which, as early as 1880, he showed could be applied to psychometric statistics. His statistical advances laid the foundations of biometrics, or the statistical approach to biological phenomena, and his Laws of Regression to the Mean and Ancestral Heredity were to govern the biometric study of heritability.

His most fruitful psychological ideas resided in the distinction he made in his *Hereditary Genius* of 1869 between general mental ability (or intelligence) and special abilities (or particular aptitudes). General ability he regarded as conditioning the whole range of intellectual performance and sometimes characterised it as a central controlling force or energy. His scheme of cognition can be seen as the starting point of the hierarchical or 'monarchic' conception of mental abilities which was to be particularly influential in

British twentieth-century differential psychology.

Galton's contributions to the practice of test construction were signal, though rather less clear-cut: in furthering the science of anthropometry (which would attempt to measure the complete man – stature, sensory responses *and* personality) he devised some of the first mental tests, but he also encouraged psychology in the largely fruitless task of correlating mental ability with sensory discrimination. Nonetheless, he seems to have been the first to suggest the procedure which eventually became the basis for modern test construction. In an addendum to an article in *Mind* on 'Mental Tests and Measurements' by his former assistant, J. McK. Cattell, Galton argued that

> one of the most important objects of measurement . . . is to obtain a general knowledge of the capacities of man by sinking shafts, as it were, at a few critical points. In order to ascertain the best points for the purpose, the sets of measures should be compared with an independent estimate of the man's powers . . .[22]

This suggestion has been seen as foreshadowing the practice of test construction by standardising against teachers' rankings of a class or estimates of the 'normal' performance at a certain age.

This by no means exhausts Galton's contributions. He was amongst the first to advocate twin study in order to determine the relative effects of environment and heredity in the development of human characteristics. Again, Burt for one saw his 'anthropometric laboratory' as furnishing the starting-point, and to a large extent the model, for the many 'psychological clinics' and 'child guidance centres' subsequently set up in Britain, America and elsewhere.

From this rather neutral recital, the fecundity of Galton's ideas might appear simply to arise from the juncture he established between statistics, psychology and the science of heredity. But though it is true that Galton provided individual psychology with many of its problems and with its statistical internal dynamic, the fruitfulness of his ideas would seem to have lain no less in their external, ideological relations. Galton achieved a synthesis of liberal individualism with Darwinism which offered a rationale for a class-stratified, but socially mobile society. In many respects he can be seen as putting forward, on natural scientific grounds, an account of the circulation of elites within a social hierarchy of constant shape similar to that later advanced by Vilfredo Pareto on sociological grounds. Galton retained from liberal individualism a belief that an individual's innate worth should determine his place in the social hierarchy and he was opposed to aristocracies of birth:

> I cannot think of any claim to respect, put forward in modern days, that is so entirely an imposture, as that made by a peer on the grounds of descent, who has neither been wholly educated, nor has any eminent kinsman, within three degrees.[23]

His ideal society was a meritocracy 'where incomes were chiefly derived from professional sources and not much through inheritance, and where every lad had a chance of showing his abilities'.[24] But Galton broke with advanced mid-nineteenth century liberal opinion in strenuously rejecting egalitarianism:

> I have no patience with the hypothesis occasionally expressed, and often implied ... that babies are born pretty much alike, and that the sole agencies in creating differences between boy and boy, man and man, are steady application and moral effort. It is in the most unqualified manner that I object to pretensions of natural equality.[25]

Galton came to regard the class stratification of competitive, bourgeois society as determined by the 'normal' distribution of innate differences in the population, and social mobility within that society as the natural selection of the more fit. The explanatory mechanism for social mobility he located in the phenomenon he observed in the correlation coefficients calculated for the stature of related individuals: the Law of Regression to the Mean. Briefly, this stated that the average deviation from the normal stature of a filial generation would be only two-thirds of the deviation of the parental generation. If this applied to the natural intellectual gifts which Galton regarded as the *sine qua non* of social eminence, then although, relative to its own size, the most able stratum was making the greatest proportional contribution to its own reproduction, in absolute terms this stratum was predominantly recruited from the strata immediately below it.[26]

As with Spencer, therefore, Galton's psychology had a crucial role, if not in a systematic sociology, then at least in a coherent view of why society had the shape it did. Social hierarchy flowed 'naturally' from individual differences. Out of the study of individual differences would come not simply a new field, differential psychology, but also the possibility of species improvement.

EUGENICS AND PSYCHOMETRICS

Galton's interests in the social, cultural and historical impact of innate differences can be traced back to his early travels in South Africa and his speculation on the causes of tribal dominance and subjugations, and the seemingly irresistible encroachments of the white race on black Africa.[27] But these speculations mainly concerned inter-racial differences and they were uttered in an intellectual context – mid-nineteenth century anthropology – highly favourable to scientific racism. Galton's reading of *The Origin of Species* encouraged him to think of human variation, natural selection and the inheritance of characters in *intra*-racial (or as he would have had it, intra-specific) terms. He was, by the 1860s, struck by the possibility of human stirpiculture or the improvement of the stocks within the race: 'If a twentieth part of the costs and pains were spent in measures for the improvement of the human race that is spent on the improvement of the breed of horses and cattle, what a galaxy of genius might we not create!'[28]

The very notion of improvement by breeding from the

better stocks (which Galton later called eugenics) was a spur
to the scientific measurement of the innate qualities of the
different stocks. Initially, Galton believed that the better
stocks could be identified by physical anthropological data,
and that this data would correlate highly with psychic
qualities. But, in his biographer's words, he quickly
'grasped that the superficial anthropometric characters
were no adequate index to the real man himself'.[29]
Nevertheless, he argued that the distribution of mental characters within a population would accord to the
same 'normal law of error' which the Belgian Adolph
Quetelet had earlier observed to govern individual variation in height and other physical characters. Furthermore, he presupposed that physical and mental characters
would be controlled by the same mechanism of inheritance.

Galton's most important contributions to psychological
theory and research were made between 1876 and 1884,
although he continued to publish minor papers on the
subject until at least 1896. The programme of racial
improvement through intervention in the evolutionary
process (which he had hinted at in *Hereditary Genius*) has
been convincingly interpreted as the original motive for his
psychometric investigations.[30] Eugenics and psychometrics
then developed interdependently in his thought. The
publicity given (by the New York Charity Organisation
Society) to the notorious Jukes family, whose sequential
generations included large numbers of paupers and
drunks, led Galton to comment in 1877, 'There can be no
more interesting subject to us than the quality of the stock of
our countrymen and of the human race generally, and
there can be no more worthy enquiry than that which leads
to an explanation of the conditions under which it deterio-
rates or improves.'[31] The prevailing 'explanation' was
environmentalist, but Galton was convinced that, with
respect to the mental characters he was attempting to define
and measure, and which he now considered of paramount
importance to the quality of the stock, only a hereditarian
explanation would suffice. In January 1880, in an article in
Nature, he wrote that

It appears to me that inquiry into the mental constitution of other people is a most fertile field for explanation, especially as there is much in the facts . . . to show that original differences in mental constitution are permanent, being little modified by the accidents of education, and that they are strongly hereditary.[32]

Its 'fertility' lay in the application of this inquiry to scientific racial improvement, and at this point Galton's choice of criteria for selection was focused on 'mental energy': 'In any scheme of eugenics, energy is the most important quality to favour; it is, as we have seen, the basis of living action, and it is eminently transmissable by descent.' In singling out the quality 'energy', Galton was drawing on his South African experience and his memories of the supposedly innate indolence of black Africans: 'energy', he believed, was 'an attribute of the higher races, being favoured beyond all other qualities by natural selection'.[33]

Galton drew together his psychological papers of the late 1870s and early 1880s in his *Inquiries into Human Faculty* (1883) and his introduction remarked that the intention of his work was to touch upon various topics more or less connected with the cultivation of race. He briefly outlined what was to be the programme of 'positive' eugenics: 'The most merciful form of what I ventured to call "eugenics" would consist in natality for the indications of superior strains or races, and in so favouring them that their progeny shall outnumber and gradually replace that of the old one.' Galton did not outline 'negative' eugenics until 1891 when he suggested the possibility of the sterilisation of those sections of the community of small civic worth but he never gave such prominence to this aspect of racial science.[34] Unlike later eugenists, Galton placed an optimistic interpretation on the implications of Darwinism for society; he saw in them the promise of improvement, rather than the spectre of racial degeneration. Much of the import of the *Inquiries* lay in its eliciting from Darwinism new ethical, indeed religious tasks for mankind for he proposed that this new knowledge should be applied to racial and social problems, and that understanding of, sympathy with, and aid in the progress of the general evolution of living forms should be accepted as religious duties.[35]

The eugenic ideology was coolly received in 1883 and significant changes in both the socio-political milieu and the scientific context were required before eugenics became influential amongst scientists and the more or less informed public. Before specifying these changes and elaborating on the relationship of psychometrics with eugenics, it is useful to further isolate two items of the Galtonian intellectual legacy for differential psychology. Perhaps the more important was Galton's insistence that scientific statements about the mind and individual differences could only be arrived at through quantification. Throughout his life, Galton exhibited 'an obsessional desire to count or classify',[36] some of his observations suggesting neurotic compulsion rather than genius. For him, calculative rationality was the sole route to positive knowledge for he believed that 'until the phenomena of any branch of knowledge have been submitted to measurement and number, it cannot assume the status and dignity of science'.[37] He and his disciples accepted the corollary that quantitative solutions to and interpretations of problems and phenomena were *ipso facto* scientific. Galton's faith in the potency of numbers alone to supply a scientific explanation of phenomena extended to the emotional characteristics of man. In an article on 'The Measurement of Character' in 1884, he wrote 'I do not plead guilty to taking a shallow idea of human nature, when I propose to apply as it were, a footrule to its heights and depths . . . . Is man . . . so different from a conscious machine, that any proposal to measure his moral qualities is based upon a fallacy?'[38] In 1906, during the twilight of his career, Galton attempted to enlist school teachers and school doctors in an ambitious proposal to repeat the British Association's anthropometric survey of 1888, but with the addition this time of a survey of psychological characteristics and with subsequent surveys to record the progress of the respondents. The scheme was intimately linked with a revived eugenics campaign and with the fears of national physical deterioration which had been heightened by the poor quality of the volunteers for

military service during the Boer War. His definition of the
scope of 'anthropometry' confirms that he regarded all
aspects of the human personality as reducible to numerical
values:

> Anthropometry is the art of measuring the physical and
> mental faculties of a human being. It enables a shorthand
> description of any individual to be obtained by recording
> measurements of a sample of his qualities. Properly cho-
> sen, these will define his bodily proportions, his health,
> strength and energy, his intellectual capacities and moral
> character, and will substitute concise numerical values for
> verbose and disputable estimates. Anthropometry thus
> furnishes the readiest method of estimating whether a
> boy is developing normally or otherwise . . . [39]

Galton's particular brand of positivism was crucial to what
its critics regard as the spurious numerology of IQ psychology. His numerical concepts of norm and standard
deviation gave psychologists the means with which they
could concretise, measure and universalise aspects of fluid
and socially-related behaviour. With his methods, the
human personality could be fragmented into negotiable
units. His concept of the proof of a causal relationship
between two phenomena by the adducement of a mathematical relationship between them was to be central both
to factor analytic psychology and hereditarian science. Yet,
as has been pointed out on a number of occasions, Galton's
most basic 'numerical' assumption – that the normal curve
of frequency applied to psychological variables – has never
been adequately shown to be true. [40] Without this assumption, ordinal scales could not be converted to equal inter-
vals, nor mental tests scaled in terms of standard deviations
or some fraction thereof, nor intelligence be conceived of as
a quantity to be measured against a norm.

The second item of the Galtonian legacy which can be
isolated is his conception of the mind and the cognitive
process. Galton posited a two-fold division of the mind:

> There seems to be a presence chamber in my mind where

full consciousness holds court, and where two or three
ideas are at the same time in audience, and an ante-
chamber full of more or less allied ideas, which is just
beyond the full ken of consciousness. Out of this ante-
chamber the ideas most nearly allied to those in the presence chamber appear to be summoned in a mechanically
logical way, and to have their turn of audience.[41]

The system of control which Galton envisaged as operating
in the mind was 'monarchic', in that he saw it as subject to
one central force which he sometimes characterised as
energy (and which, as we have seen, he regarded as critically
important for eugenics). This sovereign force mobilised
lesser but more specific abilities.

Part of the attractiveness of Galton's conception of the
mind lay in its postulating a mental division of labour
having strong affinities with the material division of labour
of the external world. Burt was later to make this quite
explicit by drawing an analogy between Galton's visualisa-
tion of the mind and the capitalist enterprise.[42] The mind
could be thought of as a factory or counting-house and its
hierarchically structured abilities as capital, management
and labour, identified according to their location and
function in the presence and antechambers. At the rear of
the enterprise, screened from public view, were the operat-
ives who provided the brute labour of industry and
commerce: these were 'the emotions and sentiments, the
fears and desires, that provide the real energy for the day's
demands'. In the front of the building resided 'the intellectual organisers who supply the necessary guidance or
direction and formed, as it were, a board of managers.'
Presiding over the board was 'a chairman' (intelligence)
whose function was the general supervision of all activities.
Under his and the board's command was a whole hierarchy
of subordinate officials, 'the special capacities or aptitudes'
of middle management. Thus, the mind was envisaged as a
hologram of the capitalist economic process, with the 'best'
minds being those best reproducing the system within
themselves.

When Galton renewed his attempt to win informed

opinion for his eugenics campaign in 1901, he found a
more receptive audience. Eugenics became a significant
influence on biologists, the sociological movement and
psychology, as well as influencing socio-political attitudes.[43]
Of cardinal importance in swaying informed opinion was
August Weismann's work on the mechanism of heredity
published in 1889. Weismann argued for a clear distinction
between the germ cells which controlled production and
the somatic cells; the former, he argued, were immutable
and not modifiable by the environment, nor by the characteristics taken on by the somatic cells. The theory disposed of
the Lamarckian concept of 'progressive' evolution through
the inheritance of acquired characteristics. Weismann's
views were rapidly accepted as the basis for biological
research and their consequences for social evolutionary
science were almost as quickly established. Benjamin Kidd
in his widely-read *Social Evolution* (1894) extracted from
Weismann the bleak moral that social Utopias were biologically impossible and that a certain result of the suspension
of selection through social struggle would be racial decay:

> If the old [Lamarckian] view is correct, and the effects of
> use and education *are* transmitted by inheritance, then
> the Utopian dreams of philosophy in the past are
> undoubtedly possible of realisation .... But if, as the
> writer believes, the views of the Weismann party are in
> the main correct; if there can be no progress except by the
> accumulation of congenital variations above the average
> to the exclusion of others below; if, without the constant
> stress of selection which this involves, the tendency of
> every higher form of life *is actually retrograde*; then is the
> whole human race caught in the toils of that struggle and
> rivalry of life which has been in progress from the
> beginning. Then must the rivalry of existence continue,
> humanised as to conditions it may be, but immutable and
> inevitable to the end. [Original emphasis]. (pp. 203–4)

As this passage suggests, Weismann's doctrine would tend
to emphasise the negative and pessimistic aspects of the
eugenics programme. In political terms it could, and by

some eugenists was, turned into a sweeping rationale for anti-collectivism, since the effect of state intervention was to suspend the elimination of the unfit. Yet here was a possible source of contradiction, since the identification and elimination of the congenitally degenerate was a task for a strong, interventionist state.

A further development in the scientific context which increased the receptivity of biologists and other scientists to eugenics was the rediscovery, in 1899, of Mendel's 1865 paper setting out his theory of gametic segregation. This served to confirm conclusions as to the principles of hybridisation reached independently by others in the field, such as de Vries. Mendelism encouraged an awareness of the covert potency of heritability. Galton had proposed that inheritance of characters was controlled by a blending mechanism, with both parents contributing equally to the traits of the filial generation. This theory provided a simple explanation for degrees of likeness (or, in another word, variation) between generations. It explained the inheritance of continuous, variant characteristics and allowed inheritance to be comprehended by the mathematics of probability. Mendelism appeared diametrically opposed to 'blended' inheritance for in simple organisms (such as the pea) inheritance was shown to be particulate and inherited traits discontinuous. Certain traits could not be bred out but were governed by 'recessive' factors. The assumption was quickly made that a large number of physical diseases, and mental and moral defects, were similarly governed by recessive factors. Alcoholism, for example, was attributed to such a physical factor. Moreover, the gametic material controlling the incidence of physical, mental and moral degeneracy was assumed to be the peculiar heritage of the poorest, yet most prolific strata of the population. What was known, in contemporary social observation, as 'the submerged tenth' was seen as carrying the seeds of a huge future burden of congenital idiocy and congenital moral turpitude.

But while Mendelism encouraged the emergence of hereditarian politics, it led to a furious wrangle between biometricians (above all Karl Pearson, Galton's leading

disciple) and Mendelians, and this split the eugenics movement even before it acquired institutional shape. Main-
stream eugenics, represented by the Eugenics Education
Society established in 1907, was strongly Mendelian; the
Eugenics Laboratory, funded by Galton and directed by
Pearson, produced a considerable literature analysing
physical and mental inheritance, and topics such as the
relationship between fertility and social status, by biometric methods. That the controversy was needless was
shown by the statistician, Udny Yule, as early as 1902, when
he demonstrated that a number of Mendelian factors could
act in such a way as to produce the effect of continuous
variation in inherited traits.[44] The two positions were
regarded as incompatible, however, until the publication of
Fisher's famous 1918 paper.[45] In this controversy there
were clear reasons for psychologists to favour the biometrical side. From Galton they had acquired the *problems*
of explaining mental variation and the inheritance of
continuous traits; many early Mendelians believed that
such traits could not be heritable precisely because they
were not discontinuous. The critical importance of biometric *methods* for differential psychology was stressed by
Charles Spearman in the first of his 1904 papers where he
bemoaned the neglect by psychologists of 'the brilliant work
being carried on since 1886 by the Galton–Pearson school'
and berated previous work in statistical psychology with the
claim that 'not once . . . has any partial correlation between
two psychological events been determined in such a way as
to provide good evidential value'.[46] The investigations of
Pearson and his co-worker David Heron into fertility and
social status provided the model for Burt's early work on
the inheritance of intelligence and its relations with social
class.[47]

Heron's investigations highlighted for eugenists –
whatever their scientific allegiance – what was their core
social problematic; the differential fertility of the social
strata. This phenomenon had been well-enough appreciated by the end of the 1880s. Professional men and
their spouses were known to be, on average, older at
marriage than working-class couples and they further

limited their completed family size by (presumably) contraception. By the early twentieth century effective fertility ratios had widened because of, on the one hand, the increasing incidence of family limitation and, on the other, declining infant mortality amongst the lower social strata. The division between the prolific and the comparatively infertile did not rest on the class divide between manual and clerical or professional labour; between the 1880s and the early twentieth century the birth rate amongst prosperous artisans fell by 46 per cent. It lay rather with the divide between the socially 'efficient' and the 'inefficient'. With some exceptions (such as the miners) the birth rate was highest amongst the casually and under-employed, the unskilled and low-paid inhabitants of the slum tenements. The feeble-minded, and the 'stock' from which they came, were believed to be exceptionally prolific. (This opinion was given official sanction in the report of the Royal Commission on the Feeble-Minded of 1908; the commission leant greatly on the evidence of the neurologist A. F. Tredgold, a leading member of the Eugenics Education Society.)[48]

For eugenists, the predicted consequence of differential fertility was an increasingly dysgenic imbalance between the more and the less innately worthy stocks. Pearson put the problem very clearly in 1903:

> We are ceasing as a nation to breed intelligence as we did fifty to a hundred years ago. The mentally better stock in the nation is not reproducing itself at the same rate as it did of old; the less able and less energetic are more fertile than the better stocks. No scheme of wider or more thorough education will bring up, in the scale of intelligence, hereditary weakness to the level of hereditary strength. The only remedy, if one be possible at all, is to alter the relative fertility of the good and bad stocks in the community.[49]

As will be discussed in greater detail later, IQ psychology provided an instrument with which this prediction could be put to the test.

The extraordinary currency gained by eugenic, and more or less related ideas, after 1901 is partly attributable to their satisfying intellectual needs created by changes in Britain's international status, and their resolving of the bewilderment caused by seemingly intractable social problems. In the late 1880s there began a period of competitive imperialism during which expansion of European (and later American) dominion over 'less civilised' coloured races was widely legitimised by a fundamentally pessimistic and brutal social Darwinism. (Kidd's work, already mentioned, was a plausible example of this thought.) Races which were not expansive were assumed by many to be decadent and, since expansion was justified, even essential, on evolutionary grounds, it contained its own twisted moral sanction. For British imperialists, the biological 'fitness' of the nation to compete for empire became a question of first importance, partly because Britain was less demographically expansive than Germany, America or Italy.[50] The connection between imperialist and bio-political thought can be illustrated by Sidney Webb's rhetorical question: 'How can we get an efficient army of the stunted, anaemic, demoralised denizens of the slum tenements of our great cities?'[51] He made the connection a rationale for state intervention: at least 'the minimum necessary for breeding an even moderately imperial race'. To the problem of biological 'fitness' to compete was added, from the late 1880s, concern for the comparative decline in Britain's international economic position as the lead in the science-based industries was taken by Germany, and in mass-production by America.

Eugenic and bio-political thought was a response, too, to a widespread feeling of helplessness when meticulous social investigation revealed the extent of apparently irremediable urban poverty. This investigation was, in truth, an indictment of the economic system, for the single most important cause of poverty, established by Charles Booth and confirmed by Seebohm Rowntree and A. L. Bowley, was low wages. But poverty amongst the lowest strata was also depicted as a biological condition. Of his Class A of occasional labourers, street sellers and criminals, Booth wrote that 'It [was] much to be desired ... that [the class] may become less hereditary in character. There appears to be no doubt that it is hereditary to a very considerable extent.' Class B – the casual poor (11 per cent of the population) he described as 'a deposit of those who from mental, moral and physical reasons are incapable of better work'.[52]

During the Boer War the internal and external sources of 'national degeneration' appeared to flow together: Britain's military weakness and incompetence was exposed in the face of a much smaller enemy; her only diplomatic friends were nations of the same 'racial stock'; a large number of the volunteers for the war were physically decrepit. Alarm over the last point led to the setting up of the Inter-Departmental Committee on Physical Deterioration, a forum which did much to establish biological 'fitness' as a major political question.

THE ORIGINS OF SPEARMAN'S THEORY OF INTELLIGENCE

The social and ideological context which has been sketched briefly is indispensable to understanding the emergence of, and the significance rapidly attached to, the theory of general intelligence produced in the first decade of the twentieth century, chiefly by Charles Spearman. It is true that elaborating the ideological conditions for the emergence of the theory will not settle its verisimilitude; but it may help us to question whether the theory constituted an epistemological breakthrough to autonomous knowledge. A theory may be unfalsified, prohibitive of certain events but nonetheless 'thin', in the sense that it does not substantially advance the causal explanation of the phenomena observed through it. To clarify by anticipating a little: Spearman inductively theorised a central factor in cognition by the mathematical analysis of test performance. But though the mathematical analysis was competent to support the theory, it was not competent to exclude others. The theory's insubstantiality lay in the heuristic weakness of relating psychological entities to mathematical data. A 'thin' theory's content may be puffed up by ideological and metaphysical considerations, as – it will be argued – was the case with Spearman's. The status of epistemological break-through is certainly claimed on behalf of Spearman's theory, and it has a central place in the internal history of psychometrics. Though there were important dis-senters – and the theory was quite quickly modified – it nonetheless dominated British differential psychology. Since the revival of the scientific debate over the nature of intelligence that was prompted by Jensen's 1969 article, Spearman's theory has come back into vogue as the starting point for discussions of the theoretical nature of intelli-gence.[53] In his *Know your Own IQ* (1962), Eysenck blithely conceded that

> It is often believed that intelligence tests are developed and constructed according to a rationale deriving from scientific theory.... In actual fact... intelligence tests are not based on any very sound scientific principles, and there is not a great deal of agreement among experts regarding the nature of intelligence. (p. 8).

In 1973, when he showed himself much more aware of the need for science to be grounded on the proper testing of theory, Eysenck cited Spearman's work as the classic instance of the hypothetico-deductive method in psychometric practice:

> Spearman postulated, on the basis of previous work and previous theories, that intelligence entered as a general factor into every sort of intelligence test fulfilling certain requirements (i.e. his noegenetic [*sic*] laws); he deduced from this hypothesis that matrices of correlation between such tests ... would in effect have a rank of unity.[54]

From Spearman's own account of the evolution of 'g' – as he styled the general factor in cognition – we know this summary to be a travesty of the internal history. Spearman began work on *g* in about 1901 when he started experimen-ting on the correlation between sensory discrimination and 'abilities commonly taken to be "intellectual" '.[55] Hitherto, this well-ploughed field of research had proved. fruitless.

But Spearman acknowledged that he was largely ignorant of previous research in this area until he had collected his own data: 'Among those who had entered the field before me – although I knew it not – had been Cattell. Had I seen his work earlier, I should certainly have thought the matter disposed of and should never have started my own work in that direction.'[56] His general intention appears to have been to further the application of exact laboratory methods to the study of higher cognitive processes. Spearman felt that experimental psychology had so far concerned itself with relatively trivial 'psychic' processes and he wished it to address itself to the problems of philosophic, introspective psychology.[57] It is, however, implausible to suggest that g was formulated within his noegenetic laws of cognition (of which more later). These laws were of much later origin – he described the whole noegenetic theory as 'complete early enough to present in my academic courses of 1920'[58] – and it is more plausible to believe that his theory of cognition was formulated to account for g.

Spearman's experiments consisted of testing two sets of children for discrimination in hearing, sight and touch and comparing their ranks with independent assessments of intellectual rank made by school teachers and, for one series, the village vicar's wife. He eventually observed that the matrices of correlation could be so arranged that their values decreased from left to right and top to bottom, and they always decreased proportionally. In statistical language, the correlations among four performances (a, b, p, q) could be shown to be

$$\frac{r\,(ap)}{r\,(bp)} = \frac{r\,(aq)}{r\,(bq)} \left[\begin{array}{l} \text{or more commonly as the tetrad equation} \\ \quad r\,(ap) \times r\,(aq) - r\,(bp) \times r\,(bq) = 0 \end{array} \right]$$

This equation would only hold good where the tests were sufficiently dissimilar and it became the criterion by which Spearman and his co-workers later included or rejected items when constructing test batteries.

In Spearman's view, the phenomenon was best explained by a 'monarchic' theory of intelligence which postulated that every mental performance involved a common g factor and an *s* factor specific to that performance. It is not the case, however, that the hierarchy of correlations was a test of a prior hypothesis, rather the observed regularity was the starting point of the theory.[59] Spearman wrote that he 'fell to brooding long over the results'.[60] The hierarchy of correlations only became clear when his data had been recalculated according to a formula he had worked out for the correction of the attenuation of correlation. The recognition of the need to purify his data was certainly *post facto* for he stated in his 1904 paper:

> when we proceed to discount the errors of measurement, it unfortunately becomes clear that our data is far from being adequate for our purposes . . . my excuse lies in the fact that at the time of the experiments I was only just beginning to realise the necessity . . . of duplication (in order to calculate the attenuation of correlation).[61]

Spearman concluded that he had demonstrated 'the existence of something we may provisionally term "General sensory Discrimination" and similarly a "General Intelligence", and further that the functional correspondence between the two is not appreciably less than absolute.'[62] Moreover, his demonstration of the common factor in mental performance suggested 'a law of the Universal Unity of the Intellectual Functions' which was 'both theoretically and practically momentous.'[63] Mental performances could be factorised to determine their saturation with *g* and the various forms of mental activity arranged into 'a stably inter-connected hierarchy' according to their different *g* loadings. The theory provided what Spearman later called 'a logical basis . . . for many of our social insitutions'.[64] In particular, it gave a rationale for the curricula of the public schools and the way men were selected to administer Britain's empire, for Spearman found that the highest *g* loading was in tests of classics. Here was a:

> long awaited rational basis for public examinations. Instead of continuing ineffectively to protest that high marks in Greek syntax are no test as to the capacity of

men to command troops or administer provinces, we shall at last actually determine the precise accuracy of the various means of measuring General Intelligence, and then we shall in an equally positive objective manner ascertain the exact relative importance of this General Intelligence as compared with the other characteristics desirable for the particular post which the candidate is to assume.[65]

In Spearman's view it was only his theory which gave scientific validity to the type of tests which Binet had devised for the identification of the intellecutally sub-normal in Parisian schools and published in 1905. (An age scale was added in 1908.) Binet had found that the most useful diagnostic tool was a heterogeneous collection of tasks and problems, graded according to age and teachers' independent assessments of an average child's performance. Thus at five a child would be expected to compare two weights, copy a square, count four coins and so on. A child successfully performing all the tests appropriate for that age, but no more, would be reckoned to have a mental age of five, and additions to the mental age would be made for correct answers to questions appropriate for a more advanced age and months deducted for incorrect answers below that age. Binet had arrived at his 'hotch-potch' of questions partly by trial and error but also as he developed a concept of intelligence as a shifting complex of interrelated functions. In Spearman's view, Binet had stumbled on a suitable method fortuitously. The very heterogeneity of the items in the Binet battery meant that the individual s's cancelled each other out so that *in toto* the battery was an adequate test of g. Spearman criticised Binet for the contradiction between his practical work with the tests and his reliance in his theoretical psychology upon a doctrine of formal faculties inconsistent with the practice.[66]

The functional identity of g with a sensory ability dependent on physical organs predisposed the view that it was largely determined by heredity. Such empirical evidence as there was for this in the early years of psychometrics came from a quite paltry piece of research by Burt.

In the concluding section to his first academic paper on 'Experimental Tests of General Intelligence' (mostly devoted to duplicating Spearman's work) he turned to the problem of how far 'the development of general intelligence' was predominantly determined by 'environmental influence and individual acquisition' or, alternatively, inheritance. Burt prefaced his discussion of this issue with the remarks:

> The gathering interest in 'the possible improvement of the human breed', the growing belief that the innate characters of the family are more potent in evolution than the acquired characters of the individual, the gradual apprehension that unsupplemented humanitarianism and philanthropy may be suspending the natural elimination of the unfit stocks – these features of contemporary sociology make the question whether ability [in the context this means intelligence] is inherited one of fundamental moment.[67]

His experimental subjects were thirteen children at an Oxford preparatory school – who were nearly all sons of dons, Fellows of the Royal Society and bishops – and thirty children at a Central school, whose fathers were small tradesmen and paid a school fee of 9d (3.75p) a week (a sufficient guarantee, Burt believed, that they were not environmentally deprived). A battery of tests ranging from simple sensory–motor to tests of higher mental processes, was given to each group, and correlated with independent estimates of intelligence. The average performances of the prep school boys were all superior to those of the central school boys with the exception of two tests of the lower senses which themselves did not correlate positively with intelligence. Hence 'we may conclude that the superior proficiency at Intelligence tests on the part of boys of superior intelligence parentage, was inborn. And thus we seem to have proved marked inheritability in the case of a mental character of the highest "civic worth" '.[68] The eugenic prescriptive linking preface and conclusion becomes even clearer when we realise that at both points Burt is quoting

Galton's lecture on the 'Possible Improvement of the Human Breed under the existing Condition of Law and Settlement', a lecture so well known by 1909 as to need acknowledgement only by the device of inverted commas. The tyro psychologist had arrived at a conception of intelligence which prescribed a task for the profession, for Burt went on in his paper: 'Parental intelligence . . . may be inherited, individual intelligence measured, and general intelligence analysed; and they can be measured, analysed, and inherited to a degree which few psychologists have hitherto legitimately ventured to maintain'. (Staggering conclusions to be drawn from the performance of forty three subjects on a few simple tests!)

The physiological interpretation which – fairly rapidly – Spearman postulated for the general factor was that it could be conceived of as the mental energy which suffused the whole cerebrum, especially the cortex, while the s's represented specific neurons brought into play during cognition. This concept of g as innate mental energy was supported by contemporary neuro-physiology.[69] But this physiological interpretation was linked to a deeply-rooted belief in an 'activist' mind. Spearman was opposed to all forms of sensationalism or mere associationism. He looked forward to the day when psychology would become 'less exclusively pre-occupied with sensations and epistemology, but turn rather to appreciating the mind or "soul" as the agent in conduct'.[70] In these more philosophical tasks, the general factor or common fund of intellective energy was 'bound to take a prominent place'.

Physiological explanations apart, there is some ambiguity in Spearman's writings as to whether g is a purely mathematical factor or whether it corresponds to truly psychological functions. There is reason to think that it was partly to settle this ambiguous status that he proposed his laws of noegenesis for 'No serviceable definition can possibly be found for general intelligence, until the entire psychology of cognition is established'.[71] These laws were the tendency to apprehend experience; the tendency, on the presentation of two items, to know relations between them; and the tendency, on the presentation of an item, together with a relation to conceive (or 'educe') the correlative item.[72] Spearman argued initially that the word intelligence must be taken to include all the processes derived from all three principles of noegenesis, but the first subsequently played little part in his discussion of the nature of intelligence. The second two corresponded closely to what were the more successful (that is g saturated items) in the early mental tests, such as Ebbinghaus's word completion test, tests for analogies and opposites and so on. Spearman looked on his scheme as providing not merely a logical taxonomy, but as 'the very basis of an effective study of function'.[73] His principles enabled psychology to fix a boundary between 'noegenetic or eductive activities' and those that were merely reproductive. Moreover, as he later wrote 'g findings do make a clean fit with the scheme of psychological laws. That which is measured by g seems to include all noegenesis, but to exclude all retentivity'.[74] Spearman made highly extravagant claims on behalf of noegenesis, arguing that there was no branch of human knowledge that could or should not be reconstructed on its principles:

> For every such reconstruction in however manifold spheres of science cannot but bring these into continually closer union, so that more and more each one of them will become quickened by the strength of all . . . all work, high or low, difficult or easy, admits of only one and always the same mode of ultimate reduction . . . as for the old question, how far mental tests can be made really to coincide with ordinary practical life, this question . . . is now answered automatically . . . . Faculties, life, tests, and world-views, so too practice and theory, nature and artifice, philosophy and commonsense, all, so to speak, dance fatally to one and the same psychological tune.[75]

Given that g was the keystone in a psychological edifice on which Spearman proposed to reconstitute much human knowledge, it is not surprising that he should have defended the theory tooth and nail. Spearman at first concluded that specific abilities were so manifold and various as to permit no significant interrelations between them, but the work of Burt and others forced him to concede the existence of group factors. The 'state of intelligence' now became a constitutional monarchy, with mighty subjects (group factors) under the rule of g whose benign reign still permitted some freedom to individual citizens (s's).[76] The criticisms of Godfrey Thomson threatened to dethrone g altogether; he showed that the hierarchy could occur by chance and there was nothing in the evidence to disprove the postulate that each test performance involved a sample from a large pool of abilities whose physiological equivalence was a 'neural bonding'.[77] Thomson's conception of intelligence had certain affinities with Binet's; although he rejected an atomised view of mind, he believed intelligence to be dynamic, fluid and multi-faceted, and he was as much concerned to identify special abilities as he was to establish a unitary function. Thomson accepted the plausibility of g but regarded it as an unnecessarily rigid convention.

The dispute between Spearman and Thomson was irresolvable. Both the g theory and the sampling theory were adequate mathematical accounts of the tendency of the hierachy of correlation matrices to have a rank of unity. The g theory demanded scrupulous selection of the items in a test battery and was therefore open to the criticism that correlations obtained in a test of g were biased by the content of the test itself. In his earlier writings on g, Spearman confidently assumed that correlation proved causation and similarly demonstrated his neurophysiological hypothesis. In a correspondence note on the Binet tests of 1914, for example, he wrote that they measure 'the constant factor, or general mental ability, or free energy of the whole cerebral cortex.'[78] Later, the picture of energy servicing individual motors of the mind became an analogy. When the existence of group factors was conceded the analogy itself became rather confused because of their elusive status between energy and engine. In his later, more mellow, writing Spearman agreed that the sampling theory was mathematically legitimate but argued that his theory was preferable because it was simpler and therefore more 'parsimonious of explanatory principles'.[79] He suggested that it was preferable for reasons analogous to those Copernicus and Kepler had for discarding the complex doctrine of planetary epicycles. Spearman's shifting grounds of defence are revealing of the scientific content of the theory. Originally put forward as a proof of general sensory discrimination/general intelligence, its final status was that of a more elegant mathematical convention.

In his pre-1914 writings there is evidence that part of attractiveness for Spearman of g lay in its accordance with his eugenist sympathies. As we have seen (above pp. 28–9) in his *Abilities of Man* of 1927 we have a plain statement of his desire to apply the measurement of intelligence in such a way as to select for the right to vote and even to have offspring, so it is clear that, if not a total eugenist (in the sense of accepting eugenics as the great scientific synthesis and a surrogate for politics) his sympathies were nonetheless deep and long-lived. His background as a former professional soldier may have particularly attuned him to the alarm over the military fitness of the nation's stocks. In 1914 he urged that the special usefulness of his g theory for eugenics lay in its giving the 'science' a firm basis for positive investigation into mental inheritance. By 1905, the most extensive investigations into inheritance had been carried out by Karl Pearson who had gathered thousands of correlation coefficients for height, weight and so on. He had also included mental estimates in his data (and thereby convinced himself that the mechanisms for physical and mental inheritance were identical). But these estimates were of such a loose and subjective nature as to render the conclusions as to mental inheritance ostentatiously valueless. Burt's first experiments in Oxfordshire were conceived partly to remedy this obvious defect. Spearman regarded the g theory as overcoming the weakness of the mental data by making possible, for the first time, 'meaningful and reliable mental measurement ... [for it admitted] not only in principle, but to a large extent in practice, of as definite measurement as the length of an arm or the circumference of a head'.[80] A testing programme using tests constructed on the g theory would yield the correlation data on which reliable statements about mental inheritance could be based. Spearman was not at this point presupposing that the general factor was largely transmitted by descent. However, his original conception of general intelligence as functionally equivalent to general sensory discrimination strongly biased him to the view that the measurement of g was the measurement of an innate quality, although he conceded the issue was not settled. William Brown had suggested that environmental conditions could influence performance on sensory tests; certain children might perform better because stricter home discipline made them more attentive.

The serviceability of g to applied hereditarian science was, almost simultaneously with Spearman's 1914 article, being argued by William McDougall, Burt's mentor at Oxford (where he held a part-time post) and Spearman's predecessor at University College, London. McDougall is now best remembered for his *Social Psychology* and theory of instincts, as well as for a racism which gained him notoriety even in America on his taking a chair there.[81] But his part in the early history of the testing movement was also significant. In the first years of the century when Galton, with the help of the Anthropological Section of the British Association for the Advancement of Science, started planning a second anthropometric survey to be carried out in schools and to include mental as well as physical characteristics, McDougall was made chairman of the psychological sub-committee. He immediately set a small group of Oxford psychology students to work on the construction and standardisation of psychological tests to measure various qualities of intellect and character. Experimental investigations in the laboratory were largely carried out by W. Brown, J. C. Flugel, H. B. English, May Smith and Cyril Burt. According to his own account, Burt was also selected to apply the tests in Oxford schools.[82] McDougall joined the Eugenics Education Society on its formation and was to the fore in formulating a 'positive' eugenics policy, namely in the form of higher salaries and family allowances for married professional men.[83] When it took institutional shape, the eugenics movement was most closely allied to the discipline of biology; McDougall urged that 'it must rely even more directly upon psychology . . . the applied science of eugenics should take pains to establish intimate relations with psychology . . . it should apply its results and adopt and adapt its methods of research for application to its own problems'.[84] In particular, McDougall argued, eugenics had to take cognisance of the field of differential or individual psychology mapped out in Stern's treatises, for eugenics required scientific knowledge of the heredity of mental qualities 'and this can only be obtained by the study of the peculiarities of endowment of related individuals . . . . It is to the application of the experimental methods in the form of mental tests that we must chiefly look for progress of our knowledge of mental heredity.' Should further research confirm the 'tentative conclusion' of the g theory then:

> we must regard it as one of the greatest importance for eugenics; for we should have discovered a measurable factor which is involved in, and is an important factor or condition of proficiency in, many mental operations; a factor which is possessed in very different degrees by different individuals.

McDougall suggested the devising of 'culture free' tests and their application to considerable numbers of individuals drawn from the different social strata to determine mean IQ in the major social groups. He also recommended applying mental tests to large numbers of near relatives, of the same and of different generations to 'determine how far such relatives show greater similarity of degrees of proficiency in various tasks than persons not related by blood'.

DECLINING NATIONAL INTELLIGENCE

McDougall wrote of 'psychology in the service of eugenics', suggesting that handmaiden relationship between subordinate disciplines and the great synthesis which was, more or less, the role ardent eugenists envisaged for the bio-, behaviourial and social sciences. Increasing specialisation, the growth of autonomous professional institutions and the identification of generic problems necessarily disrupted this relationship, for sociology and genetics, no less than for psychology. With respect to psychology, the First World War greatly encouraged a trend towards professional autonomy. The war imposed a hiatus on the development of theory, chiefly because leading psychologists were engaged in various forms of war-work, but offered an opportunity to experiment in, and validate applied psychology (most spectacularly in the group testing of one and three quarter million American Army draftees in 1917–18.) In Britain the war led directly to the institutionalisation of applied psychology (which is discussed in the next chapter). But in spite of disengagement from eugenics in this way, differential psychology retained a crucial problem from the eugenic heritage: the dysgenic consequences of demographic imbalance.

In the population question there were certain ideological reference points where eugenics, psychology and the rising science of demography could continue to meet: a concern for 'racial' balance and quality; a paranoid vision of cultural debility; and a hankering for a stable social order measured and controlled by professional expertise. Since it underlines the intellectual lineage between eugenics and mental testing, it seems logical to depart from chronology and discuss it here.

The eugenists' usual perception of the consequences of differential fertility was that the stocks congenitally endowed with the most 'civic worth' were making an inexorably decreasing contribution to the total population of the country. The political, economic and moral future was being mortgaged as the overall quality of the race deteriorated. An obvious difficulty in the argument was the amorphous and unquantifiable nature of 'civic worth'. It provided no basis for measuring the predicted deterioration. Intelligence was an ideal substitute: psychologists had established the objectivity and measurability of the term; by 1914 it was widely accepted that it was largely transmitted by descent; and it was obviously a quality of the highest 'civic worth'. Between the 1920s and the 1950s, the speculation that the mean level of national intelligence was declining was a recurrent theme of psychological literature.

For eugenists, the dysgenic consequences of differential fertility were exacerbated by upward social mobility. Social promotion of the more able from the lower classes was often combined with their adopting the deferred marriage and family limitation of the middle classes. Moreover, many eugenists saw greater competition for professional occupations as one result of upward mobility and, therefore, another reason for the middle-class retreat from parenthood. Although eugenists were on the whole committed to a social order based on innate individual worth, here was a source of considerable ambiguity towards the social liberalisation and selection from below which were prerequisites of such an order. Some of this ambiguity was to be echoed by psychologists who were otherwise engaged in creating educational opportunity for the socially disadvantaged. 'The educational system of the country' remarked Thomson in 1946, 'acts as a sieve to sift out the more intelligent and destroy their posterity.... It is a selection which ensures that their like shall not endure.'[85]

Before the First World War, much of the anxiety surrounding differential fertility trends had been couched in terms of highly speculative accounts of the causes of the decay of civilisations, particularly those of classical antiquity. Rome was commonly believed to have declined because of the low birth rate amongst her aristocracy. The war tended to increase the receptivity to this kind of speculation in certain quarters, partly because up to May 1916 Britain clung to voluntary military service which had the dysgenic effect of creaming off the most patriotic and the fittest of her future fathers and the death toll fell disproportionately on upper class junior officers. At the same time, speculation as to the cause of the decay of civilisations was, for obvious enough reasons, a European phenomenon, testified to by the success of Spengler's *The Decline of the West*. Dean Inge surveyed 'The Future of the English Race' in his 1919 Galton Lecture and foresaw 'the professional aristocracy', that special delight of the eugenist, being 'harassed out of existence, like the *curiales* of the later Roman Empire', by punitive taxation and warned that 'we are at present breeding a large parasitic class subsisting on the taxes and hampering the Government'.[86] Elsewhere, he pointed to the American Army testing results as evidence for the mental degeneration of the civilised countries.[87] Between the wars, the eugenic view on population trends expanded into a complex intellectual patchwork to which cultural distaste for liberal industrial society, 'hard' evidence from official and demographic surveys and predictions based on negative correlations between intelligence and family size all contributed. By the mid – 1930s this patchwork was by no means entirely the handiwork of the radical and romantic right. Pro-natalism was also taken up by social democratic intellectuals and proponents of state welfare, most notably Richard Titmuss and David Glass, both prominent in the Population Investigation Committee, an offshoot of the Eugenics Society. In exemplifying the main strands of the population controversy, we are necessarily ignoring much of its complexity.

Ronald Fisher's 1926 paper 'Eugenics: Can it solve the problem of the decay of civilisations?' illustrates the conservative strand which sought the causes of epochal historical change in the low fertility of the upper classes and it exposes the eugenists' ambiguous attitudes to social mobility. After a brief account of the collapse of Classical and Arab civilisation in natalist terms he then suggested that 'If we turn to our own civilisation in the hope of isolating a single cause which is capable, continually and persistently, of injuring the racial qualities of future generations, we are at once confronted with the phenomenon of the differential birth-rate . . .'.[88] In Fisher's view, intrinsic racial degeneration was being powerfully assisted by the social liberalisation and attenuation of the privileges of birth which had been accelerating since the nineteenth century. Social emancipation itself had been reinforced by that inequality in the birthrate which 'promotes an influx of persons of humble origin into influential positions.' The pernicious long-term results of the social mobility of liberal society were deduced from the argument that:

The dissolution of class barriers enables a society to draw upon ability whencesoever it may arise; it becomes a necessity for societies in which ability is becoming more and more rare. Nevertheless in plutocratic societies it completes the vicious circle, by maintaining that stream of infertile promotions by which the fertility of the upper classes is continually forced down . . . the fertility of the upper classes is only maintained at its own level by the selective promotion of the least fertile members of the lower classes.

That the threat to civilisation in the demographic trends was compounded by the above-average fertility of the mentally subnormal and defective was another strand in the population controversy. Small-scale enquiry – such as Burt's on behalf of the Birmingham Education Committee in 1921 – indicated alarming discrepancies between the returns for backwardness recorded by school teachers and the incidence discovered through psychological testing. Burt assessed the true relative amount of backwardness as five times greater in 'very poor' prolific neighbourhoods as compared with the 'very good' neighbourhoods.[89] The implication that the incidence of backwardness and mental defect was sharply increasing was confirmed by the Mental Deficiency Committee of 1929. It published the findings of Dr O. E. Lewis who ascertained a mean incidence of 8.56 mental defectives per 1000 population, almost twice as great as the 4.6 discovered by the Royal Commission on the Feeble-Minded of 1906–8.[90] Since Lewis made the first large-scale use of group-tests to discover *high-grade* defects, it seems unlikely that, in this respect, the 1929 figure was comparable with the earlier one, for then no psychological standard for the assessment of mental deficiency had been formulated; such intelligence tests as existed were not standardised and group tests (essential for the initial sorting of the high-grade defect from the merely dull) non-existent. Lewis himself believed that 'the greater thoroughness of the ascertainment accounts for a large, if not the greater part, of the increase'. But the approximate doubling of *low-grade* deficiency (that is imbecility and idiocy) had to be taken at its face-value, for it was inconceivable that the 1906 Commission had overlooked these cases in any considerable degree. The majority of mental defects were found to come from the subnormal group which formed the bottom 10 per cent of the population and whose fertility was above average. (The fecundity of mental defects *themselves* was, however, mythical; those with IQ below 70 had a fertility of one quarter the normal.)[91] A striking feature of the incidence of deficiency was its undue concentration in the countryside, from which it was deduced that nineteenth century rural emigration had drained away the more able stocks, leaving the less efficient to breed amongst themselves.

Though the growth in defectiveness was important, the critical evidence for fuelling the 'intelligence crisis' came from the frequently confirmed negative correlation between intelligence and family size. In their 1926 and 1929 papers, Thomson and H. E. G. Sutherland arrived at a negative correlation between intelligence at eleven and family size of −0.25, a value confirmed by other enquirers such as J. L. Gray and Pearl Moshinsky[92] (although Burt in *The Backward Child* arrived at the smaller figure of −0. 19). This negative correlation was quite distinct from the correlation between intelligence and occupational status for, from the testing of coalminers' children in the West Riding of Yorkshire, Thomson and Sutherland found that it held good even within a socially homogeneous group. Although environmental (including intra-uterine) factors could have explained this negative correlation, it was taken as support for the view that intelligence was largely determined by heredity. While the value was not large, extrapolation of the current fertility trends indicated a decline in mean intelligence of two Binet IQ points per generation. To the alarmists' question 'Can educational standards be maintained?' was added a prognosis of racial decline into intellectual mediocrity.[93] Two erroneous presumptions tended to sustain the controversy: firstly, that fertility rates were stable, although objective assessment of the trends would have suggested that all groups would limit family size given a certain minimum of affluence; secondly, that there was a near-perfect correspondence in intelligence between parental and filial generations.[94]

The growing number of social and demographic surveys, often on a regional basis, of inter-war Britain added another dimension to the pessimistic view of the future based on fertility. Probably the most significant was Carr-Saunders' and Caradog Jones' Merseyside Survey of 1935, for it systematically underlined a dysgenic relationship between high fertility and unskilled occupations (the unskilled manual worker was found to produce on the average a family of about five and a half children as compared with four for the skilled artisan and three for the non-manual worker), high fertility and irregularity of employment, destitution, dependence on state welfare and scholastic failure. 'So long as these conditions persist, the scales [of the population balance] become increasingly weighted in favour of the socially lower classes generation by generation.'[95]

With such results in mind, R. B. Cattell, the Leicester Area School Psychologist, set about establishing the trend in national intelligence from a 1 in 10 survey of IQ amongst eleven-year-olds in a rural and an urban district. His investigation was undertaken as a Research Fellow of the Eugenics Society and Cattell complained that it was:

> something in the nature of a scandal that an enquiry into what is a life and death matter for our national culture should have to be initiated by a private body of scientists, should depend on the unaided efforts of a single investigator and should be limited by a total expenditure of about £250.[96]

Both Fisher and Burt advised on statistical problems. Cattell's method was to group the testees of the infant generation by intelligence capacity, divide the number in any one group by the average family size of the group, multiply by two and, making allowance for the regression effect, thus arrive at a figure for the number of people at that intelligence level in the parental generation. After weighting the groups, the mean intelligence level of the

infant and parental generations could be arrived at, and –
assuming the persistence of current fertility trends – the
mean intelligence of future generations predicted. The
calculations also assumed, of course, that IQ measured at
eleven would be constant. Cattell's enquiry indicated that
there was, in round terms, a decline of average IQ for town
and country of about three points per generation, and:

> if this were to continue for three hundred years half the
> population would be mentally defective. Since the
> changes which mark the rises and declines of history are
> certainly not as drastic as to require wholesale mental
> deficiency, the present rate of change must be one of the
> most galloping plunges to bankruptcy that has ever
> occurred.[97]

Cattell's whole enquiry was coloured by the predictions of
cultural doom which had been the everyday fare of
eugenics writing and which have been exemplified in
Fisher's paper. Cattell warned:

> Under every system of civilisation yet known there has
> been an ineradicable tendency for the population to be
> recruited from the sub-men. If, generation after gener-
> ation, they have a birthrate above those of good average
> intelligence, and if the strains of high intelligence limit
> their breeding practically to the point of dying out, it does
> not require long in historical time for the quality of the
> breed to become entirely different. The unhappy country
> grows 'thin on top', loses first the fine lustre of its genius,
> then its moral culture and political stability and finally its
> arts, the material standards of living and 'civilisation'
> itself.[98]

A detailed, and quite horrendous picture of the future
consequences of the present trend in intelligence followed.
There would be an inexorable growth in delinquency
because of the connection, first established by Burt in *The
Young Delinquent*, between delinquency and low innate
intelligence. Morality and religion, Cattell reasoned, would

decay on the grounds that 'differences among religious and national groups in moral knowledge (determined by objective tests) seemed to be almost wholly a function of differences in level of intelligence.'[99] Cultural life would be diluted and vulgarised. Democratic government, responsive to intelligent public opinion would, Cattell warned, give way to 'less happy forms of authority if the landslide of intelligence continues.'[100] In an introduction, Leonard Darwin, President of the Eugenics Society, warned of the dangers of civil and external war. In spite of his claim to have adopted the 'starting point of the average socialist', Cattell's book is replete with crude social Darwinism, racism and admiration for fascist political practice. The Negro was casually written off as 'having contributed practically nothing to social progress and culture (except in rhythm) . . . even when the race is a constitutionally good-natured and lovable one, lower mental capacity means reaction, crudity and a social dead weight of conservatism.' Mussolini's imperialism in Africa won at least partial approval since 'by evolutionary morals the substitution of Italian culture for Abyssinian [was] good'. Domestic wage rates were taken to be 'symptoms of Nature's needs, i.e. of the present intelligence demands in the social organisation of the species *homo sapiens*'. Structural unemployment was biologically rooted in the 'malformation of the intellectual supply curve'. For some solutions to the dilemma of the intelligence trend, Cattell pointed to 'oligarchic Germany [where] the community boldly acts upon the wisdom of the biologist and the medical man and where eugenic laws are instantly put into operation'.[101]

Although the eugenic ideology dominated opinion on the population question, scientific advances and recoil from Nazi race policies ensured that saner voices would at least be heard in the debate. The Marxist geneticists, Lancelot Hogben and J. B. S Haldane, raised damaging criticisms of the fallacies about human heritability entangled in the 'catastrophic' view (although Haldane himself believed in the probability of a slow decline of perhaps one to two per cent per generation in the mean IQ of the country).[102] But, as Gray stressed in his thoroughly sober discussion of the 'intelligence crisis', it was political rather than scientific considerations which most markedly altered conceptions of the population question: 'The new persecution of the Jews in Germany has done more to shake the faith of English science in racialist nostrums than a generation of disinterested research.'[103]

The alarm over demographic imbalance was brought to a head with the establishment of the Royal Commission on Population in 1944 to which both Burt and Thomson submitted memoranda on intelligence and fertility. Burt argued that since 1930 the correlation between economic status and children's intelligence had, if anything, slightly increased and this had reinforced the tendency to a class segregation according to intelligence. He claimed to have direct, rather than inferred, evidence of the decline in intelligence in the recent past; 'between 1913 and 1939' he had 'endeavoured to assess the average level and variability of the London school population on three occasions ... [and] found an average rate of decline amounting to 0.87 points in 10 years, or about 1.3 points per generation'.[104] A characteristic vagueness of detail leaves one sceptical as to whether he had adequate data on which to base so positive a statement. For Burt, more important than the overall decline was the effect of the current trends on the tail ends of the distribution. Assuming an average decline of 1.5 IQ points per generation, he predicted that by the year 2000 the numbers of scholarship winners (that is children of IQ 130 and greater at eleven) would be approximately halved and the number of feeble-minded almost doubled. At this point in his career, Burt spent much of his energy defending the principles of elitist education and the tenor of his evidence to the Commission accorded with that task: national welfare was critically dependent on an elite whose innate ability had to be identified by testing and by being nourished in elite schools; this elite was threatened politically and, in a certain sense, biologically.

Thomson shared the view that average national intelligence was probably declining as a result of social selection of the able. Amongst contemporaries, Lionel Penrose was foremost in disputing this view. In a discussion following

Thomson's 1946 Galton Lecture, he suggested that the issue might be illuminated by considering the history of physique, especially mean height, in the twentieth century.[105] An individual's stature is clearly genetically determined, but optimum stature can only be achieved in a suitable environment. Stature, like intelligence, was found to be inversely correlated with size of sibship. Thus, the most populous families contained, on average, children of the smallest stature and, on the mental testers' assumptions, mean national stature should have been declining. As was well known, the true case was quite the contrary. Mean stature had improved with the amelioration of the working-class child's environment. Since physique and intelligence were positively correlated there may have been an accompanying improvement in mean intelligence. (Later, Penrose was to argue that the determination of IQ largely by heredity was reconcilable with both the negative association between family and intelligence and a permanent level of average intelligence, showing no decline. The argument supposed a genetic population in which the relative infertility of those of superior intelligence was compensated for by the sterility of the mentally defective.)[106]

Thomson in his lecture called for empirical investigation of the problem and this was duly undertaken under his direction by the Scottish Council for Research in Education. In 1933 the Council had published the results of the hitherto largest group intelligence test administered in Britain when scores were obtained from nearly 90 per cent of eleven year-olds, while a smaller sample was individually tested. This survey was itself partly a response to the 'generalisations of an alarmist nature [which had] frequently been made regarding the increase of mental deficiency in the population as a whole'.[107] In 1947, the Council repeated the survey specifically to confirm or refute the inferences of Cattell's and others' indirect predictions. It found not only no fall in the average score on the self-same test but an increase – quite a substantial increase from about 34.4 to about 36.7 points in a test with a maximum of 76 points.[108] Even convinced environmentalists must have feared a fall, and logically so, since most of the 1947 cohort would have had their education disrupted by teacher shortage, evacuation and so on. 'Undoubtedly' Thomson wrote 'this strengthens the environmental side of the argument' unless it could be adduced to 'test sophistication' acquired through greater prominence of the test-type situation in schools, children's culture and on the radio in the intervening fifteen years. (In 1932, children were very rarely exposed to tests in Scottish schools and a control comparison with Halifax children, familiar with tests because they figured in the English eleven plus exam, suggested that 'test sophistication' could result in an apparent difference of 3 points in IQ.) 'Test sophistication' was a useful saving clause for hard-core hereditarians: they could postulate that a 'real' fall in mean IQ had taken place and that this was temporarily masked by environmental improvement. An additional saving clause was already suggested in Burt's evidence to the Royal Commission: the average might be rising but the size of the socially essential elite was falling. In 1949, Cattell put his own thirteen-year-old prediction to the test and found a significant increase in average measured intelligence of 1.28 IQ points. However, amongst children with IQ above 130 the decline in intelligence had occurred at about the predicted rate and the overall gain was produced by a shift to higher test scores among those of average and below average intelligence.[109]

The Scottish mental survey did not pronounce a quietus over the issue of declining national intelligence; the question lingered on into the 1950s, though the topic became increasingly barren. Despite the sterility of the controversy, it is – ostensibly at least – of interest from the point of view of the critique of the scientific rationality of psychometric history. A group of scientists had, as it were, made themselves hostage to Popper's famous demarcation criterion: they had specified a test of certain hypotheses which, if failed, they should either have abandoned or radically revised. Admittedly even the 'hard' physical sciences scarcely work like that; rather they bury anomalies and 'failed' investigations in the obscurity of academic journals.[110] Notwithstanding, that things did not happen as the

Popperian conception of critical tests suggest they should is at least some further indication that the testable scientific issues were not the heart of the matter: 'declining national intelligence' provided a focus for a bundle of political and social anxieties whose roots lay in the changing pattern of social promotion and class privilege. Less directly, it contributed towards a surrogate explanation for national economic and political decline. By the late 1940s the demographic context of the controversy had altered considerably. The cultural pessimism of earlier decades had been overtaken by an immediate horror in which eugenic and racist nostrums were tainted by association. 'Declining national intelligence' was an intellectual and moral panic peculiarly of its time.

3

Mental Testing and Society – II: Individual Psychology, Industry and Education

PSYCHOLOGY, INDUSTRY AND VOCATIONAL SELECTION

Earlier, it was suggested that the psychometric movement can be seen as responding to an interrelated group of problems concerning race and empire, industry and human efficiency. Before 1914, British psychometrics had scarcely touched the second part of this problematic, although on the eve of the First World War Münsterberg's classic text *Psychology and Industrial Efficiency* became available. The war proved decisive in the development of applied psychology, because of both the immediate needs of the 'warfare' state and the longer-term effects of the war on capitalism. In all the belligerent countries, the war brought into being a powerful industrial-military complex charged with expediting production, most commonly by the use of machine-tool technology and 'flow' techniques, and securing the maximum efficiency of labour. In Britain, this complex was centred on the war-time Ministry of Munitions whose officers spread the gospel of scientific management, recruited scientific, professional and business expertise to the service of the state and enforced the 'dilution' of labour (that is the more frugal use of skill in production). Under the auspices of a welfare agency of the Ministry, the Health of Munition Workers Committee, and, later, the Industrial Fatigue Research Board, psychologists were employed to study the relationship between hours and output, analyse the causes of labour turnover and undertake time and motion study. Psychological testing was stimulated by the Ministry of Munitions and other government departments (most notably the Admiralty) setting psychologists to work devising selection tests for special tasks, such as hydrophone work and piloting aircraft. Charles Myers, head of the Cambridge Psychological Laboratory and editor of the *British Journal of Psychology* was the most prominent of the psychologists engaged in this way and he was later to write: 'The more scientific development of vocational selection was greatly favoured by the recent war.'[1] Originally trained in medicine, he set industrial psychology the tasks of disowning its kinship with Taylor's mechanistic notions of scientific management and adopting the diagnostic perspective of the doctor attending the human needs and neuroses of industry. Though we should not doubt his forceful, and often repeated, repudiation of Taylorism's labour-degrading methods, the objective of industrial psychology was much the same: the maximisation of profitability. A close colleague later wrote: 'the human sciences of psychology and physiology have now entered the industrial field to ensure that the physical and mental energies of man are used to the best economic effect.'[2]

In a slightly longer-term, and wider perspective, the war can be seen as having given a marked impetus to social rationalisation, in Weber's sense, in Britain. It led to a closer relationship between science, industry and government, encouraged the growth of industries dependent on advanced technology and promoted vertical and horizontal integration in industry and finance. Many of the features of the modern corporate economy took shape during the war. A cluster of managerial professions, such as cost accountancy and actuarialism, found their services increasingly called upon by industry and government while industrial and vocational psychology were born in its aftermath. From these were later to develop personnel management and consumer psychology.

A diagnostic and therapeutic posture was felt essential for industrial psychology, not solely because of the ingrained hostility of organised labour to 'speed-up' and the further erosion of craft status, but also to a greater sensitivity to the effects of nervous debility on labour efficiency and a widespread misapprehension that industrial unrest had socio-psychological causes.[3] Seen from this angle, industrial psychology was partly a response to industrial militancy created by the dislocation of normal collective bargaining, the rise of rank-and-file movements attempting to encroach on managerial control and the impact of inflation on earnings and wage differentials. It was, of course, a modest response, favoured by the more enlightened employers. Its institutional origins can be traced back to October 1918 when H. J. Welch, a director of Harrisons and Crosfield, approached Myers with a view to initiating some scheme whereby the results of physiological and psychological research might be used for vocational selection and guidance, and for the improvement of human conditions generally in commercial and industrial life.[4] Welch was apparently moved to do so by two lectures which Myers had earlier given to the Royal Institution on 'Present Day Applications of Psychology'. This initiative led eventually to the founding of the National Institute of Industrial Psychology, a body which was to be an important source of group intelligence tests for schools in inter-war Britain, of selection tests (which included intelligence tests) for industry, commerce and government, and of scientific vocational guidance for school leavers. Although its relations with the Board of Education and the Ministry of Labour were often uneasy during the inter-war years, the Institute was also important as a source of psychological dogmatism on which quasi-official bodies (such as the Spens Committee) drew.

The meeting between Myers and Welch resulted in the creation of an organising committee of former members of the Industrial Fatigue Research Board (Myers was himself a Board member) and interested industrialists, and the committee's initial expenses were chiefly met by the Bradford Dyers' Association. Burt and Eric Farmer, who had both undertaken Ministry of Munitions' work in the war, were committee members. Promises of financial support for the proposed Institute were obtained from Cadbury Brothers, Rowntrees, Tootal Broadhurst Lee and other firms (most of them with strong links with schemes for labour co-partnership, financial support for social enquiry and so on). Through the good offices of W. L. Hichens, the Chairman of Cammell Laird, the claims of the proposed Institute were advanced to the Carnegie UK Trust and its financial viability secured by a yearly grant of £1000. From its beginnings, the Institute was to place considerable emphasis on maintaining good relations with organised labour and, in February 1919, its objectives were discussed with representative trade union leaders at Fabian Hall. But Myers' most significant achievement in these early days was to gather together a representative scientific committee which included most of the distinguished names in British psychology at that time. Professors Collis, Nunn, Pear, Spearman, Thomson and Valentine, and Doctors Drever and Burt were present at its first meeting. Between July 1922 and July 1924, Burt had a part-time post in charge of the Institute's vocational guidance section, and maintained a connection with the NIIP until 1931.

The vigorous expansion of applied psychology in Britain in the 1920s – of which the activities of the NIIP formed a major part – contrasts strongly with the stasis in experimental psychology. Myers, described in an obituary notice as 'the businessman's psychologist,'[5] was distrustful of theory, including the g theory, and his wholly utilitarian conception of psychology had an important influence on the development of the discipline in universities and colleges in the 1920s and helped shape its impact on education. The NIIP was recognised as a teaching institution by London University and certain local education authorities. Its staff taught on the Academic Diploma course in (Industrial) Psychology at London University and teachers and training college students were instructed in test administration, among other things, at the Institute.[6] One of its officers, E. P. Allen Hunt, was seconded to Birmingham Education Committee and established a training course for teachers wishing to gain a certificate in the

theory and technique of test administration.[7] Together
with the City's Vocational Guidance Officer he undertook
long-term studies of the validity of scientific vocational
guidance, in which the employment histories of groups of
children 'scientifically' advised on the choice of career after
being subject to a battery of the Institute's tests were
compared with those of control groups.[8] The more important of the experiments, whose subjects were given the
NIIP's Group Intelligence Test No. 34 and a number of
'performance' tests of intelligence and special abilities,
appeared to confirm the superiority of scientific over more
conventional guidance. Adolescents taking up 'accordance'
posts were more stable in them, happier and gave their
employers greater satisfaction. But an experimental study
of the prognostic value of objective tests for the selection
of skilled apprentices in the engineering trade, eventually
cast some doubts on the inclusion of a linguistic intelligence
test (Group Test 33) in the battery (largely consisting of
'performance' intelligence, spatial comprehension and
sensori-motor co-ordination tests). Excluding the linguistic
intelligence test improved the battery's prognostic value.
This, and similar results, reinforced Myer's belief that there
was a 'concrete' intelligence distinct from 'verbal' intelligence.

Sceptics of the major enquiry pointed out that it was of
the nature of a self-fulfilling prophecy: special efforts were,
in effect, made to place adolescents in 'accordance' posts
and a corresponding effort was not made with the control
group. For enthusiasts, the results confirmed that the
psychological tests provided 'a rational bridge between
school and industry'.[9] Although objective testing was not
the sole difference between scientific and conventional
vocational guidance, it was by far the most important, and
Myers' main strategy for 'spreading his gospel' lay in the
training of teachers and juvenile employment officers in
testing technique. Just how successful this strategy was is
difficult to assess. Just as important as the numbers who
brought the testing movement into the classroom was the
fact that psychometrics was inscribed on the social consciousness through the vocational guidance movement.

Myers and others used the radio[10] to popularise the topic while psychological testing for vocational guidance was quite extensively discussed in both the popular and specialist press, as well as at meetings of local Juvenile Employment Committees.

Burt's active engagement in vocational selection and guidance and his commitment to business rationalisation were part of the practice of the theory of intelligence of which he was becoming the most fluent exponent. In the early 1920s, some of his most trenchant statements on the nature and distribution of intelligence and the proper function of differential psychology were made while elaborating the principles of vocational guidance. It can be argued that, at this time, he considered the threshold of employment, rather than the educational system, the point where intelligence testing would achieve its optimum social validation. In brute numerical terms, the greatest impact of group intelligence tests in the early 1920s was made in the field of vocational selection as a result of the Civil Service Commission's adoption of an intelligence test for candidates for clerical posts. By 1923, some 30 000 had been selected in this way.[11] Furthermore, Burt and his fellow evangelists in the NIIP saw the intelligence test as only one (though the most important) of the instruments of a testing society. They devised aptitude tests for typists, shorthand writers, dressmakers, milliners, engineering apprentices and other grades of labour. In the later 1920s, the NIIP adopted American tests, and constructed its own, non-verbal or 'performance' tests of intelligence, largely to assist selection procedures for that expanding sector of employment requiring types of skill not reproduced by traditional and archaic apprenticeship. Burt's commitment to scientific vocational selection and guidance derived from the Galtonian notion that the supposedly normal distribution of innate intelligence was replicated in its distribution in the occupational hierarchy, was, indeed, a cause of that hierarchy. The duty of scientific guidance and selection was to match innate ability with its appropriate occupation. Burt developed this view in a paper on 'The Principles of Vocational Guidance' given to the Seventh International

Congress of Psychology held under Myers' Presidency in Oxford in July 1923 and in an address to the Psychological Section of BAAS in the same year. (It is an indication of the dominance of applied over experimental psychology in Britain that Boring, at the Congress, found it 'easier to find a British psychologist from a coal mine than from a psychological laboratory.')[12] Both are worth extensive citation, for they display with great frankness the social teleology of psychometrics, their conclusions were soon incorporated into the teaching literature and they are clear prototypes for the better-known paper on 'Ability and Income' of 1943.

'Of all pyschological capacities,' Burt began

> general intelligence is the easiest to measure; it is also the most significant for the purposes of vocational guidance .... A certain degree of general intelligence ... differing in different instances, is needful – and in theory assignable – to the ability to adapt oneself quickly to new tasks and situations. Hence, for any trade which does not demand mere repetition of routine movements, or the mere reiterated application of knowledge and skill already acquired, general intelligence must be fundamental. In view, therefore, of the present difficulties of measuring other mental qualities, I am inclined to suggest that for the time being the chief (though not the sole) provisional guide in making vocational recommendations should be the degree of the candidate's intelligence.... As a principle of guidance ... a candidate should always be recommended to aim at the highest form of employment of which his intelligence is capable, as a principle of selection out of a given batch of candidates the most intelligent will always give the most satisfaction .... It is probable that for most occupations there is an optimal range of intelligence with an upper limit as well as a lower.[13]

Burt then went on to claim that material gathered in his capacity of LCC School Psychologist enabled him to divide the whole population, according to their intelligence, into eight sections or grades:

Grade 1 mental ratios 150 + ... 'rarely found in elementary schools; almost entirely confined to families from higher social and professional classes'.
Grade 2 130–150 '1 to 2% of the elementary school population'.
Grade 3 115–130 'usually drafted in London to "central" schools'.
Grade 4 100–115 '38% of the total'.
Grade 5 85–100 '40% of the total'.
Grade 6 70–85 '10% of the total'.
Grade 7 50–70 1%.
Grade 8 imbeciles.

'Is it possible' Burt then asked 'to arrange the occupations of adults, by strata, as it were, in any corresponding series?' From the data collected by the US Army, the Civil Service and the NIIP, Burt claimed it was. He then went on to describe an eight-fold occupational classification, with each class grouped about an average mental ratio. At the top of the hierarchy was a group conforming suspiciously closely to Burt's own: Class 1. 'These are ... for the most part highly educated, and either following the higher professional careers (University lecturers, lawyers, medical men), or holding the higher administrative posts either in business or the service of the State. They have a mental ratio of over 150 ... averaging about 165.' Burt then progressed inexorably down the occupational scale, making his eighth class 'defective adults certified for institutional care'. Just above them was 'casual labour of the poorer types, the lowest class of domestic service and of rural labour [who] show an intelligence little if at all above that of the high-grade feeble-minded child, and have a mental ratio which is often below 70'. The origins of this classification lay in Booth's epoch-making London survey which when corrected by the latest census figures gave the following proportions amongst the total population:

Vocational category	Mental ratio	% of total population
1. Higher professional	150+	0.1
2. Lower professional	130–150	3.0
3. Clerks and highly skilled workers	115–130	12.0
4. Skilled workers; most commercial positions	100–115	27.0
5. Semi-skilled labour; poorest commercial	85–100	36.0
6. Unskilled labour	70–85	19.0
7. Casual labour	50–70	3.0
8. Imbeciles, idiots	–50	0.2

Burt put forward the parallel between occupational and mental classification, not 'as a scientific deduction from a concrete survey' (although subsequent papers were to purport to do that) but as a 'rough and concrete illustration'. (In a psychology textbook for teachers they appear as facts.)[14] He conceded that 'vocational categories overlap enormously; nor is there sufficient data yet available to define with any exactitude the limits of each class'. But he stressed that the 'proportions of the vocational categories show a fair correspondence with those of the different intellectual categories among the school children. But the distribution is less symmetrical. The percentages in the lower groups are too large, and those in the higher groups, too small, for a perfect correspondence.' The function of scientific vocational guidance and selection, and indeed of social mobility generally, could be said to be ironing out those asymmetries. Bearing this in mind enables us to grasp the unity of Burt's academic and practical preoccupations. The search for the causes of juvenile delinquency, the identification of the vocational 'misfit', the use of psychological tests for streaming in elementary schools and selection for secondary education were all based on 'the positive foundations [of] a practical psychology of individual differences'.[15] The three basic tenets of this psychology were the distinctions between intellectual and emotional characteristics, between inborn and acquired mental tendencies and between special and general capacities. Burt could not deny the theoretical question marks hanging over the g theory,[16] but the notion was 'of the greatest value in practice'.[17] From it could be derived

> a simple aim alike for educational administration and for vocational guidance. It is the duty of the community, first, to ascertain what is the mental level of each individual child; then to give him the education most appropriate to his level; and lastly, before it leaves him, to guide him into the career for which his measure of intelligence has marked him out.[18]

INDIVIDUAL PSYCHOLOGY AND EDUCATION

Let us now consider the impact of psychological testing on the British public education systems. At first sight, this might appear a relatively easy task, since the most public face of IQ has been that presented to millions of children who have sat a group intelligence test as part of the examination for a secondary (or grammar) school place. Furthermore, the fiercest public debates about the merits, and validity (both terms are for the moment ambiguous) of intelligence testing have arisen in the context of a wider controversy over selection in education. In fact, the 'publicity' is deceptive. Tracing the growing influence of psychometric theory on the public policy statements of the Consultative Committee of the Board of Education during the inter-war years (and the loosening of that influence on analogous bodies in the 1960s) is relatively simple, as is noting the major additions to the research evidence which under-pinned that theory. But it is false to presume that policy statements determined practice in the schools – often they merely recorded its changes – and our frequent ignorance about that practice must be frankly acknowledged. Local education authorities enjoy considerable autonomy in selection procedures and they have been absurdly secretive about the methods used.[19] Though the main outlines of

English and Welsh practice from the late 1940s to the 1960s are clear, there was a great deal of variety between authorities which is still obscure. The quite distinctive Scottish education system, where historically there has been no sharp line of division between primary and secondary education, no Special Place examination, and where a large number of children attended multilateral type schools, has meant that intelligence testing for 'promotion' has been less widespread there, and where it has taken place less decisive in the individual child's education. In the late 1930s about ten out of the thirty five Scottish authorities made some use of intelligence tests in their promotion schemes.[20] By 1939, a majority of the larger English authorities were making regular use of IQ testing for selection[21] (ironically most were using a Moray House, Edinburgh, test!). The autonomy of English authorities from their political masters, and their secretiveness, is underscored by the ignorance of a Board of Education official who in 1943 noted:

> As regards . . . the development of intelligence and other tests for children at the age of 11 to 'select' . . . my own feeling is that too little is known about the value and working of intelligence tests to make it likely that they will be generally adopted at the present time. I doubt whether, except in individual areas, there is much likelihood of courses being required for teachers in the use of these tests.[22]

Even if 'grossing out' the growth of routinè testing in education were easier than it is, critics of the practice would rightly insist that this would give a quite inadequate account of its impact. We need to gauge its influence on the organisation and curriculum of the primary school and its ideological function in validating and sustaining a selective secondary school system. On the other hand, many would object that to emphasise the latter is to over-politicise IQ: they would argue that the tests appeared in the selection methods long after the principles and outline of a selective secondary system had been established, that the tests were less discriminatory against the working-class child than conventional tests of attainment and that if children had to be selected, then the typical battery of objective tests in English, arithmetic and verbal intelligence was the best means to do it. For evidence of the essential political neutrality of IQ testing they could point to its use by Gray and Moshinsky, and Douglas to expose educational inequalities that arose from working-class environmental deprivation[23] and to the commitment of the principal tester, Godfrey Thomson, to the democratisation of secondary education. In the 1950s and 1960s, certain individuals – such as D. A. Pidgeon of the National Foundation of Educational Research – both defended the objectivity and prognostic value of the eleven plus examination and advocated comprehensive education. In principle, the issues were separable.[24] Obviously, analysing the impact of psychological testing on public education is only apparently easy.

The publication in 1911 of the last of Binet's revised mental age scales excited worldwide interest and in Britain led to their translation by Cyril Burt. Consistent with their original purpose, the first widespread use of the new tests was for the identification of mentally sub-normal, but still educable children, as opposed to the merely educationally backward.[25] The problem of identifying the sub-normal was by no means a new one; it dated back at least to the 1890s when special schools and classes for the mentally defective had been established, initially by the London School Board, and then by other authorities. Difficulty lay first in defining a norm between non-educable imbeciles and the simply dull or backward and secondly in devising the diagnostic tools to select the group. The establishment of the School Medical Service in 1907 (it did not become comprehensive for a number of years) may have introduced briefly the diagnosis of sub-normality by cranial and facial 'stigmata', a technique derived from the Lombroso school of criminology. Certainly, Burt was wont to claim that this method was extensively employed before the adoption of the London Revision of the Binet–Simon scale[26] (although this may be yet another instance of self-esteem distorting the historical record). The value of the Binet–Simon tests for the medical examination of children for mental defect was impressed on school doctors by the Chief Medical Officer of the Board in his Annual Reports for 1911 and 1912, where the principles of test construction and mental age calculation were set out. He specifically did *not* recommend their routine use:

> in the ordinary school as the means of primary selection and diagnosis. The teacher should select all retarded and backward children and the school doctor should determine by careful examination which children need subsequent examination by the Binet tests ... these apparently simple tests should not be applied by anyone not fully understanding how to use them ... [27]

More pressing legislative obligations on local authorities to identify and make provision for the mentally sub-normal presumably encouraged greater use of the tests (although still within the CMO's guidelines) and helped familiarise educational administrators and school doctors with the principles of psychometrics. Before the publicity given to Binet's work, for example, the common belief was that defectiveness could be categorised into distinct types; acquaintance with his research spread the notion of a gradient of ability from which only the brain-damaged were excluded. By convention, an IQ of below 70 became the measure by which children were selected for segregation in special schools or classes, but any doctor administering the Binet tests in the spirit intended by their author (and reiterated by the CMO) would have treated this convention flexibly. The problem of identifying sub-normality was clearly not one which allowed psychometrics great scope in educational administration and growth. Although in the 1920s psychologists (prone to believe in the over-fecundity of the sub-normal) recommended greater segregation and the Mental Deficiency Committee favoured an extended school life within special classes in the ordinary school, neither had any serious impact on an educational system starved of finance.

The routine use of intelligence tests for the normal does not appear to have been extensive before 1930, but then spread rapidly in conjunction with other standardised tests. E. P. Allen Hunt and P. Smith, both employees of the second largest educational authority with special responsibilities for introducing psychological tests (and therefore in a position to know) wrote in 1935 that:

> Intelligence tests are now accepted as such an integral part of school organization that it is difficult to realise that 15 years ago such tests were rarely met with in ordinary school work, and it is only during the past five years or so that they have been used to any appreciable extent. The rapid growth of this type of examination has perhaps been one of the greatest dangers. Intelligence tests are not, however, the only psychological tests in which teachers are interested, and tests of attainment and special abilities are commanding their attention to an increasing extent.[28]

A mix of objective tests of educational attainment and intelligence was becoming the normal pattern of the free place (or after 1931, special place) examination by which a scholarship could be won to the fee-charging grammar schools (the change of name signified the means testing of the scholarship). Not, however, until 1936 did the Board's special place regulations specifically recommend this mix.[29]

While Hunt and Smith mentioned educational selection at eleven as one cause of more extensive intelligence testing, they placed as much emphasis on the growth of educational guidance (streaming) in both the junior and senior classes of the elementary schools. (At that time, the public elementary schools usually catered for children from five to fourteen and many of the rural ones did so in two classes: boys and girls. In the large towns and cities provision of special centres for older elementary school children became more common from the late 1920s.)

Following the recommendations of the Hadow Report of 1926 on the Education of the Adolescent, the elementary schools slowly began to reorganise to allow for a definite break in school life at eleven. The Report envisaged a wide-range of post-primary schools – junior technical,

selective and non-selective 'modern' schools – in addition to
the traditional grammar school. Allocation to these would
itself necessitate estimating a child's ability and, in borderline cases, the Report suggested psychological tests might be
employed. More important, the move towards a general
identification of children's abilities at eleven encouraged
classification in the junior forms although Hadow made no
explicit recommendation about streaming.[30] The 1931
Report on the Primary School hastened the trend. Rather
optimistically, it hoped that extended provision of the
different types of post-primary education envisaged by
Hadow would lessen the incidence of an educationally
distorting competitive selection at eleven and it deprecated
the falsification and distortion of 'the conception of the
primary school and its curriculum . . . by any form of school
test whether external or internal'.[31] Nonetheless, classification by some method was recognised as inevitable if full
advantage was to be taken of the break at eleven and,
according to Hunt and Smith, 'guiding into different
streams has been one of the main causes for the rapid
increase in the use of tests of "general intelligence" in the
elementary schools'.[32]

The ideal map of educational segregation, based on the
psychometric cartography, was:

IQ	Educational category	% of the population
< 50	Ineducable idiots; occupation centres	0.2
50–70	Mentally defective; special schools	2.0
70–85	Dull and backward; 'C' classes in senior schools	10.0
85–115	Normal pupils; 'B' and 'A' classes in senior schools	76.0
115–130	Bright pupils; selective central schools	10.0
130–150	Scholarship pupils; secondary schools	2.0
150 +	Scholarship pupils; secondary schools ultimately university honours	0.2

Why the routine intelligence testing of normal children was
not more common before 1930 is itself an interesting

question. The map had, after all, been there for some years. Immediately after the First World War, it appeared to many psychologists that the way was open for their profession to exert an influence on education both more practical and immediate than its traditional place in pedagogical theory. Percy Nunn, then an educational theorist of repute, addressed the Educational Section of the British Psychological Society in April 1919 and spoke 'of the immense increase in prestige which has accrued to our studies during the war. The psychologists have been mobilised side by side with their fellow men of science...'[33] He noted that educational thought had already responded to the discrediting of the faculty doctrine and he hoped it would learn from Freud's and McDougall's theories. Of more direct import, however, was Spearman's work: 'My faith in the essential soundness of Spearman's doctrine of the central intellective factor is confirmed by the growing evidence of the practical efficiency of "intelligence tests"; for it seems difficult to explain this efficiency on any other basis.' The biggest body of evidence came from the American Army programme and with this example 'the use of such tests as a means of grading County Council scholars and other entrants to Secondary Schools has received a very great impetus...' although he warned that 'if this outburst of faith in psychology is not cautiously and capably guided, it may end in disillusion...'

Not only had the war put group testing on the map, it had also greatly encouraged the demand for secondary school places, and put a corresponding pressure on the scholarship system by which able children were selected from the public elementary schools. This system dated from the Board's 1907 Regulations for Secondary Schools which made it a condition of grant (that is financial aid) that 25 per cent of the pupils admitted to secondary schools should be admitted from the elementary schools without payment of fees. As originally conceived, the free place regulations were not framed with the intention of instituting a scholarship system for the intellectual elite of the elementary schools, but – despite the Board's protests – they did just that. The demand for free places was such that tests of admission were almost invariably more stringent than those placed on middle-class fee payers from the preparatory schools. Moreover, with the very marked improvement in the hygiene and social tone of the elementary schools which began around 1910, this demand no longer came solely from the working-class child. The 1907 Regulations assumed that attendance at a public elementary school was in itself sufficient indication of inability to afford secondary school fees, but the greater attractiveness of the public elementary schools encouraged middle-class parents to send their children there until the age of eleven when they were entered for the free place examination and if unsuccessful were still sent to the secondary school as fee-payers.[34] The increased demand for secondary school places can be gauged from the fact that, in 1908–9 in England, there were a total of 135 800 pupils at 804 secondary schools; by 1914–15, this had risen to 180 500 at 929 and by 1919–20 to 282 000 at 1 002.[35] Unfulfilled demand, measured by the numbers who passed a local authority qualifying examination, but failed to obtain a secondary school place was, in the immediate post-war years, considerable. Methods of selection for free places varied both between local authorities and individual schools. Some authorities established a common entrance exam – usually conventional tests of attainment in English and arithmetic and an essay – and entered all children at eleven. Secondary schools were then obliged to award free places to successful candidates. But other authorities left nomination for the examination to the elementary school headmaster or the parents, while elsewhere certain secondary schools ran their own examination and included a headmaster's interview which was sometimes frankly discriminatory against the working-class.[36]

This confusion, and the regional and social inequalities it involved, clearly offered an opportunity for group intelligence testing to play some part in the free place examination. It would be more meritocratic, less arbitrary and cheaper. When the Departmental Committee on Scholarships and Free Places reported in 1920, it suggested the consideration of 'psychological [that is, IQ] tests' be given when auxiliary methods were being sought for the selection process although it stressed the experimental status of testing.[37] A year earlier, Bradford, one of the most progressive education authorities in England (and at the time the only one under Labour control) had introduced a group test into its free place examination. According to Burt's account the test adopted was one first used in 1911 for his research in Liverpool.[38] In 1921, Godfrey Thomson devised a set of group tests at the request of the Northumberland Education Authority to be used in its scholarship examination. Here, the tests served to even out some of the educational disadvantage that arose from the geography of the region. Many of the smaller and isolated rural schools presented no candidates for the traditional form of scholarship examination and it was presumed that overcrowded classes and the cultural deprivation of rural life handicapped them, particularly with respect to essay writing and tests of English. When tested for intelligence, the incidence of children of scholarship ability (coming to be thought of as IQ 130) was just as great in the remote areas as it was in the cities, although in country areas contiguous to the towns the incidence was only half (suggestive evidence, Thomson believed, for the 'draining-away-of-talent' hypothesis).[39] The successful secondary school careers of children selected by this means persuaded the authority to use the tests in a routine fashion.

Contemporaneously with these developments, the Consultative Committee of the Board of Education had been considering the 'possible use of psychological tests of educable capacity in the public system of education' and it reported in 1924. In spite of an historical and theoretical chapter written entirely by Burt and his obvious influence on other sections of the report as well as the co-option of Ballard, Spearman and Myers to a special sub-committee it was by no means an unambiguous endorsement of psychological testing for educational selection. The Report spelt out the claims of intelligence testing: that it 'afforded a more objective, more systematic and more trustworthy means of discovering the existence of inborn intelligence and educable capacity in pupils than the ordinary . . . exams', that IQ was tolerably constant and adult levels could be predicted, and that it would 'neutralise to a very considerable extent the effects of bad teaching and unfavourable surroundings'.[40] Without seriously contesting these claims, it recommended only that the value of intelligence tests to the free place examination 'should be investigated by tentatively adding group tests to the customary written examinations'. The Report argued that the case for the general use of intelligence tests as adjuncts to the free place examination would be correspondingly weakened if the existing written and oral examinations were reconstructed 'on sound psychological lines'[41] (which presumably meant the use of standardised tests of attainment) and this was obviously a solution it preferred. With respect to the use of intelligence tests within the elementary schools, it argued that, if 'applied by adequately trained teachers and inspectors' they would chiefly assist in classifying pupils at entry and the transference of pupils to classes or schools of different types. The Report suggested the appointment (where possible) of educational psychologists to local authorities and the organisation of short courses in educational psychology for teachers with special reference to the theory and application of group intelligence testing.

The Report's rather lukewarm recommendations were clearly disheartening to the more vocal advocates of intelligence testing[42] and the absence of more positive guidance from the centre may have been one reason for the only modest spread of intelligence testing of the normal child in education before 1930. (In the Board's 1928 pamphlet on free place examinations, for example, the use of intelligence tests received little support.) Another, and much more important stumbling block, was the reluctance of the teachers to see examining wrested from their professional control and a fear of the derogation of the elementary school headmaster's role in selection procedure. The National Union of Teachers consistently advocated that the school record should play a large part in selection methods. School psychologists were apt to depict the conservatism of teachers with respect to selection methods as a Luddite reaction to progressive technology.[43] A more sympathetic view would have been that the teachers in the elementary school system had little stomach for the pessimistic and elitist pedagogy which arose from a doctrine of more or less constant innate general ability. This doctrine subordinated their teaching to a fixed index of mental capacity. If consistently applied it would skim off all the most able children at eleven and curtail the development of advanced instruction in higher elementary classes.

Unequivocal support from the centre for intelligence testing in education and the whole gamut of psychological theory on which it rested came with the Report on the Primary School (already alluded to) and the Spens Report of 1938. The former published an appendix written by Burt giving the psychometric rationale for classification (or streaming) in the junior school from about the age of eight: since IQ was constant, he argued, the disparity in mental age between children increased as they grew older and the range of individual differences became inexorably an impediment to the successful functioning of the un-streamed class.[44] During the infant period, the range was sufficienty small 'to allow them to be grouped together without much regard to their different degrees of mental endowment'. By the age of eight:

> to put together in a single room all those who are of the same age would be to organise a class that was extremely heterogeneous ... by the age of twelve the range has become so wide, that a still more radical classification is imperative. Before this age is reached children needed to be grouped according to their capacity, not merely in separate classes ... but in separate types of schools.

The Report recommended three-track streaming in large primary schools. The Spens Report on secondary education enshrined the psychometric orthodoxy in its purest form. During the making of the Report the differences between Thomson, who supported multilateralism in secondary education and the hardline psychometricians were overridden. Representative of the latter were the spokesmen for the NIIP who in their evidence to the committee asserted that:

the group intelligence test afforded a trustworthy instrument for the selection of children at the age of
11 + ... 'intelligence' remained constant throughout life
and they would be prepared to reject a candidate [for
grammar school] if the results of the group tests were
poor, even though the candidate had secured high marks
in the tests of English and Arithmetic.[45]

The Report, in a passage drafted by Burt, assured its
readers that application of mental tests to children at
successive years of school life had shown that intellectual
growth was remarkably uniform and

> appears to progress as if it were governed by a single
> central factror ... that can be measured approximately
> by means of intelligence tests ... it is possible at a very
> early age to predict with some degree of accuracy the
> ultimate level of a child's intellectual powers, but this is
> true only of general intelligence and does not hold good
> in respect of specific aptitudes or interests.[46]

The major policy implications of the Report were to
confirm that the basic shape of adolescent state schooling
should be the selective tripartite system, that multilateralism should be confined to the experimental and
peripheral (valid, possibly for sparsely populated rural
areas) and that an important, even overriding function of
the junior school would be the preparation of children for
the eleven plus.

It would clearly be an error to see all these implications as
determined by the hard-line psychometricians' consensus
which is spelt out in the Report. Tripartism arose from the
ad hoc incorporation of the old grammar schools into the
state education system through 'the scholarship ladder' and
the building, by the local authorities, of their own selective
secondary, technical and 'modern' schools. The Spens
Report rejected multilateralism for the reason that it 'would
be too subversive a change to be made in a *long established
system* ...'[47] [our emphasis] and, though it was doubtless
comforting to know that selection was underwritten by the

psychometricians' consensus, it was a rationale after the fact. While it can be tellingly argued that the consensus reinforced the narrow limits in which secondary education would be allowed to develop, those limits were set up by different forces.

With respect to streaming within the junior forms of the elementary schools (which, as later research by Douglas and others was to show, had the effect of a self-fulfilling prophecy) and the deforming influence of selection methods on the junior curriculum, the psychometric consensus appears to have been a culpable agent, rather than merely an accessory after the fact. By 1938, according to Ballard, most of the important education authorities had added to the two customary papers in English and arithmetic of the free place examination a third consisting of intelligence tests which was, as a rule, considered co-ordinate and allotted one-third of the total marks. Moreover, psychological techniques aimed at standardisation of marking and a 'normal' distribution of results had been applied to the academic papers, transforming them from papers with a small number of questions requiring long answers to a large number requiring brief answers.[48] There would have been little to object to in this had it not been the case that 'The education of junior children is dominated by the scholarship system.'[49] The premium paid for standardised assessment at eleven was, in the view of many critics, a curriculum biased against creativity and in favour of the acquisition of a narrow range of measurable skills. This development was reinforced by the widespread abandoning of the essay in the free place exam.[50]

Streaming, on the basis of measured ability, in the upper classes of the elementary schools had also by the late 1930s produced curricular changes which the psychometricians smugly assumed demonstrated the soundness of their science. Thus Cattell stated that:

> through the application of psychological knowledge, the curricula of these A, B and C classes is tactfully graded to the interests normal to the mental capacities drafted into each stream. Where the A child revels in geometrical

problems and the finer points of history, the C child enjoys simple shopping arithmetic, handwork and the story of a few battles . . . we may congratulate ourselves on this improvement in educational understanding.[51]

The precise extent to which selection by psychologically designed tests at eleven had exerted its deleterious backwash effects on the junior curriculum and organisation before 1945 is unclear, and could only be decided by painstaking archival research. But the frequent reiteration in official and authoritative sources of the dangers of these effects, and generalised statements as to their presence, suggest they were real enough. The 1943 White Paper on Educational Reconstruction, for example, regarded the eleven plus arrangements as even more serious in their effects on the junior schools and their pupils than the prevalence of very large classes:

There is nothing to be said in favour of a system which subjects children at the age of eleven to the strain of a competitive examination on which, not only their future schooling, but their future career may depend. Apart from the effect upon the child there is the effect on the curriculum of the schools themselves. Instead of the junior schools performing their proper and highly important function of fostering the potentialities of children . . . the curriculum is too often cramped and distorted by over-emphasis on examination subjects and on ways and means of defeating the examiners. The blame for this rests not with the teachers but with the system.[52]

Similar statements and warnings culled from documents dating from subsequent years indicate that such round condemnation of the eleven plus for its effects on the junior schools was largely unheeded by educational administrators. The NUT's Report, *Transfer from Primary to Secondary Schools* (1949) devoted some of its strongest passages to 'the Freedom of the Primary School', voicing the conviction 'that the traditional examination in English and arithmetic exercises a harmful influence on the work of the primary schools; and that the matter is not mended but in some ways made worse by the substitution of standardised objective tests . . .' The harm arose from an undue concentration upon a limited part of the curriculum which was treated in a narrow way, based on drill in the types of question which were expected to appear in the examination paper. Because performance in attainment tests could be notably improved by continuous and intensive practice (as, to a lesser extent, could performance in IQ tests), cramming in the six months prior to the exam was a significant feature of junior school teaching. It was encouraged by the standardisation of IQ scores and attainment scores for an educational area which led to junior schools with low average IQ scores attempting to hold their own in competition with schools with higher IQ scores by improving their performance in tests of English and arithmetic. 'We are satisfied that there are many primary schools in which the work is unduly and harmfully influenced by examinations or attainments tests . . . as they are now used.'[53] Much later, the Plowden Report was no less emphatic; though the assessment of the Schools Inspectorate was that the backwash effects of selection were lessening (in the early and mid-1960s), nevertheless 'the less enterprising primary schools are what they are now partly, at least, because of the influence of the selective system'.[54]

The psychometric consensus which, as we have seen, embedded itself in the inter-war reports of the Board's Consultative Committee was strengthened by the gathering body of evidence as to the predictive value of IQ testing for later educational achievement (one of the most important ways in which it was held to be 'valid'). Research by Emmett in the West Riding in 1935 into the predictive value of testing at eleven found IQ to be significantly superior to the traditional unstandardised type of examination then still commonly used in selection. A more authoritative study was William McClelland's, undertaken for the Scottish Council for Research in Education and published in 1942 as *Selection for Secondary Education*. This sought to establish the predictive value of teachers' estimates, ordinary exams, IQ tests and standardised scholastic tests. It confirmed 'the view that

able attack from 1940. R. S. Wood, Deputy Secretary at the Board, sensed in 1941 that the war 'is moving us more and more in the direction of Labour's ideas and ideals'.[57] Officialdom itself remained unconvinced of the merits of alternative educational models (such as multilateralism and the common school) but it recognised the likelihood of having a different set of post-war political masters and the need to plan accordingly. Consequently, the Board was much more open to criticisms of the psychometric consensus from bodies such as the Labour Party, the NUT, the TUC and the WEA. As we have seen, the Board's 1943 White Paper on Educational Reconstruction – in many ways a progressive document –explicitly condemned competitive examination at eleven and did so partly because of its undesirable 'backwash' effects. It went on to suggest that:

In the future, children at the age of 11 should be classified, not on the results of a competitive test, but on the assessment of their individual aptitudes, largely by such means as school records supplemented, if necessary, by intelligence tests, due regard being had to their parents' wishes and the careers they have in mind.[58]

Here was a marked concession to the teaching profession.

In the same year, the Norwood committee reported on the Curriculum and Examination in Secondary Schools and though it reinforced the case for tripartism, it rejected the psychology of selection on which Spens had relied. Norwood leant far less on expert psychological testimony; it did not call witnesses, but received memoranda from interested bodies and individuals and circulated a questionnaire. Its recommendations reflected the conservative-elitist pedagogy of its chairman (a former headmaster of Harrow). On the basis of a woolly reasoning that harked back to the old faculty psychology, the Report hazarded the now notorious recommendation that adolescents could be grouped into three types of mind, each with its appropriate curriculum. With respect to how these groups should be sorted at eleven, the Committee was, from an early stage in its deliberations, sceptical as to the claims of the intelligence testers; it sought to restore the authority of the teacher and the headmaster as opposed to that of the psychologist and the official. The Report recommended selection on the basis of school records, headmasters' Reports and, if thought desirable, supplementary intelligence tests, though it slightingly suggested that the tests were somehow still 'experimental'.[59] In so doing, it was closely following the advice of bodies such as the Incorporated Association of Head Masters, and may, too, have been influenced by the opinion of the WEA that 'precaution should be exercised in the use made of current "intelligence tests", which are still in their infancy and require years of experiment before they can be regarded as wholly satisfactory'.[60] Although the NUT was highly critical of the Committee's proceedings and its report (for rejecting multilateralism and the common school) it too recommended transfer from junior schools on the basis of school records. The NUT executive was 'of the opinion that any use which may be made of intelligence tests, as an additional criterion for the classification of pupils, should not result in children with the highest intelligence quotients being allocated to one type of school . . .'[61], a view with which the White Paper had some sympathy. Although they approached the problem in entirely different ways, both the Norwood Committee and the White Paper were, then, proposing to select or differentiate children at eleven in terms of individual abilities and aptitudes (rather than 'general ability') and both placed great emphasis on teachers' assessments (rather than psychological testing).

1943 was a critical year in the history of British psychometrics because it witnessed both these assaults on its consensus and the onset of Burt's career in fraud. The two were not unconnected. G. Sutherland and S. Sharp have pointed out that Burt's work is slipshod and difficult to document from the time of his appointment to the LCC in 1913.[62] Nonetheless, the manufacture of research assistants and the witting deployment of suspect (and probably mendacious) data to bolster the hereditarian case date from the 1943 paper 'Ability and Income' whose publication immediately preceeded that of the Government's White

Paper. Though a technical paper, it was explicitly conceived of as a rebuttal of the progressive demand for 'equal educational opportunity for all' which in Burt's view could only be achieved in violation of the psychological facts.[63]

Leon Kamin first drew attention to the scientific spuriousness of Burt's data and Professor Leslie Hearnshaw has, since then, acknowledged that 'Ability and Income' marks a watershed in Burt's career.[64] Hearnshaw explains Burt's misdemeanour primarily in personal terms: Burt's marriage was foundering, many of his papers had been destroyed in the Blitz, he was ill and isolated in Aberystwyth; and he places much less weight on Burt's response to what had become a hostile socio-political environment. From the timing of his paper, it would appear much more plausible to reverse the order of explanation and envisage Burt as primarily setting out to restore the reputation of the pre-war psychometric consensus and its prestige amongst educational policy makers. This interpretation appears more plausible, firstly, if we re-examine the 'Ability and Income' paper, not for its scientific credibility, but for its sociological perspectives and the social policy objectives identified in it and, secondly, if we consider it in relation to some of the less specialist papers Burt produced at that time and in the years immediately after 1943.

'Ability and Income' was a highly sophisticated defence of an elite society and elitist education. Much of the paper is inspired by the elite theories of the Italian sociologist, Vilfredo Pareto,[65] and the paper attempts to prove that income inequality is a function of variability in innate ability. This is scarcely obvious from the known distribution of income which in no way corresponds to the supposedly normal distribution of innate ability. But Burt argued that ability above the norm would have a 'multiplier', rather than simply an incremental effect on an individual's 'output' and output would, in most fields, correspond to income. There are a number of 'practical corollaries.'

The first politico-economic corollary is that the nation's wealth is crucially dependent on the recognition and sustenance of the nation's 'natural' elite (that is those with abnormal innate ability):

The tacit habit of treating the symmetrical curve of mental ability as entailing a corresponding symmetry in the curve of mental output has hitherto led us to underrate, and to underrate very grossly, the extraordinarily high output [in industry, in commerce, or in any intellectual field] of which the super-normal child should eventually be capable. It follows that the ultimate return to the community that would be gained by investing public funds in the tasks of discovering and educating those super-normal individuals is far above what we have hitherto been inclined to expect.[66]

This, in a nutshell, was an argument for concentrating educational resources on the elite schools, the grammar schools. Since Burt deployed his own, and Howard's (*sic*), data to show that this elite was located predominantly in the professional and middle-classes, it also legitimised their existing economic and educational privileges. This first politico-economic corollary was itself underpinned by the evidence Burt advanced to the effect that sibling IQ correlation was greater amongst more, rather than less, intelligent children; for Burt this meant that high ability and a privileged educational environment reinforced each other. While this is doubtless true, Burt then turned it into an additional argument for directing a disproportionate share of educational resources to the able:

the influence of a good environment appears most conspicuous where the influence of good heredity is also most conspicuous. There is an obvious practical corollary: *it is far more urgent to provide brighter children with an education appropriate to the ability of each than to do so for the dull, the backward or the defective.*[67] [Original emphasis]

More simply, this warranted a policy of public munificence for the able and parsimony for the average and less than average.

A further practical corollary was the need for a selection system designed to identify members of the 'natural' elite in the lower social classes. According to Burt's own logic this system would have to be based principally on tests of innate ability which, as far as possible, were culture-free. Though both a hereditarian and an elitist, Burt remained consistent to the Galtonian principle that a hereditary elite defied the Galtonian Law of Regression to the Mean. A properly scientific method had to be found to ensure the recruitment and circulation of members of the 'natural' elite coming from the lower socio-economic strata.

Burt was able to confront the arguments in the Government's White Paper much more directly when he published the results of an 'Inquiry into Public Opinion Regarding Educational Reforms'.[68] At the close of 1942, the Home Intelligence Division of the Ministry of Information had prepared a departmental report on public feeling with regards to post-war reconstruction and Burt was asked to examine the report and the methods and materials on which it was based. He suggested a supplementary study of *expert* opinion on educational reconstruction and this became a weapon with which to flay the ignorance of the man in the street and attack the proposals in the White Paper. For example, the widespread demand, revealed by the Ministry of Information, for more or less open access to any type of secondary education displayed the 'popular ignorance of the limitations imposed by children's innate capacities'. Burt was able to set against this ignorance, and the White Paper proposals

> the expert opinion of teachers, with a wide experience of the great variation in innate ability shown by children, who laid great stress on the need for assessing a child's ability, before admitting him to the 'type of school which a fond or ambitious parent might be tempted to suggest.' Nearly all now appear to appreciate the value of intelligence tests in this connection.

Burt found that a majority of his 'educational experts' favoured a non-competitive examination turning on innate ability rather than acquired attainments (that is an intelligence test) as the method of selection for secondary schools.

Moreover, it was particularly the younger – and by implication more progressive – teachers in the elementary
schools who 'now appreciate the value of intelligence tests as
a method of selection àt this stage . . .'.

The technicalities of Burt's 'Ability and Income' suggest
that it was addressed to the small, statistically inclined,
audience in his own profession. He followed it in *The British
Journal of Educational Psychology* with 'The Education of the
Young Adolescent: the Psychological Implications of the
Norwood Report' which appears to have been aimed at a
wider audience of educational psychologists, teachers and
local authority officials. In it, he skilfully recapitulated the
psychometric consensus of the inter-war years with its core
propositions that 'analysis of mental measurement has
demonstrated beyond all doubt . . . the supreme importance during childhood of the general factor of intelligence',[69] that this was innate and constant, that its distribution in the population led to inexorably increasing intellectual distances between the bright and the dull child, and
that, therefore, a streamed and selective system of education was the only one consonant with the psychological
facts. Burt had little difficulty in holding up to ridicule
Norwood's amateurish speculations on different types of
mind and the Report's jejune reasoning made it easier for
him to defend secondary selection by, above all, intelligence
testing. He argued that, although psychological theory
recognised the existence of special abilities and aptitudes
such as Norwood and the White Paper were proposing as a
basis for selection, identifying them by objective testing at
eleven was a far more hazardous business than identifying
general ability. (Of course, neither Norwood nor the White
Paper had actually proposed this.) He dismissed the notion
of selection by teachers' assessments and the school record
on the grounds of their poor predictive value (a claim
scarcely warranted by McClelland's report!). The core
social policy recommendation of his paper was for 'a
well-conducted external test' which would reduce the
unwelcome backwash on junior schools to 'negligible proportions'.[70] His ideal examination would consist of (i) a set
of group tests for elementary scholastic knowledge and skill

(particularly in English and arithmetic) which would eliminate all who did not possess a requisite minimum of
attainment in the basic subjects, (ii) a set of group tests for
innate intelligence for which no coaching was possible (then
an article of faith amongst IQ psychologists) which would
pick out the ablest children and earmark borderline cases,
and (iii) a supplementary investigation chiefly for these
borderline cases, consisting of individual tests, oral interviews and special records or reports from the pupil's own
teachers.

During the immediate post-war period, Burt organised a
symposium on the selection of pupils for different types of
secondary schools and in his contribution advocated a
greater emphasis in selection procedure on tests of innate
ability as compared with tests of attainment. Here, he
reiterated the elitist notion that 'in the present stage of our
national civilization, this [the grammar school] group of
children form in many ways the most important, as well as
the most neglected members of the community'.[71] This
'present stage', we should bear in mind, was marked by the
accession to power of the first Labour government with a
working majority and by a popular demand for a sustained
assault on socio-economic inequality. Burt has a reputation
for being 'slightly pinkish', almost Fabian. This reputation
should not dispose us to think that Burt ever had any
serious sympathy for the political objectives of the
working-class movement or even much sympathetic understanding of the disadvantages of class. In fact, he was typical
of a generation of intellectuals before the First World War
who acquiesced in social inequality and took, as their major
political objective, social efficiency, to be achieved by
scientific and bureaucratic expertise. In an earlier context,
Burt's position had meritocratic implications. The social
context at the time of the symposium revealed the shallow-
ness of these meritocratic pretensions:

a realistic policy [of selection] must take frankly into
consideration the fact that a child coming from this or
that type of home may as a result be quite unsuited for a
certain type of education, occupation or profession,

which lies at an excessive 'social distance' from those of his parents and friends.[72]

Teachers and educationalists must, in Burt's view, take account of 'traditional taboos, class conventions and proverbial wisdom current in the particular *Kulturkreis* to which the parents belong' when giving advice on the type of school a child should attend. (A suggestion which he illustrated by quoting without disapproval the anti-semitic remarks of a junior school head on the inappropriateness of a grammar school education for bright working-class Jewish children.)

That the bright working-class child might fail to realise his educational potential because of socio-cultural disadvantages duly became a research topic for a Burtian acolyte. W. J. Campbell produced evidence to show that bright children who ranked low on a scale designed to measure the social and cultural level of the home did less well than expected at grammar schools. On the other hand, less bright children ranked higher on the socio-cultural scale, did better than was to be expected at central schools (that is schools of a secondary modern type). Campbell concluded that misplacements would be reduced if the assessment of home environment was used in a particular way when children were being transferred from junior schools; in other words, the working-class scholarship child would have to be outstandingly bright to compensate for the lack of motivation and encouragement in grammar school work which presumably went with the working-class home. Campbell (as had Burt) conceded the political difficulties which obviously stood in the way of this preposterous notion, but he went on to make the astonishingly mealy-mouthed suggestion:

> Much might be accomplished by means of tactful individual talks with the parents in those cases where children would otherwise be allocated to grammar schools in which they would almost certainly be failures. The withdrawal of these children from the grammar school entrants, accomplished in a sympathetic and tactful manner, would allow education authorities to allot places to children who would otherwise have been allocated to

central schools, but whose home backgrounds were such that they would almost certainly be better placed in grammar schools.[73]

It was suggested above that the onset of Burt's career in fraud can be most plausibly interpreted as a response to an intellectual environment which had become hostile to his views. This cycle of responding to attacks on the psychometric consensus with spurious 'scientific' papers, whose conclusions had a marked bearing on educational policy, was repeated in 1955 when Burt published 'The Evidence for the Concept of Intelligence' in the *British Journal of Educational Psychology*. All commentators now agree that the data ostensibly derived from twin studies is valueless. The social and political intent of the paper becomes a little clearer if we read it as a response to the growing dissent from the psychometric consensus within the psychological profession, the gathering evidence for the fallibility of the eleven plus examination and the popular discontent with its operation. Burt compounded dishonesty with delusion for, basically, he was contending that issues such as the structure of secondary education – a matter for legitimate political debate – could be settled by an expert and apolitical assessment of the 'scientific facts'. His intellectual adversaries were portrayed as politically inspired, while he himself had no political axe to grind. That his own intellectual position derived from, and helped sustain, a politically elitist perception of the social structure, he refused to acknowledge.

EDUCATION AND PSYCHOMETRICS
AFTER THE SECOND WORLD WAR

For many of the left, the bewildering paradox of post-1944 educational development was that tripartism entrenched itself in the secondary education system during a period of Labour's political dominance. Typical of their bewilderment was Robin Pedley's complaint: ' . . . a Labour Government, with massive electoral backing for social reform, chose the segregationist course . . .'[74]. There was no legislative compulsion to do so, since the 1944 Act neither prescribed the form secondary education should take (it merely demanded its universal provision) nor did it lay down that children should be tested at eleven. Pedley, Brian Simon and others have laid the blame for this squarely on the psychometric consensus:

> the outlook of most professional educators had for a generation taken on a new slant under the influence of a school of educational psychologists whose prime concern was mental measurement .... Fundamentally, secondary school organization at this vital period (1945–51) was befogged and bedevilled by the tremendous hold on almost all educationalists which the movement for intelligence testing had acquired.[75]

While there is undoubtedly merit in the argument, it also masks a failure on the part of the Labour movement to make, during the inter-war period, a comprehensive alternative to a segregated secondary system a matter of political priority and urgency. Many in the Labour movement had achieved social mobility by climbing an educational ladder whose first rung had been the scholarship at eleven plus. They were inclined, therefore, to look on the ladder – for whose broadening and strengthening they themselves were sometimes responsible – as a good enough guarantee of the social equity of the selective system. Nor was it obvious to them that the use of intelligence tests in the mechanism of selection in itself biased that mechanism against the working class, and in this they were perfectly correct. The abolition of intelligence tests in the eleven plus examination by the South West Hertfordshire authority in the mid-1950s led to a small but persistent diminution of opportunity for working-class children and a corresponding increase in opportunity for those at higher social levels. Had selection for grammar school been based solely on measured intelligence, the proportion of working-class grammar school entrants in the 1950s would have been higher than it was.[76] Far more glaring than the inequalities of class were those of geography, for the availability of grammar school places varied from region to region in a way which had no connection with the distribution of intelligence. Grammar school places were 9 per cent of total secondary school places in Gateshead and 39 per cent in Gloucester.[77]

The attraction of the psychologists' doctrine of innate inequality for Conservative political philosophy and the sanction it provided for selection and unequal provision after the age of eleven scarcely present any paradoxes. The only danger was that, with the eleven plus creating popular discontent by the mid-1950s, it would prove an electoral liability. For David Eccles, long-time Conservative Minister of Education, the problem in 1955 was:

> how to convince parents that the secondary school which is educationally suitable for their children is one which they would choose for themselves. It is defeatist and unprincipled to deceive parents by pretending that all secondary schools can, and should, be equal, and, there-fore no choice need be made. The honest policy is to admit that we are not born equal, and to build up each secondary school with its own distinctive character and fitness to serve a range of ability and aptitudes. As this happens, and as it is explained to parents, a growing number of them can be offered a satisfactory choice. Our aim is to work towards selection for everybody.[78]

Nevertheless, there is a degree to which Simon and others offer an over-simplistic account of the relations between psychological theory and educational administration. Theory was mediated through a chain of bureaucracy in which the psychological profession was not well rep-resented. Local authorities, for example, were markedly reluctant to enlist the services of educational psychologists in devising and administering their selection procedures; only about a quarter of them did so in the mid-1950s.[79] The same chain of bureaucracy, we might suggest, made educa-tional administration slow to respond to changes in psychological theory.

In spite of its trenchant defence by Burt, the psychomet-ric consensus crumbled considerably in the late 1940s and

1950s, though this crumbling had no appreciable effect on the use of psychological tests in secondary school selection (see Table 3.1) nor any effect on the practice of streaming

TABLE 3.1 *Percentage of local education authorities using standardised tests of intelligence, arithmetic and English in England and Wales*

	1952	1956	1960	1964
Standardised intelligence*	84.5	88.4	92.5	93.8
Standardised arithmetic	69.8	73.6	80.8	69.7
Standardised English	69.8	72.1	80.8	71.0

*After 1956, designated standardised tests of Verbal Reasoning.
SOURCES: A. Yates and D. A. Pidgeon, *Admission to Grammar Schools* (London: Newnes, 1957); National Foundation for Educational Research in England and Wales, *Local Authority Practice in the Allocation of Pupils to Secondary Schools* (London: NFER, 1964).

by ability. (In 1962, only 4 per cent of junior schools were unstreamed; this is not to imply that intelligence testing was widely used to stream.[80] Indeed, had that been the case, middle-class children would not have congregated in the 'A' streams of the junior schools in numbers disproportionate to the distribution of measured ability amongst the social classes. As with selection at eleven, streaming solely by intelligence would have been more equitable for the working-class child. However, this does not substantially detract from the argument that psychometrics 'forbad' mixed-ability teaching, that children were streamed on the basis of assumed performance at eleven, that for many this created the future it predicted and in this fashion working-class children were effectively discriminated against in large numbers.[81]) Strong criticisms of the post-Spearman theory of intelligence were raised by, among others, G. H. Kent, Julian Blackburn and Alice Heim[82] while objective selection at eleven was shown to be far more prone to error than had previously been believed. In 1952, Vernon demonstrated that improvements brought about by coaching (amounting to 12 to 15 points IQ in some cases) were large enough to make a considerable difference to children on or near the selection borderline, although he added that such improvements were definitely limited and that they were achieved as a result of quite small amounts of coaching and practice.[83] Furthermore, even the most efficient system of objective testing produced a large percentage of borderline candidates and, inevitably, a goodly proportion of 'misplacements' with which the arrangements for transfer between secondary schools were quite inadequate to deal. Assuming that the predictive accuracy of the test battery was 90 per cent and that one in five secondary school places was at a grammar school (as was the average for English local authorities) then it was statistically certain that one quarter of the grammar school entrants did not 'deserve' their place.[84]

The crumbling of the psychometric consensus is particularly evident in the scepticism with which the major reports on education from the late 1950s treated its claims. From the time of the Crowther report on the raising of the school leaving age (1959) – stressing the close association between a father's level of occupation and the educational achievement of his children at school – it was evident that the burgeoning sociology of education was displacing psychology as the major influence on the Ministry's advisory committees. Robbins, reporting on higher education in 1963, was particularly scathing about the notion of a fixed 'pool of ability' which was implicit in the psychometric consensus. It dismissed the belief

that there exists some easy method of ascertaining an intelligence factor unaffected by education or background as 'outmoded'. Years ago, performance in 'general intelligence tests' was thought to be relatively independent of earlier experience. It is now known that in fact it is dependent upon previous experience to a degree sufficiently large to be of great relevance . . . there is a vast mass whose performance, both at the entry to higher education and beyond depends greatly on how they have lived and been taught beforehand . . . . If there is to be talk of a pool of ability, it must be a pool which surpasses the widow's cruse in the Old Testament, in that when more is taken for higher education in one generation more will tend to be available in the next.[85]

FACING 'THE FACTS'

There are no conclusions to contemporary history; it is a process without an end although one of its goals is, we hope, the emancipation of men and women from beliefs which fragment their total personalities and confirm their dominant and subordinate roles in a class society. Differential psychologists almost invariably confront such a social objective, and the policies required in education and elsewhere to attain it, with an injunction to 'face the facts'. Progressive educational principles and policies wrote Burt, 'are advocated – as they always have been – not on the basis of experimental trial or factual evidence, but as deductions from certain ideological theories'.[86] In 1978, Jensen was saying much the same thing.[87] Some of the 'factual evidence' and the arguments deployed against progressive 'ideological theories' are frankly risible. Burt, for example, included in a learned journal article in 1963 'guesstimates' of the IQs of mid-Victorian men of genius in order to strengthen an argument that the distribution of intelligence was skewed at both ends of the normal curve.[88] Jensen invokes the warranty of the ancients to support an argument for the concept of general mental ability having a history throughout recorded time; it is to be found, we are told, in the psychology of classical Greece and ancient India.[89]

Doubtless classical Greece and ancient India had many concepts which show close affinities with those of modern technologically-advanced class societies; love, honour and the natural inferiority of women and ethnic outsiders might be amongst them. But the differences in these concepts would be quite as striking as the affinities; the Greek concept of love, for example, was far more tolerant of homoeroticism, that of honour was one appropriate to a martial society. Greek love and honour were concepts which stood for certain socially and historically contextualised types of loving and honourable behaviour. It is no less the case that the modern concept of intelligence stands for a socio-historically specific type of behaviour. Vernon – by no means a critic of psychometrics – has conceded as much when writing that the 'complex intelligence of the western middle-class is not the only one'. He suggests that 'the major differences between African and Western intelligence probably arise from the emphasis on conformity and social integration as against individual responsibility and internal controls; and from the acceptance of magical beliefs which inhibit analytic perception and rational thinking'. He hints too at the historical specificity of (western) intelligence in suggesting that it is 'reasonable to regard the Puritan ethic of the western middle-class as producing the greatest development of intelligence'.[90] We do not mean to endorse Vernon's ethnocentric views on the stimulus of the Puritan ethic for developing a 'higher' intelligence, or the inhibition of rational thinking among Africans, but to simply point out that his views represent a belated and rather half-hearted recognition that psychometricians have attempted to define and measure a social construct as if it could be abstracted from time and society.

The objectivity assumed on the part of the psychologists is extraordinarily difficult to attain if not altogether chimerical. They are not free from the constraints of time and society and cannot step outside their social beings. The social construct of intelligence has both contributed to their social beings – for they are 'bright', 'able', 'successful', 'intelligent' people – and has done much to consolidate their professional identity. Intelligence testing is one of the most important ways in which psychology has established a professional relationship with society, in the sense of offering a calculative service whose principles are guaranteed by the corporate honour of the profession.

Finally, the injunction to 'face the facts' has for too long been advanced within the delusion that 'the facts' are there and have merely been 'discovered' by psychometry. The facts do not exist, like trees or lumps of rock, subject to easy counting and measurement. The 'facts' are ideational constructs made by a statistically powerful but theoretically weak science and the facts belong largely to a period of scientific immaturity and insecurity. An object lesson of Kamin's book is the extent to which IQ psychology consists of unexamined encrustations from the past. Unfortunately, the lesson has not been taken fully to heart; IQ psychology still rests on 'facts' out of their time. To give one example, Jensen in his previously quoted 1978 article cites, as evidence for a hereditary component to social class IQ differences, the positive correlation between a child's IQ and the social class of his or her biological parents found in Evelyn Lawrence's study of adopted children in orphanages, completed by 1928.[91] This fifty year-old study was made under great difficulties (particularly that of assigning a social class to a – putative – father on the basis of adoption papers) and is remarkable for its anomalies as well as its conclusions. In some instances, the correlation coefficient of children's intelligence with the mother's class was actually higher amongst children separated from their parents than it was for a control group of elementary children living in their own home.[92] All the adopted children of high IQ (135 plus) came from low social classes[93] (yet the study is never cited as showing a relationship between high IQ and low social class!). The investigator had no information whatsoever about parental IQ and therefore produced only dubious inferential evidence for a hereditary component in the small positive correlation between class and IQ. Finally, even if we concede that the evidence is satisfactory, what reasons have we for believing that this component is still present half-a-century later? IQ psychology subsists on a thin gruel of theory produced (in a way typical of the pre-paradigmatic sciences) under great ideological constraints in turn of the century Britain. Let us now turn from a historical critique of its practice to a scientific one.

4

The Scientific Issues – I: the Measurement of Individual Differences

In the history of the mental testing movement, IQ tests have clearly played the central role. The claim that psychometrics has gone beyond mere testing, to the scientific measurement of individual differences rests largely on factor analytic techniques, and especially on the apparently ubiquitous 'factor of general intelligence'. The claim that psychometric research is relevant to great social issues is based mainly on the evidence that IQ can predict educational achievement and occupational success. Although many other types of psychometric test have been developed, and although many psychometricians believe that IQ tests have received an unfair share of the limelight, it remains true that no other type of test has a comparable basis of apparent theoretical support or social significance.

The importance of the g factor in providing the theoretical underpinning for IQ tests has not always been fully appreciated by psychometricians. We have already seen that Eysenck was only recently converted to this view. The same can be said of Jensen. In his recent writings[1] he has placed great emphasis on g, but in his influential 1969 paper he treated the subject in ambiguous terms (see below, page 126), preferring to rely on an 'operational definition' of intelligence:

We *can* measure intelligence. As the late Professor Edwin

G. Boring pointed out, intelligence, by definition, is what intelligence tests measure. The trouble only comes when we attribute more to 'intelligence' and to our measurements of it than do the psychologists who use the concept in its proper sense.[2]

Boring's dictum is probably best thought of as a psychometrician's joke. As Alice remarked to Humpty Dumpty in *Through the Looking Glass*, the question is, whether you *can* make words mean what you choose them to mean. Is it not the man in the street rather than the psychometrician who uses the term 'intelligence' in its 'proper sense'? But the operational definition of intelligence certainly has been taken seriously. It is usually associated with the view that IQ tests tap a sample of cognitive abilities, just as the decathlon event taps a sample of athletic abilities. It is then argued that the operational definition has proved to be satisfactory because psychometricians have gone on to show that IQ has clearly demonstrable statistical relationships with other things which can also be operationally defined and measured, such as educational achievement and occupational success. Intelligence, thus measured, may not mean everything that the man in the street means by intelligence; specifically, and as Neisser has suggested, it may be synonymous with 'academic intelligence', but not with the many different forms of everyday intelligence[3]. But this need not disturb us, so it is argued, provided that everyone remembers that the psychometricians are using the term in a special technical sense.

This may seem reasonable enough, but in fact it is very naive to suppose that psychometricians are using the term only in a technical sense. Usually when scientists want to introduce a technical term, they invent a new word like 'positron' or 'allele', When they do borrow from ordinary language they do so in such a way that confusion is unlikely to result. No-one is likely to be misled when quantum physicists talk of 'charmed particles'. On the other hand, confusion is positively encouraged by the way the term 'intelligence' is used by IQ psychologists, as Block and Dworkin point out:

At the same time, many of them (Jensen and Herrnstein included) actually use 'smart', 'stupid', 'bright', 'dull', 'intelligent', 'unintelligent', in stylistic variation with 'high/low IQ'. They thereby transfer to IQ all the emotional and conceptual associations the reader has to intelligence. All this after we are disarmed by being told that after all, 'intelligence' is just a word like any other word, and how a scientist chooses to use it is just a matter of stipulation. Thus, they manage to have their cake and eat it too – that is, they have their new 'scientific' concept of intelligence at the same time retaining the social importance of the old 'prescientific' concept of intelligence.[4]

Quite apart from the question of ordinary usage and technical usage, there are further objections to the operational definition of intelligence. As has frequently been pointed out, the operational definition makes the meaning of the term 'intelligence' dependent on which particular IQ test the operationalist has in mind.[5] IQs as assessed by different IQ tests, are far from perfectly correlated, even when allowance is made for the imperfect 'reliabilities' of the tests.[6] Indeed, IQs for different tests are intercorrelated at a level no higher than their correlations with educational achievement scores, or the intercorrelations among different types of achievement scores. To assert, for example, that the Stanford–Binet test and Raven's Progressive Matrices test both measure the same thing is akin to asserting that height and weight both measure the same thing (and called 'bigness', say), on the grounds that the two measures are substantially, although imperfectly, positively correlated. The use of a common label may merely disguise important differences.

To those who believe that IQ tests tap a sample of the cognitive skills which make up 'academic intelligence', the problem may not seem as crucial as in fact it is. After all, it could be argued that the different IQ tests tap slightly different samples, some perhaps weighted rather more heavily towards verbal skills, others towards logical reasoning, and so on. Variation in the weighting of different abilities by different tests thus explains the imperfect intercorrelations among them. The difficulty here is concerned with the notion of sampling. In order to obtain any kind of representative sample of anything, one must have a clear definition of what the population is from which the sample is to be drawn. Sampling the cognitive skills which make up 'academic intelligence' presupposes that psychologists or educationalists have a reasonably clear understanding of what these skills actually are. But this is palpably not the case. One has only to survey the state of theoretical confusion in comparatively restricted but presumably relevant domains, such as the investigation of the cognitive processes underlying reading, to appreciate this.[7] And yet, without this type of preliminary understanding, it would seem that cognitive abilities can only be 'sampled' in an entirely arbitrary manner.

Operational definitions of intelligence are unsatisfactory because scientific measurements must be embedded within scientific theories. The Harvard astronomer David Layzer, in the course of a very thoroughgoing critique of IQ psychology, has made essentially the same criticism:

> The 'operational stance' recommended by Jensen is thought by many social scientists to be the key ingredient in the 'scientific method' as practised by physical scientists. This belief is mistaken. The first and most crucial step toward an understanding of any natural phenomenon is not measurement. One must begin by deciding which aspects of the phenomenon are worth examining. To do this intelligently, one needs to have, at the very outset, some kind of explanatory or interpretive framework. In the physical sciences, this framework often takes the form of a mathematical theory. The quantities that enter into the theory – mass, electric charge, force, and so on – are always much easier to define than to measure. They are, in fact, completely – if implicitly – defined through the equations that make up the theory.[8]

Layzer goes on to point out that psychometricians who

subscribe to the operationalist doctrine have failed entirely to appreciate this. Their scientific methodology originates in the Baconian philosophy, now universally rejected by physical scientists and philosophers of science, that meaningful generalisations emerge spontaneously from systematic measurements. The revived fashion for the g factor perhaps indicates a belated recognition among psychometricians of the shortcomings of operationalism, and the need to ground IQ psychology in a theory of intelligence. The question to which we now turn, is whether g does provide IQ psychology with its theoretical base.

THE FACTOR OF GENERAL INTELLIGENCE:
BIOLOGICAL CONSIDERATIONS

g is a theoretical construct used to explain the co-variation among test scores. The abilities assessed by different types of test item (for example, vocabulary questions, immediate memory tests and so on) can be regarded as a function of g together with further, more specialised factors. Test items are assumed to differ in their 'g loadings', the extent to which g predominates over the other factors. By incorporating a battery of different types of items, IQ tests provide reasonable estimates of g, because the more specialised factors will tend to cancel each other out, leaving the aggregate score, from which IQ is calculated, with a relatively high 'g loading'.[9]

This hypothesis appears, on the face of it, to dispose of our previous criticisms. The imperfect intercorrelations among different IQ tests can now be explained by proposing that they differ in their 'g loadings' and in the residual effect of placing different emphases on different more specialised factors. Thus all tests can be thought of as biased estimators of g, but the fact that they are biased does not necessarily mean that they are completely useless. A reinterpretation of the relationship between 'intelligence', as assessed by IQ tests, and 'intelligence' in everyday usage is also provided for by g. 'Intelligence', and words like 'bright', 'dull', 'clever' and 'stupid' are used to characterise all kinds of different human activities and the people who perform them, but these activities, so it can be argued, probably all have some 'g loading'. Thus IQ tests, with their high 'g loadings', can be regarded as providing an improvement on everyday usage, rather than a gross violation of it. Looked at in this way, IQ tests can be compared with early thermometers, providing, from a scientific point of view, an improvement on everyday subjective judgements of temperature, but somewhat biased and still awaiting further development based on a greater theoretical understanding.[10]

This is all very well, but we have already seen that the history of psychometrics provides a confusing picture of the theoretical status of g. Once Thomson had shown that any set of correlations which could be factor analysed to yield a g factor could also be generated by his own model, which did not contain g, it was never again clear whether g was an arbitrary statistical convention of questionable usefulness, or a genuine scientific hypothesis awaiting critical testing against alternative hypotheses such as Thomson's. This remains true today. Before examining the statistical issues, and in order to throw some light on them, we shall begin by assuming that g is, in some sense, real, and consider how this might be interpreted given our present knowledge about cognition and the human brain.

Neurobiologists and neuropsychologists conceive of the brain as a complicated set of interconnected structures with distinct functions. Those relevant to the operation of intelligence might include various distinct types of memory, attentional systems, systems concerned with the production and comprehension of language, pattern recognition systems, and so on. The study of these systems involves the co-operation of specialists from a number of disciplines, including neurophysiology, linguistics and psycholinguistics, computer science, and cognitive psychology. Cognitive psychology should not be confused with psychometrics. It is a comparatively recent (post 1950) development in experimental psychology which has now replaced behaviourism as the dominant 'paradigm'. Its theories are concerned with the basic cognitive processes which we all share, rather than with the measurement of individual differences.[11]

Although the interdisciplinary study of brain systems is still in its infancy, there has already emerged a fair degree of agreement about the location and function of a number of systems. The most compelling evidence comes from clinical case studies where localised brain damage has been shown to lead to the loss of certain cognitive skills, while others remain intact.[12] If IQ tests are given to these patients the typical finding is that there is abnormally poor performance for certain types of test question, but normal performance for the remainder. Damage in different regions of the brain has selective effects on different IQ subtests, but there does not appear to be any area which can be regarded as a location for g. Damage to such an area would have to have a similar deleterious effect on all test items having a high 'g loading', but it now seems unlikely that any such area exists.

An instructive comparison can be made between the role of the brain in cognitive abilities and that of the body in physical abilities. The human body can be measured in countless ways, but there is no one measurement which stands supreme. Even if we restrict ourselves to an extremely narrow class of abilities, such as athletic abilities, there are many measurements which can be made, and the relevant ones vary greatly from one athletic event to another. For example, runners in any distance over 400 metres require cardio-respiratory efficiency. Such events require super-efficient transportation of oxygen through the body. The throwing events, on the other hand, involve body bulk, especially in the upper body. Here muscles require efficient thick fibres as opposed to effective blood capillaries for explosive movements. One does not need to breathe any more efficiently than the average man to propel a javelin or discus. In the same way, body bulk is of no help to a runner who has to carry his body over the ground at speed for a long time. In the jumping events the ability to use oxygen is outweighed by the need for a good power-weight ratio, the ability to handle one's own body weight in the form of tremendous leg power or spring. Consider here also the role of heredity and environment.

Genetically influenced physical differences have varying effects on different abilities, and the extent to which each can be overlaid, so to speak, by different types of training also varies greatly. The overall picture is multifaceted, and it would be implausible to suppose that this complexity could be eliminated by proposing the existence of a general factor of athletic ability which is x per cent inherited.

Present day knowledge about the human brain and cognitive abilities is very limited and the appropriateness of the comparison may be questioned, but it is not unreasonable to suppose that a similar kind of picture may one day emerge from this field of enquiry. As an alternative to the conception of a highly heritable g factor, we shall see that it is a useful picture to have in mind when evaluating the statistical arguments of IQ psychologists.

Since g does not appear to have any specific location in the brain, the only alternative way to provide a physical identification seems to be to suppose that it is some general characteristic of neural efficiency which varies between individuals and which influences the functioning of all of the cognitive brain systems. There has in fact been a long lasting tradition of unsuccessful attempts to find correlations between intelligence and various aspects of neuro-anatomy, such as brain size, a tradition which received its greatest disappointment when the post-mortem examination of Einstein's brain showed it to be remarkable only in its very ordinariness. Correlations between IQ and brain characteristics have be found to be zero or very low. The highest among them is .30,[13] a figure far too low to make the characteristic in question a candidate for g (it would have to be at least .70 to qualify).[14] The solitary example of a really substantial correlation between IQ and any physical characteristic has been located by Eysenck. It came to light when a 'junior sergeant tester' in the British Army, lacking anything better to do, decided to obtain the correlations between the soldiers' IQs and just about every measurable characteristic for which he could obtain the necessary information. In the course of his computations he discovered a correlation of −.63 between IQ and number of missing teeth. Eysenck comments, in one of his occasional moments of disarming frankness, 'This correlation of −.63 was quickly verified by correlating the same variables on other samples and still constitutes the highest correlation between intelligence and a physical feature of the human organism that has ever been discovered.'[15]

According to the usual psychometric criteria this means that the number of missing teeth is a fairly good inverse measure of intelligence! The example illustrates the main problem inherent in the correlational methods upon which psychometrics is based, the problem of interpretation. One interpretation would be that IQ and patterns of dental care are both a function of social class background and educational level. An hereditarian interpretation would be that people with high intelligence are much more likely than those with low innate intelligence to take good care of their teeth. It could even be interpreted by proposing that having your teeth removed lowers your IQ (although it would be relatively easy to investigate, and, no doubt, dismiss this interpretation). Whatever the true interpretation may be, it should be borne in mind that the correlation implies a level of predictive power (predicting the one variable from the other) over four times greater than anything found among the few positive correlations between IQ and brain measures.

It remains possible, of course, that there is some as yet unknown or unresearched brain characteristic which really does correspond to g. This is Jensen's current position,[16] but it obviously amounts to no more than the idlest of idle speculations. In considering the objective status of g, the factor analytic arguments have to stand up on their own. Bearing this in mind, let us now consider them.

FACTOR ANALYSIS AND g

Factor analysis and other related techniques are statistical methods which can be used to analyse the pattern of intercorrelations obtained when a battery of psychometric tests has been administered to a large sample of testees. An example of data for factor analysis is provided by the

Wechsler intelligence tests which, like their close cousin the Stanford–Binet, consist of a number of distinct subtests, including tests for vocabulary, general knowledge, immediate memory for strings of digits, identifying the missing part of a picture, copying a design with coloured blocks, and so on. There are eleven subtests and the test manuals give the correlations obtained for the standardisation samples between each subtest and each of the others. These 55 correlations were obtained for 6 different age ranges yielding a total of 330 correlations. The vast majority of them lie in the range from .20 to .75, there being just eight less than .20 and six greater than .75. The higher correlations tend to occur in the older age groups for subtests which would appear to be most strongly associated with general educational level and subsequent life style, the highest of all being .85 between the vocabulary and general knowledge subtests for the oldest age group (45–54). The lower correlations tend to occur for children for dissimilar 'performance' subtests, the lowest being .10 between digit memory span and picture completion for ten and eleven year-olds. The array of subtests and the pattern of intercorrelations, all positive but mostly not particularly high, is typical of the type of data base which forms the natural stamping ground for factor analysts.

In Spearman's original model g was the sole cause of intercorrelations among subtests. The varying size of the correlations was explained with the additional assumption that the subtests differed in their g loadings (if the g loadings were all the same the model would predict that all the correlations would be the same, which is never actually found). In Thomson's model, each subtest was assumed to sample a large subset from an even larger pool of 'mental bonds'. The varying correlations were then explained by proposing that the subtests overlapped to varying degrees in the bonds which they sampled, although it would be unlikely that any particular bond or subset of bonds would be sampled by all subtests.[17]

The different views of Spearman and Thomson have a striking parallel in the distinction in linguistic philosophy between 'universals' and 'family resemblances'. In his famous analysis of the concept of a game Wittgenstein[18] pointed out that we tend to assume that there must some defining characteristics which all games have in common, otherwise how do we come to call them all games? On the other hand, if we actually examine particular games, we find only a criss-crossing pattern of family resemblances with some characteristics common to some groups of games but not to others, and none common to them all. Spearman's g factor amounts to proposing that there is a universal in different intelligent activities, while Thomson's is a simple version of a family resemblance view. The family resemblance analogy can be extended by considering a large group of siblings, say a dozen. Each will have some characteristics in common with each of the others, but there will probably be none common to them all. From a genetic point of view this is certainly the case. Each sibling inherits half of its forty six chromosomes from each of its parents. On the average each pair of siblings will have twenty three chromosomes in common. For a large family it is mathematically very unlikely indeed that there will be any one chromosome common to all siblings, or that there will be any two siblings with no common chromosomes.[19] Substituting 'mental bonds' for chromosomes, one obtains essentially the same picture for Thomson's model when applied to the correlations between psychometric tests. The model is slightly more difficult to grasp, but, mathematically speaking, it is just as simple as Spearman's.

Spearman's original model did not provide a mathematically unique solution, but it does not follow from this that it was not falsifiable in the Popperian sense. It was necessary to estimate mathematical parameters (the g loadings) from the data before theoretical intercorrelations could be calculated and compared with the observed values, but it turned out that the data was not completely exhausted by this procedure. It is possible to invent a matrix of positive intercorrelations which cannot be satisfactorily 'fitted' by Spearman's model however the parameters are set, and it soon became apparent that this was true also of many observed correlation matrices. The gradual elaboration of hierarchical factor models with group factors of varying degrees of specificity eventually enabled factor analysts to 'fit' the data, but, like the epicycles of pre-Copernican geocentric astronomy, they made the model increasingly inelegant and they effectively exhausted the capacity of the data to test the model. The procedure is rather like mathematical curve fitting where one wants to find a functional relationship between x and y which fits an observed curvilinear relationship between the two variables. This can always be done if one adds in and estimates enough free parameters (the a's, b's, c's and so on) in a function of the form:

$$y = a + bx + cx^2 + dx^3 + ex^4 + \ldots$$

The procedure is frowned upon. It works even if the true function is of a quite different nature (for example, $y = \sin x$). The old joke is that, with enough free parameters, it is possible to fit a curve the shape of an elephant. The procedure adopted in hierarchical factor analytic models is in fact very similar to mathematical curve fitting.

The manner in which modern psychometricians interpret the g factor is confusing, to put it in the mildest terms. This is illustrated by the varied use of the concept which occurs within the space of a few pages in Jensen's 1969 *Harvard Educational Review* paper:

> We should not reify g as an entity, of course, since it is only a hypothetical construct intended to explain co-variation among tests . . .

> As the tests change the nature of g will also change . . . . In other words g gains its meaning from the tests which have it in common.

> Despite numerous theoretical attacks on Spearman's basic notion of a general factor, g has stood like a rock of Gibraltar in psychometrics defying any attempt to construct a test of complex problem solving which excludes it.[20]

It is not easy to see how a hypothetical construct whose nature changes from one set of data to another can be said to have stood like 'a rock of Gibraltar'. To gain a slightly clearer impression, compare the following remarks of the geneticist Lewontin, a particularly hostile critic of IQ psychology, and those of Butcher, a sympathiser. Lewontin writes:

> Without going into factor analysis at any length, I will point out that factor analysis does not give a unique result for any set of data. Rather, it gives an infinity of possible results among which the investigator chooses according to his tastes and preconceptions of the models he is fitting. One strategy in factor analysis is to pack as much weight as possible into one factor, while another is to distribute the weights over as many factors as possible as evenly as possible. Whether one chooses one of these or some other depends upon one's model, the numerical analysis only providing the weights appropriate for each model.[21]

Butcher, in a widely used textbook which is broadly sympathetic to the aims and methods of IQ psychology, and which includes an appendix written by Burt, mentions a number of limitations of factor analysis, the most important being the following:

> A third qualification about the technique of factor analysis is that in itself it does not provide a unique and objective description of the structure of abilities or about any other data to which it is applied. It can provide a number, in fact an infinite number, of mathematically equivalent answers. To select one of these and say that 'such and such is the structure', that general intelligence, for instance, accounts on the average for 50% of success at a particular task, and spatial ability for a further 20%, depends on extra assumptions, either mathematical or psychological. Mathematical considerations may indicate one kind of answer as most elegant and economical but psychological considerations may suggest an alternative solution as more easily interpretable in terms of existing concepts.[22]

The two views are virtually identical. If g has any meaning at all, it is a queerly shifting meaning in a very rarified statistical atmosphere. It has been shown by Thomson that it can be dispensed with altogether, and there appears to be no alternative neurobiological evidence to support it. Why, then, does it continue to exert such a strong fascination on psychometricians?

One reason is that, as Wittgenstein suggested, it may be a natural habit of thinking to suppose, when one finds resemblances among a number of particulars, that there must be some universal running through them all. The correlations in the matrices investigated by factor analysts all tended to be positive, so what could be more natural than to assume that there is a 'factor' common to them all? Proponents of g also derived much comfort from the problems experienced by the American factor analyst Thurstone, who dispensed with g altogether and attempted to analyse the correlations by factoring out a number of distinct factors called 'primary mental abilities'.[23] When this was done the primary ability factors were themselves found to be intercorrelated and a g factor could still be extracted from them. This has often been represented as a great triumph of the g hypothesis over a rival,[24] and so indeed it may have been, but the real challenge to the g hypothesis had already been issued by Thomson with his sampling model. As Thomson pointed out, if his model was correct, then it was just as misleading to construe intelligence as a small number of primary abilities as to construe it in terms of g.[25] In the end the only response the proponents of g had to Thomson's model was to ignore it.[26]

We have already argued that the g hypothesis seems inconsistent with the findings of contemporary neurobiology and cognitive psychology. The same can partly be said of Thomson's model since it seems to imply a rather amorphous conception of the brain.[27] On the other hand, stripped of its mathematical rigour, something of the flavour of his idea is retained if we consider how a cognitive psychologist might interpret a factor analyst's correlation matrix. If cognitive processes are multifaceted, involving complex interactions between various subsystems, then it seems natural to interpret the correlation matrix in terms of 'family resemblances', different pairs of test items tending to 'overlap' because they share certain cognitive processes, although there need be none common to all. If this picture is correct then it should, in principle, be possible to devise a series of cognitive tests each of which taps distinct cognitive systems, and which yield scores which are not mutually intercorrelated. There are now beginning to emerge some signs that this can indeed be done. In a recently published study, Stevenson and his co-workers investigated the inter-correlations among measures of children's performance on a range of different tasks based on contemporary cognitive theories. They found that the median (middlemost) of 220 correlations was approximately .11 a figure which is non-zero but trivially small, and they concluded that 'Because an individual's performance on each task was only weakly related to performance on other tasks, it is clear that differences among the children must be characterised in terms of an array of skills rather than in terms of a few general abilities.'[28]

The correlations between IQ tests and subtests in the usual factor analyst's matrices are much higher than this, and it can be asked why this is so? One reason is that they are not selected on the basis of any theory about cognitive processes, so that it is very unlikely that by sheer chance they will tap clearly distinct processes. Another reason is that the mutual intercorrelations were built in as a consequence of the manner in which the tests were first constructed. For example, regarding their development of the Stanford – Binet test, Terman and Merrill stated, that 'Tests that had low correlation with the total were dropped even though they were satisfactory in other respects.'[29]

The procedure is valid if g exists, since it would then follow that the rejected tests had low g loadings, but it clearly presupposes that g does exist. If not then the practice simply ensures that the Stanford–Binet test taps a more narrow range of abilities than would otherwise have been the case. A further reason why IQ tests and subtests are intercorrelated may be that they all share a similar cultural bias. We shall examine this criticism in the next section. Suffice it to state here, that if IQ test constructors did have a predisposition to invent questions which are unfairly loaded in favour of those coming from a similar middle-class cultural background to that of their own, and against those coming from other backgrounds, and if the tests were administered to a representative sample of the population, as factor analysts usually attempt to do, then a general factor is bound to be present in the intercorrelations, although it would be a 'factor of general cultural bias', and certainly not the kind of factor which proponents of g have in mind.

There is clearly more than one way of accounting for the intercorrelations among IQ tests and subtests. The postulation of a g factor is one way, but it is open to more than one interpretation, and, as a scientific hypothesis, it is remarkably insubstantial, far too insubstantial to lend serious support to the proposition that IQ tests provide scientific measurements of intelligence. We shall now turn to the second limb of the IQ psychologists' argument, which may be stated thus: 'However one chooses to appraise the scientific status of IQ tests, the fact remains that the tests are very good at predicting educational achievement and subsequent success in life. IQ research therefore has considerable social significance.' Before considering the specific issue of IQ–achievement correlations, we shall first consider more generally the cultural context of IQ testing and also the criticism that the tests are culturally biased.

THE CULTURAL CONTEXT OF IQ TESTING

A *prima facie* case for the allegation that IQ tests are culturally biased can readily be made by considering some of the questions which are incorporated in the widely used Stanford–Binet and Wechsler tests. For example, the vocabulary subtests ask the meaning of words such as catacomb, vesper, chattel, traduce, perfunctory, casuistry and parterre. The information subtests ask, among other things, what is a hieroglyphic, what is a lien, and who discovered the South Pole. A similarities subtest asks what certain words have in common, such as liberty and justice. It is difficult to believe that the inventors of these questions really thought that they were fair to children and adults of all social classes, that they would all have been equally likely to have come across the information required to answer them correctly. Some even more extraordinary examples occur in the 'comprehension' subtests, which include the following questions:

Why is it good to put money in the bank?
Why is it generally better to give money to an organised charity than to a street beggar?
What's the thing to do when you are on your way to school and notice that you are in danger of being late?

To obtain maximum points for the first question it is necessary to appreciate the intrinsic virtuousness of saving money, the importance of security and the advantage of obtaining interest. To answer the second correctly one must make the questionable assumption that organised charities ensure that money goes to those most in need. A correct answer to the third question must include the idea of hurrying, and listed incorrect responses include 'Go on to school and tell my teacher why I am late', 'Not stop', 'Just keep on going', and 'Get a late card'. One could spend some time arguing whether the listed correct answers to these questions really are correct answers, but it is clear that they involve value judgements which almost certainly differ among social classes.

Both the Stanford–Binet and the Wechsler tests also include 'performance' subtests which are not so obviously culturally biased, but since the verbal subtests, including those cited above, account for fifty per cent or more of the total, it seems ridiculous to suppose that the overall IQ scores for these tests are not culturally biased, or to put forward a genetic explanation for differences of 15 points in the average scores of different social classes and ethnic groups. IQ psychologists are sometimes prepared to go along with these criticisms. They concede that the Stanford–Binet and Wechsler tests are not entirely free of bias, but they argue that the criticism does not apply to certain other IQ tests which they have labelled as 'culture fair'.

A major problem with 'culture fair' tests is that it is not easy to see why they should be regarded as intelligence tests, even when adopting the lenient criteria of the mental testing movement. In the case of the Stanford–Binet, Wechsler, and other conventional IQ tests, the argument is firstly, that by including a range of different subtests they ensure that the aggregate score has a high *g* loading, or, at least, that the tests sample a good range of abilities; and secondly that the tests are demonstrably good at predicting educational achievement. However, most 'culture fair' tests meet neither of these criteria, and none meets both.

The most well known 'culture fair' test is Raven's Progressive Matrices, in which the problem always involves choosing the geometrical figure which completes a matrix of figures according to a logico-mathematical rule which can be discovered by examining the remaining figures. A typical rule would be of the form, 'take the number of triangles from the number of squares to obtain the number of circles'. Blum has recently noted that, more than thirty years after the publication of this test, unequivocal evidence of its predictive validity is still lacking. The same is true of the other well known 'culture fair' test, which was designed in 1940 by Cattell.[30] In general, when the designers of 'culture fair' tests seek validation evidence they are content to cite correlations with other IQ tests, usually the Stanford–Binet or the Wechsler. This is a most unsatisfactory criterion to adopt because, if these conventional tests are as culturally biased as they appear to be, then tests which have a similar bias would be likely to correlate better with them than those which have not. On a survival of the fittest principle, one would expect new tests to have a similar bias to the old ones.

The 'validation' correlations between 'culture fair' tests and the Stanford–Binet and Wechsler tests are moderate rather than high. They inhabit the range from .4 to .7 and a similar range is found for the intercorrelations among different 'culture fair' tests. This is also similar to the range of intercorrelations among the subtests of the conventional tests, and since most 'culture fair' tests consist of a single type of problem, it is probably best to think of them as akin to extended versions of single subtests from the conventional tests rather than as IQ tests in their own right. To reiterate from our previous discussion of factor analysis, it appears to be merely a matter of personal preference whether or not one discerns the presence of g in these correlations.

Why do psychometricians refer to certain tests as 'culture fair'? The obvious reason would be that testees from different cultures or different social classes have the same average scores, but this is not the case for any test. In any event, this criterion would not be acceptable to those who believe that average levels of intelligence really do vary from one group to another, whether for genetic or for environmental reasons. This has presented the mental testing movement with a very real dilemma. Can one formulate an objective criterion of culture fairness? Responding to recent litigation where civil rights groups have been successfully challenging the use of IQ tests on the grounds that the tests are discriminatory, American psychometricians have suggested a number of abstruse statistical criteria of culture fairness. However, they have been unable to agree among themselves on the issue and the controversy has produced fundamental objections to all of the suggested criteria.[31] These recent criteria were, of course, not available to the constructors of 'culture fair' tests, who obviously relied on the subjective criterion that the questions seemed fair to them. This sometimes had absurd consequences, as in the case of the Porteus Maze Test, which consists of a series of pencil and paper mazes. Its designer used it to test Australian aborigines and concluded, from their low average scores compared with whites, that they had low 'innate intelligence'. Recently, even committed hereditarians have been able to find flaws in the logic of this comparison. Thus, Richard Lynn has commented,

To return now to Porteus's finding that the Australoids

[*sic*] have mean IQs in the range of 50–70, we probably ought to conclude that the Australoids tested by Porteus were too far removed from Western culture for the test to give a valid index of their mental ability. The reason for this lies in the lack of familiarity of Australoids with the task presented in the test. The essential concept required for the Maze Test is that of the cul-de-sac, as contrasted with the through road. These are familiar enough concepts to people brought up in houses and in towns but not to people like the Australoids reared in the Australian bush. There are no cul-de-sacs in the deserts of central Australia.[32]

Lynn reviews all international comparisons of IQ and he concludes, with obvious regret, that cultural explanations for the observed differences cannot be ruled out, and could not be ruled out using existing tests and techniques. In this respect he probably speaks for his fellow hereditarians, who nowadays tend to restrict themselves to group comparisons among those receiving full-time state education within one country, usually the USA. The reason for this restriction is that it is becoming increasingly obvious that it is not possible to devise tests which do not depend heavily on knowledge which varies greatly between cultures. For example, some 'culture fair' tests involve the production or interpretation of figurative drawing, but the conventions of figurative drawing and the extent to which it occurs, if at all, are subject to enormous cultural variation. Raven's Progessive Matrices involves mathematical skills which are unlikely to be familiar to anyone who has not attended school. These skills may also depend very much on the quality of education a person receives.

It is possible to take the argument a little further, and ask whether it is useful to conceive of human intelligence as a property of individuals which can be detached from the culture to which they belong. Many aspects of human intelligence, such as writing a poem, designing an experiment, solving a mathematical equation, or preparing a balance sheet, can be regarded as both the work of an individual (or sometimes a group of individuals, or even of a computer) and as the product of a cultural tradition. Looked at in this way the construction of a culture fair test of intelligence, and also the implicit assumption that intelligence is a measurable property of individuals, may be simply a vanity on the part of psychometricians.

In considering the cultural context of IQ testing one must bear in mind not only the nature of the questions included in the tests, but also the fact that the administration of a test is a social event. Even a simple procedure, such as measuring a person's height is a social event, of course, but it is not one in which the relationship between tester and testee is likely to have much effect on the outcome. In the case of IQ testing the problem is obviously a great deal more serious and it has been the subject of much discussion in recent years. Whether stated in terms of psychological variables such as self-confidence, anxiety, and motivation to perform well, or in broader terms, such as the meaning which the testee ascribes to the test-taking ritual, there is clearly a case to be made for supposing that individual and group IQ differences involve factors other than purportedly culturally neutral cognitive skills. Once again, the point is sometimes conceded by hereditarians. In his *Harvard Educational Review* paper, Jensen wrote:

> When I worked in a psychological clinic, I had to give individual intelligence tests to a variety of children, a good many of whom came from an impoverished background. Usually I felt that these children were really brighter than their IQ would indicate. They often appeared inhibited in their responsiveness in the testing situation on their first visit to my office, and when this was the case I usually had them come in on two to four different days for half hour sessions with me in a 'play therapy' room, in which we did nothing more than get better acquainted by playing ball, using finger paints, drawing on the blackboard, making things out of clay, and so forth. As soon as the child seemed to be completely at home in this setting, I would retest him on a parallel form of the Stanford–Binet. A boost in IQ of 8 to 10 points was the rule...'[33]

It is most instructive to consider the way in which Jensen employs this anecdote. He introduces it while discussing the efficacy of compensatory education schemes which have sought to boost IQ. The reported gains, he argues, may be a consequence of greater familiarity with the test situation from first to second testing, and they might have occurred in the absence of any intervening compensatory education scheme. While this is a perfectly valid criticism of poorly conducted research where no test – retest control group was included, it is notable that Jensen does not consider the possibility that similar test sophistication factors might go a long way towards explaining the average IQ difference of 15 points between US blacks and whites, or between social classes, differences for which he favours a genetic interpretation.

An influential discussion of cultural differences has been given by the linguist William Labov.[34] Labov is highly critical of cultural deprivation theorists who have studied the language of black ghetto children in the USA, and who interpret the monosyllabic responses of the children in interviews as evidence that they are linguistically deprived. His own studies of black ghetto language in more natural settings produced findings in complete contrast to this, and he argues that the monosyllabic responses found by the deprivation theorists occurred because the children found the interviews a very intimidating experience. Labov's conclusion is that ghetto children speak a dialect of English governed by rules which differ from those of standard English, but which are equally rich when it comes to expressing fine shades of meaning. To the linguist, black ghetto language is not a primitive form of English, but simply a strong local dialect.

Labov's arguments are convincing because they are based on the reasonably advanced state of theory in modern linguistics. This has also enabled linguists to dispel the myth, disseminated by earlier generations of anthropologists, that some of the world's languages are structurally more primitive than others. In the field of cognitive studies, it is doubtful whether there have been theoretical advances sufficient to permit cultural comparisons which are not ethnocentric. There have been some pioneering cross-cultural studies of human reasoning in natural settings (for example in disputations) by Cole and his co-workers,[35] but as yet they are extremely cautious in interpreting their research. It may of course be that it is not possible in principle to produce theories of cognition which are free of cultural values in the sense that this can be said of the phonetic and syntactic theories of modern linguistics. It is not at all easy to find good arguments either for or against this position, but, unless the problem can be solved, the subject of 'culture fair' tests of intelligence seems destined to remain in limbo.

IQ-ACHIEVEMENT CORRELATIONS

IQ, as assessed by the Stanford–Binet, Wechsler and other conventional IQ tests, has been shown to be substantially correlated with a variety of indices of educational achievement. It is not, however, the best predictor of educational achievement. It is now generally acknowledged by psychometricians that the best predictor of a child's future achievement in any particular subject is a test of present achievement in that subject, and that the best predictor of all round future achievement is a test of all round current achievement.[36] This can apply even for children arriving at school for the first time. For example, Stevenson and his co-workers in the study cited earlier,[37] gave a wide variety of psychometric tests as well as tests for specific cognitive processes, to children starting at school and investigated the correlations between each test and many combinations of tests, and the children's later reading ability. They found that the best predictor by far of reading ability even several years later was the children's reading ability on arrival as assessed by the simple device of finding out how many letters of the alphabet they could name correctly.

As with all correlational studies, the problem with IQ–achievement correlations is the problem of interpretation. This has not often been appreciated by psychometricians who have tended to amass correlations between IQ and achievement indices without stopping to consider the possible alternative interpretations of the correlations. They have assumed that the correlation must be explained by the common causal influence of g or at least of some common pool of basic cognitive abilities. In fact there are a number of possible alternative explanations.[38] For example, many of the reported correlations involve the achievement of children who have previously been 'streamed' or 'tracked' on the basis of their IQ scores. Thus, if children with high IQs are placed in classes aimed at high levels of achievement, while those with low IQs are placed in lower standard classes, then the occurrence of a subsequent IQ–achievement correlation has something of the character of a self-fulfilling prophecy. The importance of this artefact has never been properly investigated, although it certainly should have been. It may very well be that IQ–achievement correlations are, to a considerable extent, a consequence rather than a cause of educators' confidence in the tests.

A second problem arises from the fact that IQ tests are only able to predict achievement when they are administered to children who are already attending school. Attempts to devise infant IQ tests have been a failure. Now, as we have already illustrated, the IQ tests are composed of questions which lean quite heavily on certain types of language skills, mathematical abilities, and general knowledge, all of which are taught in schools. To what extent, one can ask, do IQ–achievement correlations reflect differences in the quality or type of education which different children receive, rather than differences in ability which may exist when the children first arrive at school? To give an example, children whose schooling is heavily geared towards test taking, and who are repeatedly tested, may perform better on IQ tests and achievement tests than those whose schooling is not so geared, thereby contributing a spurious component to IQ–achievement correlations.

A third problem occurs if we consider the influence on test performance of factors whose origins lie outside the specific character of a person's schooling. Consider cultural, subcultural and family differences in acquired knowledge, skills, self-esteem, attitudes to schooling and test taking, as well as individual differences in personality and motivation. Although it could be argued that some of these factors may themselves be associated with the hypothetical *g* factor it would be absurd to suppose that the association is a perfect one. These differences presumably have some independent role to play in accounting for IQ–achievement correlations, and, once again, the question is, how much?

Some attempts have been made to provide statistical answers to the above questions, but they are inconclusive and the subject is generally acknowledged to be a methodological quagmire. Each possible influence is likely to be associated with each of the others to such an extent that it is probably not possible to assess the independent contribution of any one influence either to IQ or achievement, let alone to assess its contribution to the correlation between the two. A more productive approach to the problem of 'validating' IQ tests has been to investigate the extent to which IQ can predict success outside the educational sphere, especially occupational success. The argument is as follows. If IQ tests really do measure something as basic as is implied by the term 'general intelligence', then we should expect the tests to predict occupational success, especially in intellectually demanding occupations, over and above their ability to predict educational achievement. A number of studies have investigated the subject and the results cast grave doubt on the validity of the tests.[39]

The problem is not entirely a simple one, because educational credentials play a very large role in determining initial entry into occupations. Since the social structure enforces the existence of a substantial correlation between educational achievement and subsequent occupational status, it follows that anything else which correlates with educational achievement is also likely to correlate willy-nilly with occupational status. IQ is indeed correlated with occupational status, as proponents of the tests constantly affirm, but the real point, established by more recent studies, is that this correlation is entirely dependent on the correlation with educational achievement. Thus for a set of individuals with the same educational level but varying IQs, IQ is not correlated at all with occupational status; on the other hand, for a set of individuals with the same IQ, but differing educational levels, educational level remains closely associated with occupational status.

Investigations which have been concerned with finding the correlations between IQ and indices of success within particular occupations have produced strong evidence against the predictive power of the tests, even for occupations which most people would consider to be especially intellectually demanding. Studies of lawyers, engineers and chemists have found, in each case, a range of IQs from about 100 to over 150 and, again in each case, approximately zero correlations between IQ and assessments of success within these occupations. It remains reasonable to argue that a certain minimum level of IQ is required for success within these occupations, but this has not been tested and, in any case, the minimum certainly appears to be quite low, no higher than the average for the total population. The fact that IQs within the upper half of the overall range are not at all predictive of success even within intellectually demanding occupations suggests strongly that IQ has very little social significance outside the confines of educational testing.

THE CURRENT STATE OF PSYCHOMETRICS

Judged according to commercial criteria, psychometrics is in a very healthy state. There has been a huge proliferation of psychometric tests and the tests are used extensively by applied psychologists. On the other hand, judged according to scientific criteria, psychometrics is in a bad way. Attempts to place psychometrics on a sound scientific footing have been a failure. Factor analysis still has its devotees, but it has remained essentially an hermetic art, and there are signs that it is on the decline. For example, the *British Journal of Educational Psychology*, long a receptacle for factor analytic studies, has been publishing fewer and fewer of them in recent years. In November 1974 an editorial listed three types of paper most commonly rejected, one of them being 'factor analyses of intercorrelations where tests had not been selected according to any systematic design and results were essentially a list of the author's interpretations of his factors'. The editor placed the blame on the widespread availability of computers.

Other attempts to provide a theoretical foundation for psychometric tests have also fared badly. These attempts originate from the traditional preoccupation of psychometricians with the concepts of 'validity' and 'reliability'. 'Validity' is taken to mean, whether a test really does measure what it sets out to measure. Thus the validation criterion for an IQ test would either be correlations with educational achievement, or correlations with a well established IQ test. We have already discussed the shortcomings of this approach. In general, the validation of any psychometric test is impossible unless an independent and 'valid' measure already exists of whatever it is that the test purports to measure. Correlations with existing tests may simply perpetuate previous errors.

'Reliability' is a concept drawn from the fact that physical scientists assess the accuracy of their measuring instruments by repeatedly using them to measure the same quantity and noting the variation in the readings of the instrument. Psychometricians attempt to crudely approximate this procedure by devising an 'alternative version' of the test under consideration, replacing each question with a similar question which is roughly equally difficult, and then obtaining, for a sample of testees, the correlation between the two versions of the test. The procedure is unsatisfactory because the two versions of the test are really two slightly different tests. One particularly invidious use of reliability coefficients, dating back to Spearman, is the practice of 'correcting for attenuation'. To illustrate, suppose that an IQ psychologist obtains the IQ correlation between twins for a sample of identical twins. The reliability correlation may then be used to 'correct' the twin correlation to a new higher value, supposedly an estimate of the correlation between the twins' 'true IQs', a kind of platonic ideal score which differs to an unknown extent from the obtained score. The lower the reliability of the test the more the obtained correlation is increased. This thoroughly unscientific procedure has been much criticised in the psychometric literature,[40] but it is still often used, and anyone wishing to examine psychometric research literature would be well advised to be on the lookout for attenuation corrections.

Various attempts have been made to replace the concepts of validity and reliability by alternative statistical models based on the idea that a test can be said to 'sample' from some population of cognitive abilities (or 'behaviours'). Although these models have been developed into elaborate mathematical formulations, they have not been successfully connected up with the practical business of test construction because, as we have already noted in the case of IQ, it does not seem possible in practice to specify the 'population' from which the test is supposed to 'sample'.

The present state of 'test theory' has recently been rather well summarised by a practitioner. After reviewing developments in the period 1970–74 in the prestigious *Annual Review of Psychology*, James Lumsden concludes:

> The picture revealed is grim. Little of any consequence has been achieved during the review period; nor can we look with any great pride at the cumulative result for this century. It is only slightly unfair to say that test theory has failed as a theory. In most areas it does not act as a set of propositions which generates testable propositions in the content area of interest. It fails in the minimal demand that can be made of a theory: that it acts as an aide memoire.[41]

The applied psychologists who actually use psychometric tests do not worry much about test theory. Many of them are sceptical about the scientific foundations of the tests, but regard them as useful rough and ready practical tools of their trade. They consider the tests to be helpful when they have to make educational or clinical decisions about individuals. This is not necessarily as harmless a philosophy as it appears to be. For example, IQ scores often form the basis

for decisions to place children in 'remedial' classes. However, as was argued in the recent Californian court case,[42]
'remedial' education may simply mean abandoning any
attempt to instil anything in the child other than the most
rudimentary educational skills. Thus, the IQ test, with its
scientific connotations, is used to justify placing the blame
for educational failure on the child, when it might better be
placed elsewhere.

The IQ test is not the only culprit. In a recent and
detailed critical review, G. S. Coles makes the same point
about another widely used collection of psychometric tests
known as the 'learning-disabilities test battery'. His conclusion is:

> There is little question that eventually the tests reviewed
> here will be discarded; the evidence against them is
> mounting. The central question is really whether recog-
> nition of the invalidity of these tests will result in the
> abandonment of an untenable professional dogma, or
> whether it will merely result in the test battery being
> replaced by other equally questionable instruments. I
> have sketched the context of the test battery because I
> believe that the answer lies in the political and social
> realm and not in the worth of other less well-known
> instruments that are standing in the wings; these tests, in
> any case, do not yet exist. The future of the learning-
> disabilities test battery will depend upon how we answer
> the following questions: How catastrophic then will it be
> for the dependent industries, institutions, and profes-
> sionals to acknowledge that, so far as we can tell, Johnny's
> neural connections are intact? If we do not 'blame the
> victim', where then does the blame lie?[43]

We do not wish to imply that all uses of psychometric tests
are necessarily bad. For example, they may prove quite
useful in helping teachers to monitor their pupils' progress,
say in learning to read, although even here the subject is
fraught with difficulties. There is the usual psychometric
problem that the tests are based on inadequate theories.
Reading theorists constantly complain that reading tests are

based on intuitive and wrong conceptions of the nature of reading,[44] and teachers often assert that they can find out more about how well a child is reading by spending ten minutes with the child than by administering any number of reading tests. It may be that psychometricians under-estimate teachers. In a study of the efficacy of psychometric tests in identifying kindergarten children who were likely to experience difficulty in learning to read, Seymour Feshbach found that 'a kindergarten teacher's ratings can predict first grade reading achievement at least as efficiently as a psychometric battery that had been designed for this purpose'.[45]

Psychometric tests may very well have their uses, but the hypothesis that they can be dispensed with without disadvantage needs to be thoroughly investigated. Our primary concern in this chapter has not been with the practical uses of psychometric tests, but with their scientific background. Our conclusion is that there is no justification at all for the psychometricians claim to have established the 'scientific measurement of individual differences'.

5

The Scientific Issues – II:
The Potency of Heredity

The question of hereditary influences on test scores can be considered independently of the question as to what the tests actually measure. The methods of investigation used by psychometricians, if they are sound, can theoretically be used to estimate the heritability of any quantifiable characteristic; to borrow an example from the humourist J. B. Morton, they could be used to estimate the heritability of the ability to roll a pea up the side of a hill using only one's nose. Psychometricians have investigated the heritability of a number of different types of test score, and some other quantifiable characteristics, but by far the largest part of their research effort has been concerned with IQ. It is therefore appropriate to examine the validity of their methods by concentrating on this subject. Our reservations about the significance of IQ should still be borne in mind, however. There are countless seemingly trivial physical characteristics which appear to be heavily genetically influenced, and there is no reason why this should not also apply to behavioural characteristics, or cognitive skills; but, to attach profound significance to research concerning the heritability of any particular characteristic, it must first be established independently that it is a profoundly significant characteristic. And this has not been done in the case of IQ.

Although some of the more vociferous hereditarians continue to make extravagant claims about what IQ tests measure, the majority of psychometricians have moved a considerable distance towards accepting the criticisms made in the last chapter. Nevertheless, many of them are still prepared to defend the practical use of the tests and the investigation of hereditary influences. Their position, which merits serious discussion, may be put as follows:

It is true that IQ tests only measure a limited range of cognitive abilities, but this does not entirely detract from the usefulness of the tests. One can argue about the possible past or future significance of these abilities; but abilities which are predictive of scholastic success are certainly of considerable significance at present. Heredity–environment research provides further evidence in favour of using the tests for the following reasons. Although there is room for disagreement about the exact figures, the evidence is consistent with the view that heredity is of greater importance in the case of IQ, but that the environment is of greater importance in the case of educational achievement. The predictive power of the tests is limited precisely because achievement *is* influenced by environmental factors which IQ tests were designed to minimise. This is, in fact, a strength rather than a weakness; because, if IQ tests were abandoned, and current achievement formed the sole basis for educational selection, then this would ensure that those who had experienced an advantageous environment up to the point of selection, would continue to do so thereafter, even despite the fact that they might have little natural ability. On the other hand, using IQ tests gives a relatively greater chance to the individual who has greater natural ability, but who has experienced a disadvantageous environment. Thus, although IQ tests may not be completely fair to all underprivileged groups, they are likely to be a good deal more fair than the obvious alternatives. The importance of genetic factors in accounting for group differences in average IQ is less certain at present, but there are good reasons for investigating the subject; because, if genetic factors are present, then it would be unreasonable to expect group differences in achievement to be entirely eliminated by egalitarian policies.

The evidence in support of this comes primarily from the analysis of kinship data to arrive at estimates of 'heritability', a statistic designed to measure the proportion of the variation in a characteristic which can be attributed to genetic differences as opposed to environmental differences. A number of studies of IQ heritability have arrived at estimates of the order of 70 per cent or 80 per cent, while those for the heritability of indices of educational achievement have been much lower. In a sophisticated mathematical treatment which has received a great deal of attention, Jinks and Fulker estimated heritability for three IQ measures as 71 per cent, 73 per cent and 86 per cent, while their single estimate for achievement was 'uncertain but probably less than thirty per cent'.[1] Jensen has provided similar estimates for IQ, and summarises his own review of achievement heritability as follows:

> The heritability of measures of scholastic achievement is much less, on the average, than the heritability of intelligence. In reviewing all the twin studies in the literature containing relevant data, I concluded that individual differences in scholastic performance are determined less than half as much by heredity as are differences in intelligence.[2]

As we shall see shortly, there are some very strong grounds for rejecting the above heritability estimates. Before doing so we shall point out briefly a serious flaw in the psychometricians' argument which applies even if we accept the estimates as they stand. This concerns the correct interpretation of IQ–achievement correlations. Given an heredity–environment ratio of say 70–30 for IQ, and 30–70 for achievement, to what extent are the IQ–achievement correlations attributable to common genetic influences and to what extent to common environment? Hereditarians tend to assume that it is the genetic factors which hold sway, but the situation is quite symmetrical, and it is equally reasonable to suppose that the correlation is mainly attributable to environmental factors. Since IQ–achievement correlations are only moderate, they admit of a wide range of interpretations in this respect.

The problem applies equally to the interpretation of other test correlations, such as the intercorrelations among subtests of standard IQ tests, among different IQ tests, and among different indices of educational achievement. For example, childrens' scores for reading tests are correlated with their scores for mathematics tests. Are common genetic factors at work here or are both scores influenced in the same direction by factors of upbringing and education?[3]

In principle it should be possible to answer this type of question by extending the research methods to be discussed in this chapter. In practice, this has not been done, and it is a serious omission from the hereditarian research literature. This applies particularly in the case of IQ–achievement correlations. It means that hereditarians who make strong claims about the social significance of heritability studies are arguing from research into one partially heritable characteristic (IQ) to conclusions about another (educational achievement) merely on the grounds that the two are partially correlated.[4]

THE ESTIMATION OF HERITABILITY

The heritability of IQ has been a central concern in the history of the mental testing movement, but although the subject has been discussed *ad infinitum*, there are still no signs of general agreement on any major issue. The critics, including many leading biologists, continue to argue that existing heritability estimates are worthless, that it is not practically possible to obtain accurate estimates, and that, in any case, hereditarians have misunderstood the meaning of the concept of heritability and greatly exaggerated its significance. These criticisms will now be considered in detail.

Heritability estimates have a very restricted range of potential usefulness in the study of human populations. The main reasons for this were made clear at least as early as 1933, by Lancelot Hogben in an outstanding paper which is still worth reading today.[5] Since that time, whenever the subject of IQ heritability has provoked controversy, geneticists have repeatedly made the same points, adding a few more details and providing further illustrations. For a thorough and up to date treatment the reader is referred to recent papers by Richard Lewontin.[6] In order to emphasise the consistency with which successive generations of geneticists have viewed the issue we will quote from early papers as well as recent ones.

In a general sense it is not possible to assign percentages to the contribution of nature and nurture to a measurable characteristic. Recently Sir Peter Medawar explained this point as follows:

> The reason, which *is*, admittedly a difficult one to grasp, is that the contribution of nature is a function of nurture and of nurture a function of nature, the one varying in dependence on the other, so that a statement that might be true in one context of environment and upbringing would not necessarily be true in another.[7]

J. B. S. Haldane made the same point in 1938, and gave the following illustration:

> Let *A* be Jersey cattle and *B* Highland cattle. Let *X* be a Wiltshire dairy meadow, and *Y* a Scottish moor. On the English pasture the Jersey cow will give a great deal more milk than the Highland cow. But on the Scottish moor the order will probably be reversed. The Highland cow will give less milk than in England. But the Jersey cow will probably give still less. In fact, it is very likely that she will give none at all. She will lie down and die. You cannot say that the Jersey is a better milk-yielder. You can only say that she is a better milk-yielder in a favourable environment, and that the response of her milk yield to changes of environment is larger than that of the Highland cow.[8]

In a 1950 critique, J. A. H. Waterhouse gave the following example from human genetics:

Rickets is a childhood disease now well known to be due to a deficiency in vitamin D which may result from an insufficiency of sunshine whose ultra-violet rays can cause synthesis of the vitamin on the skin. Susceptibility to the disease, in some cases at least, is also governed by a genetic factor, so that in a suitable environment lacking both in the vitamin and in sunshine, the condition would appear to be determined mainly by heredity. Control of the environment, however, . . . can entirely negate the expression of a deleterious gene.[9]

A recently discovered example is phenylketonuria, a condition produced by a conjunction of genes which causes an inability to handle the dietary ingredient phenylalanine. Under normal circumstances children who inherit this condition become severely mentally deficient; but if they are fed on a specialised diet excluding phenylalanine they grow up perfectly normally.[10]

Heritability estimation methods were first developed by R. A. Fisher.[11] They are used by plant and animal breeders to estimate the contribution of various aspects of genetic variation to a measurable phenotypic characteristic (for example, milk yield) of a particular population (for example, Jersey cows) subject to a clearly specified and rigorously controlled range of environments (corresponding perhaps to the conditions under which it is proposed to graze them). Using complex statistical tools it is possible to partition the variation of the phenotypic characteristic into a number of components associated with genetic and environmental variation, as well as 'non-additive' effects of the type illustrated in an extreme form in Haldane's example. They enable the breeder to determine what breeding strategy to adopt.[12]

Estimates based on one set of environments would be of no use to a breeder who is concerned with a different set of environments, which is why Lewontin refers to heritability estimation as a 'local perturbation analysis' rather than a global analysis.[13] This is why it is of comparatively little interest to experimental geneticists. In his 1933 paper, Launcelot Hogben put it as follows:

From an experimental standpoint what do we mean by making the environment uniform? We can do so in an infinite number of ways, some tending to bring out genetic differences which were not previously measurable, others tending to obscure genetic differences which were measurable before. A balance sheet of nature and nurture has no meaning in this sense . . . [14]

In other words, the only balance sheet which could be obtained would apply only to the particular set of environments included in the experiment and the genetic variation in the population under study. Turning now to the investigation of human populations in naturally occurring environments, consider the heritability of height. If accurate estimates could be obtained, the heritability of height for the adult population of England would probably be much higher than for the adult population of the world, since the latter would include somewhat more gentic diversity, and also a far greater range of nutritional 'environments', including much severe malnutrition. Heritability might also vary from one region of England to another, partly because of slight genetic variation, partly because of variation in diet. It would probably be different for men and women, and a current estimate would probably differ from one made thirty years ago. One can go on multiplying examples indefinitely.

If we now turn to the subject of IQ heritability the problem becomes acute. Whereas any person's height can be measured unambiguously, the same cannot be said of IQ. Indeed it would be pointless even to attempt to give a standardised IQ test to a substantial proportion of the world's population, such as those who are illiterate. In practice estimates have only been attempted on subpopulations, usually local subpopulations, within a few countries in Europe and the USA. A further problem lies in choosing which test to use, since there is no reason for supposing that heritability is the same for different tests.

Some hereditarians believe that all of the above considerations amount to no more than nit-picking criticisms. They argue that they have a perfectly legitimate interest in IQ heritability for populations that have received full-time education, for whom it is quite reasonable to administer an IQ test. They agree that heritability is likely to vary between tests and for different populations, but claim that it has been a consistent finding that heritability is greater than 50 per cent for quite a number of populations, and tests. Thus, they argue, it can be asserted with a fair degree of generality that genetic differences play a greater role than environmental differences in accounting for individual differences in IQ.

This point of view, common especially in the popular writings of hereditarians,[15] is simply not supported by the facts. Estimates made before 1970 are now acknowledged by hereditarians to be unsatisfactory, because they were based on incorrect methods. Estimates made since then have ranged fairly evenly from 16–86 per cent, and the highest estimates are based largely on Burt's faked data.[16] So great are the discrepancies in the literature that it is impossible even to guess how much differences in heritability estimates are the result of using different tests, studying different populations, or are due to methodological differences in methods of estimation.[17]

THE QUALITY OF THE DATA USED TO ESTIMATE IQ HERITABILITY

The inadequacies of the original data which are used for heritability estimation have been shown in detail by Kamin.[18] The basic problem can be explained very simply. In order to obtain estimates it is necessary to obtain IQ data for relatives with varying degrees of genetic similarity (for example identical twins, ordinary siblings, cousins, and so on). Under normal circumstances these data are of no value because the degree of genetic resemblance is obviously closely correlated with environmental similarities (for example, twins share a common environment far more than do cousins). If psychometricians were to follow the appropriate procedures used in animal studies, they would have to take a large random sample of babies from their mothers at birth, then re-allocate them among the parents at random, and then test them fifteen or twenty years later. Obviously they cannot do this, and so they try to circumvent the problem in various ways.

The most intuitively appealing method is to study adopted children, and quite a number of adoption studies have been conducted. One serious drawback of these studies is that adopted children do not experience anything like a typical range of social environments. Because the demand for babies to adopt greatly exceeds the supply, and because the adoption agencies try to place the babies with what they consider to be the best adoptive parents, the vast majority of adopted children experience social environments which are very much at the upper end of the socio-cultural spectrum as assessed by a variety of indices.[19] It immediately follows from this that estimates of heritability based on adoptees are not valid as estimates of heritability for the general population. An interesting side effect of this bias is that it produces an unusually clear and unambiguous demonstration of social environmental influences on IQ. Adoption studies have invariably found that the adopted children have above average IQs, as an environmentalist would predict; however, from the point of view of a hard line hereditarian who denies that there are any significant social environmental effects on IQ, this is a serious anomaly, because the natural parents of adopted children tend to come from the lower end of the socio-cultural spectrum, which leads to the hereditarian prediction that the children should have below average IQs.[20]

Social environmental effects can, in principle, also be discerned by finding the correlations between the childrens' IQs and those socio-cultural characteristics which do vary significantly among the adoptive homes; and hereditary effects can, in principle, be discerned by finding the correlations between the childrens' IQs and those of their natural parents. In practice, these interpretations come up against the problem of 'selective placement', which Leon Kamin describes as follows:

The adopted children have not been delivered to their

foster homes by storks. They have typically been placed
there by adoption agencies, and such agencies attempt to
'fit the child to the home'. The agencies are also keenly
aware of the mental testers' assertion that IQ is heritable.
They often strive to place a child with 'good heredity' in a
similarly 'good' home. The agencies may have knowledge
of the true mother's IQ, and they almost always have
knowledge of her socio-economic and educational status.
They invariably have, by law, detailed knowledge of the
characteristics of the would-be adoptive parents. Thus, if
children of high IQ biological mothers are systematically
placed into homes conducive to the development of high
IQ, such selective placement would guarantee the development of a *non-genetic* correlation between adopted
child and biological mother.[21]

It should be emphasised that the phenomenon of selective
placement is separate from, but co-existent with the upward
bias in the socio-cultural characteristics of adoptive parents
described previously. Roughly speaking, being adopted is a
form of upward social mobility, but children whose natural
parents have the lowest socio-cultural status are not placed
in such 'good' homes as those with higher status natural
parents. Selective placement is generally acknowledged to
be a serious problem for adoption studies. Just as environmentalists like Kamin use it to provide a non-genetic
account of IQ correlations between the children and their
natural mothers, so hereditarians use it to provide a
non-environmental account of the correlations between the
childrens' IQs and characteristics of the adoptive homes.[22]
The two competing explanations cannot easily be disen-
tangled. The theoretical separating of the effects of heredity and environment, which was the original aim of
adoption studies, is not adequately manifested in practice.

In the original research reports of the major adoption
studies, the authors have usually been careful to point out
their limitations, but this certainly cannot be said of the
hereditarians who have reviewed this research area and
argued that the studies provide overwhelming evidence of
the potency of heredity. Both Kamin and Arthur

Goldberger have documented at length the lack of objectivity which has been displayed by the present day hereditarians Jensen, Herrnstein and Munsinger.[23] For example, Herrnstein's much publicised book *IQ in the Meritocracy* contains a description of an adoption study by Burks in which he reports that Burks found that 'the foster children's IQs correlated with their natural parents' IQs more than with their foster parents'. . . . The control-group correlations, for parents raising their natural children, were only slightly higher than the true parent–child correlations in the experimental group, comprising adopted children.' As Kamin observes, these statements are wholly false. Burks did not obtain the IQs for the natural parents. Furthermore no study has ever reported IQ correlations between adopted children and their natural fathers. At the time Herrnstein was writing (1973) only two studies had reported adopted child–natural mother IQ correlations, and neither of these reported the corresponding correlations for the adoptive parents.

Of the two studies which did report adopted child–natural mother IQ correlations, one had disappeared from the hereditarian literature until it was rediscovered by Kamin. In this 1938 study, Snygg found that, for a Canadian sample of 312, the correlation was .13, much lower than the correlations for normally reared children which are variable but mostly over .40. The other study, by Skodak and Skeels, is the one which has been reported by hereditarians, but it has been reported in a highly selective fashion. The study was reported originally on a number of occasions with varying sample sizes as new cases were added and others dropped out. The adopted child–natural mother correlations varied from .00 to .44, probably attributable to peculiarities of the shifting samples, but, as Kamin notes, hereditarians have shown a preference for the figure of .44.[24]

In the case of adopted child–adoptive parent IQ correlations, hereditarian selectivity has operated in the reverse direction, in favour of low correlations. Kamin points out that most reviews cite two studies, by Burks and Leahy, yielding correlations of .18 and .20 between the children's

IQs and the adoptive midparents' IQ (the average of the IQs of the two adoptive parents), but ignore a third large-scale study by Freeman, Holzinger and Mitchell where the same correlation was found to be .39.

Since 1973 further adoption studies have yielded figures which, for each of the two types of correlation, are roughly intermediate along the ranges given above.[25] When one bears in mind the problems of sampling and selective placement, it is apparent that, taken together, adoption studies do not provide any clear-cut evidence of the potency either of hereditary influences or of environmental influences.[26]

A different, but also intuitively appealing method of investigating hereditary influences is to study identical twins who have been separated and reared in different homes. If their home environments are uncorrelated, then any IQ correlation between the twins would appear, on the face of it, to be attributable only to their identical genes. Here again Kamin shows that hereditarians have given a highly misleading impression of the original research. The problem is that of correlated environments. Separately reared twins are an extremely rare phenomenon. What usually happens in these cases is that the biological parents retain one twin, and hand over the other (rarely at birth and frequently after several years) to a close relative or friend. This can obviously produce a non-genetic IQ correlation. The only study which appeared to have overcome the problem was Burt's, now known to be fraudulent but previously considered by hereditarians to be the knock-down argument in favour of high IQ heritability. The remaining three studies account for a total of 71 twin pairs and the largest of them (40 pairs) was a British study conducted by James Shields.[27] The problem of correlated environments is illustrated by the following examples from Shields' detailed case histories:

> The paternal aunts decided to take one twin each and they have brought them up amicably, living next door to each other in the same Midlands colliery village. . . . They are constantly in and out of each other's houses.

Brought up within a few hundred yards of one another. ... Told they were twins after girls discovered it for themselves, having gravitated to one another at school at the age of five.... They play together quite a lot.

Among the 40 pairs there are at least a further five similar cases.[28] Most of the 40 pairs were reared in related branches of the same family, or one was brought up by a relative and the other by a family friend. In four cases the twins were not separated at all until they were over five, and in eight cases they were reunited in childhood. 14 pairs attended the same school for most of their childhood.

In his report, Shields was quite frank about the weaknesses of his study but, as Kamin notes, hereditarians have ignored these weaknesses and, inexcusably, cited the twins' IQ correlations as direct evidence of hereditary influences. It is obviously scientifically indefensible to obtain heritability estimates from these correlations on the assumption that there is no environmental contribution to them, but this has been done by Jensen and others.[29] We have already mentioned the sophisticated mathematical treatment of heritability by Jinks and Fulker in which they obtained three heritability estimates of 71 per cent, 73 per cent and 86 per cent.[30] The first two estimates were based on Shields' twins, for two different tests, and the third on Burt's fraudulent data.

The remaining two studies of separated twins consist of an American study of 19 pairs and a Danish study of 12 pairs.[31] In both studies the twins' environments were again correlated. The amount of separation appears to have been rather greater in the American study but even here the authors wrote that 'the effective environmental differences for some of the separated cases were not much greater than for those reared together'. The majority of the twins were not separated at all until they were between one and five. Kamin has pointed out many further weaknesses of the studies but they need not concern us here, since it should by now be obvious that separated twin correlations cannot be used to estimate IQ heritability.[32]

The one remaining source of IQ heritability data which is

worth mentioning comes from studies of normally reared identical and non-identical twins. The argument is that, since both types of twin share a common environment, any increase in the IQ correlation for the identical twins compared with the fraternal twins must reflect their greater genetic similarity. Making a number of simplifying assumptions, it is possible to obtain heritability estimates from this type of data. Kamin and others have questioned the validity of these simplifying assumptions,[33] but they need not concern us here. The most straightforward objection to the methodology concerns the assumption that identical twins share a common environment to the same extent as fraternal twins. As Hogben put it in 1933:

> On account of their greater physical resemblance identical twins may tend to work together, play together and be exposed to the same sources of infection to a greater extent than fraternal twins. There is therefore an element of legitimate doubt concerning the correct interpretation of the greater intellectual resemblance of the former.[34]

Kamin reviews the few studies where this has been investigated and shows that there is indeed an element of legitimate doubt. For instance, in one study, 43 per cent of the identical twins reported that they had never spent a day apart compared with 26 per cent of like-sex fraternal twins. In another, 40 per cent of the identical twins reported that they studied together compared with 15 per cent of like-sex fraternal twins. Kamin ironically observes that 'There is some possibility that studying together might tend to produce similar test scores'.[35] Kamin gives a number of further examples, and goes on to argue that the observed correlation differences are fully consistent with a strictly environmental interpretation. He also notes that heritability estimates based on this type of data are highly variable with some sets of data producing theoretically absurd estimates less than 0 per cent and greater than 100 per cent.[36]

The current vogue among hereditarians is for fitting

elaborate mathematical models to large sets of kinship data in order to arrive at estimates of heritability. There are three different types of model, based respectively on methods first introduced by R. A. Fisher, Sewall Wright and Christopher Jencks. The data to which the models are fitted includes the adoption and twin data discussed above, together with further data from normally reared individuals which the models attempt to account for with a combination of genetic and environmental parameters. These models have recently been analysed at great length by the American econometrician Arthur Goldberger,[37] who points out that different models, when applied to the same sets of data, yield grossly varying heritability estimates. In a series of detailed mathematical analyses, he shows that the models are either 'overdetermined', or that they incorporate highly questionable simplifying assumptions. An 'overdetermined' model is one which has more mathematical parameters than equations which can be applied to the data, so that the parameters cannot be estimated. In order to bring the models into contact with 'reality' the model fitters have to reduce the number of free parameters by imposing constraints on them. Goldberger shows that these simplifying assumptions are unsatisfactory, often flying in the face of common sense or ignoring influences known to be present in the data following Kamin's analysis (for example, correlated environments for separately reared twins). The imposing mathematical edifices presented by the models and the subtlety of the discussions between their adherents combine to give an impression that this area of enquiry is free of hereditarian bias, but Goldberger argues that this is not really so, and he writes, 'It strikes me that the ordinary canons of scientific research and scholarly discourse are not being observed in biometrical – genetic writing on the heritability of intelligence.'[38]

BURT'S KINSHIP STUDIES IN PERSPECTIVE

There is no more eloquent testimony to the shortcomings of hereditarian science than the manner in which Burt's fraudulent kinship studies came to occupy the centre of the stage in hereditarian writings from 1969 until 1974, when Kamin's demolition of them was published. Most of Burt's kinship studies were published between 1955 and 1966,[39] in an attempt to rekindle interest in hereditarian science when it was in the doldrums, and when there was mounting criticism of the eleven plus examination in Britain. They did not attract a great deal of attention at the time, but they succeeded in the long run, because they played a key role in converting Jensen to hereditarianism,[40] and Jensen was undoubtably the key figure in revitalising the subject from 1969 onwards.

We have already noted that hereditarians have acquired the knack of turning a blind eye to kinship data which do not lend support to their views, and also to the cautions and provisos expressed in the original reports of data which do appear to support the hereditarian position. This is not necessary in the case of Burt. All of his correlations are consistent with high IQ heritability and, when they are analysed collectively with mathematical models, they pro-duce much higher heritability estimates than most other sets of data.[41] Furthermore, in Burt's reports there are no cautions and provisos concerning the interpretation of the correlations. What rapidly does become apparent when inspecting the original papers is that they are so grossly deficient as scientific reports that it is difficult to see, from a purely scientific point of view, why they should ever have been taken seriously.

Burt's first report of kinship correlations is in his 1943 paper on 'Ability and Income'.[42] In the space of just over one page he provides the results of a large study of orphanage children (over 172), a study of 157 adopted children conducted at Burt's behest by the ubiquitous but apparently non-existent Miss Conway, and kinship corre-lations for 167 first cousins, 86 second cousins, and either 189 or 218 twins (Burt's figures are inconsistent in succes-sive sentences). Out of 62 identical twins (or 77 depending on how one reads Burt) located in a survey, he states that 15 were reared separately, an absurdly high proportion. The amassing of all this information would have involved a prodigious amount of work. If the previous studies of orphanage and adopted children are anything to go by, Burt's report might have consisted of a large book or several monographs; and yet his account is restricted to a few short paragraphs in a paper written on a different topic!

Burt did not write on the subject for another twelve years, and then, during his retirement, he published a series of papers from 1955 to 1966. As Kamin shows,[43] these papers are also grossly deficient. In them, Burt published the results of kinship studies which he claimed to have been carrying out over a period of fifty years, and which, if genuine, would be by far the largest set of kinship data ever to have been amassed by a single investigator; and yet it is not even possible to determine from them which IQ test was used, or whether the same test was used on different occasions. The few procedural details which are given serve only to invalidate other aspects of his work. For instance, he states that he relied frequently on subjective 'assessments' of intelligence rather than tests. In the case of the separately reared twins some of the correlations are for 'final assessments' which had been adjusted 'to reduce the disturbing effects of the environment to relatively slight proportions'. Scores which have been adjusted to reduce environmental effects are obviously useless for estimating heritability, which is supposed to measure the relative influence of heredity and environment, but this has been conveniently overlooked by heritability estimators.

Of the many bizarre features of Burt's reports pointed out by Kamin, the one most strongly suggestive of fraud is the fact that a number of the reported correlations remain the same to three decimal places as the sample size changes. For example, the correlation for separately reared twins using a 'group test of intelligence' was reported as .771 in 1955 (sample of 21 pairs), .771 in 1958 ('over 30'), and .771 in 1966 (53 pairs). From a statistical point of view this is nothing short of miraculous. When it was first pointed that this might indicate fraud, and before Hearnshaw had found that the separated twin data had indeed been fabricated, (from a perusal of Burt's personal diary),[44] hereditarians were quick to defend Burt's reputation; but the nature of the defence again speaks volumes about the shortcomings of hereditarian science. The most favoured explanation was that Burt had not bothered to recalculate the correlation after obtaining more data, a regrettable mistake, but not really fraud.[45] The explanation scarcely bears contemplation. It is evident from the other twin studies that tracking down separately reared twins is an intolerably difficult and time consuming business. To have located 32 fully separated pairs from investigations in the London area from 1955 to 1966, as Burt purported to have done, would have been an extraordinary achievement. On the other hand, the computation of the IQ correlation for 55 pairs of twins which would have been the main purpose of the study, is a trivially simple statistical exercise. One must either be exceptionally charitable, or else have a heavy prior investment in the matter, in order to accept such an explanation.

Kamin's inquiries appear to have prompted Jensen to conduct his own re-examination of Burt's data,[46] with very much more charitable interpretations, although concurring that the data had to be rejected. Jensen concludes with the slightly cryptic remark that 'It is almost as if Burt regarded the actual data as merely an incidental backdrop for the illustration of the theoretical issues in quantitative genetics, which, to him, seemed always to hold the center of the stage.'[47] This remark should be compared with Dorfman's subsequent demonstration that Burt faked the results of a 1961 paper which purports to present IQ data for 40,000 father–child pairs obtained from 'a London borough selected as typical of the whole county'. In a detailed analysis Dorfman shows that many aspects of the data are too statistically good to be true, and he goes on to show how they were in fact faked using standard statistical tables and the constraints imposed by Burt's theories. The data were not, however, presented to illustrate theoretical problems in quantitative genetics but, as Dorfman puts it, 'to test deductions from his genetic theory of social class and to answer criticisms of previous work.'[48]

It has also been asked why, if Burt was being deliberately dishonest, he made such a botch of it?[49] Now that we know that he was being deliberately dishonest the question can again be posed. The obvious answer is that Burt was only too well aware of the low critical standards to be found in this field of enquiry. If so, he probably died with this opinion intact, since it was not until some months after his death that Kamin first expressed his misgivings. It is also clear that the two leading hereditarians had no misgivings at that time. In one obituary notice Eysenck, who was once a student of Burt's, wrote that he 'was a deadly critic of other people's work when this departed in any way from the highest standards of accuracy and logical consistency' and that 'he could tear to ribbons anything shoddy or inconsistent'[50] Jensen was even more fulsome in his praise especially for 'his unflagging enthusiasm for research, analysis and criticism ... and, of course, especially his notably sharp intellect and vast erudition – all together leave a total impression of immense quality, of a born nobleman.'[51]

Kamin's critique received a great deal of publicity. Once it became clear that Burt's data had to be rejected and that many of Kamin's criticisms of the remaining heritability literature could not easily be dismissed, hereditarian science was thrown into disarray. A recent response has been to conduct new kinship studies, especially adoption studies, which are enjoying a revival in the USA for the first time since the 1930s. It is already becoming clear, however, that the new studies are dogged by the same problems that beset their forerunners.[52] Selective placement has again been demonstrated to exist. Although some ingenious methods have been devised for controlling out this effect in order to arrive at estimates of heritability, it has also been found that there are serious discrepancies in the estimates which are obtained from different features of the data. Furthermore, since it has again been found that the adoptees experience an atypical range of social environments, it remains a valid criticism that the obtained heritability estimates would not apply to the general population. Following the barrage of criticism concerning the basic concept of heritability which has been mounted by geneticists led by Lewontin,[53] it is not easy to see why psychometricians should continue to show such enthusiasm for the subject. The most likely reason is that, despite protests to the contrary, they are continuing to confuse the notions of heritability and plasticity. This merits some further discussion.

HERITABILITY AND PLASTICITY

The considerable public interest in IQ heritability studies, and their political impact, derives from a tendency to confuse the concepts of heritability and plasticity, to assume that a highly heritable characteristic is largely genetically fixed and impervious to attempts at environmental modification. Our discussion of the concept of heritability should have made it clear that this is incorrect. Since any heritability estimate is based on a particular set of environments, it cannot tell us how the characteristic will behave when a new element is introduced into the environment, or when deliberate attempts are made to modify it. The point has been made repeatedly by the geneticists but it has been largely ignored by hereditarians.

To illustrate the distinction between heritability and plasticity consider the heritability of adult height and weight. A number of kinship studies have also reported correlations for height and weight. If they are taken at face value they indicate that both have high heritability, somewhat higher for height than weight but both higher than for IQ.[54] For the reasons already discussed this is not necessarily a sound inference but, for the sake of argument, let us make it. Now consider the plasticity of height and weight. An adult who wished to increase his or her height would not meet with much success. As was pointed out in the Sermon on the Mount, it is not possible by taking thought to add a cubit to one's stature, although it is possible that a suitable programme of physical exercise might produce some small increase for most people. On the other hand, a person's weight can obviously be increased or decreased within wide limits by excessive eating or fasting. In a famine great decreases in weight occur rapidly. The difference in plasticity is not discernible, however, from the heritability estimates, even despite the fact that the two characteristics are themselves quite highly intercorrelated. It is notable, incidentally, that hereditarians, when they want to borrow a simple example from physical anthropometrics, choose height but not weight.

The heritability–plasticity fallacy is not restricted to psychologists. Karl Pearson, the pioneer of statistics and biometrics, was deeply impressed by some dubious evidence for the high heritability of susceptibility to tuberculosis, so much so that he opposed the widespread introduction of TB sanatoria, believing that the disease could only be eliminated by stern eugenic measures. He did so even despite the fact that the infectious nature of the disease was already known.[55] We can be grateful that the medical profession was unimpressed by his arguments. Similarly, today's children who have inherited the phenylketonuria gene complex but who are growing up normally on a phenylalanine-free diet, can be grateful that the indisputable evidence of genetic determination did not deter researchers from investigating environmental influences.

Hereditarians have frequently opposed educational reforms, such as the expansion of higher education and compensatory education schemes, by citing the evidence for high IQ heritability and arguing that the reforms were attempting to improve the achievement of individuals who lacked the necessary innate ability. In a singularly unpleasant comparison which perhaps reveals his underlying attitude, Jensen has compared some of today's educationalists with alchemists attempting to transmute base metals into gold.[56] Since he clearly regards IQ heritability studies as relevant, indeed central, to the issue, there can be no doubt that he has confused the notions of heritability and plasticity.

The distinction should by now be clear enough. The plasticity of a characteristic can only be investigated by attempting to modify it and, since there are an infinite number of possible ways of modifying any characteristic, plasticity can never be fully understood. Following recent criticism there are signs that hereditarians are now beginning to appreciate the distinction. Jensen, for example, now concedes the general point, but argues that high heritability does at least show that only limited effects would be achieved by 're-allocating existing socio-economic and educational or other existing environmental advantages or disadvantages.'[57] To put it more precisely, if heritability studies were based on a representative sample of environments (which they are not) and if IQ can be shown to have high heritability (which seems unlikely), then it would be possible to calculate the effects of re-allocating the existing range of environments, effects which would then probably turn out to be quite small. A complete re-allocation of environments would involve randomly re-allocating babies at birth. We are presumably supposed to infer that, since any practicable redistribution of environments would be restricted to school environments (for example, the controversial 'bussing' programmes), then this would have an even smaller effect, perhaps a trivially small one.

The reply to this is that educational and social environments are continually changing, not simply in statistical terms, but *qualitatively*. To take just one type of example, new methods of teaching are frequently being devised and introduced. Children today learn branches of mathematics which were previously thought to lie within the grasp only of university mathematics students, and only a few of them. Any new method of teaching introduces a novel element into the environment, and its effect cannot be known until it has been tried. A few years ago the Harvard astronomer David Layzer concluded a critical review of IQ psychology by putting forward the 'hypothesis of unlimited educability' and pointing out that there exists no theoretical or experimental basis for rejecting it.[58] Indeed it is difficult to see how there could be such a basis. Paradoxically, it seems both reasonable and desirable to view educational research and reform as an attempt to test this untestable hypothesis, just as medical research can be viewed as a test of the hypothesis of the unlimited curability of diseases.

The plasticity of IQ has been debated recently in the context of the American Headstart programmes of compensatory education in which the aim was, among other things, to boost the IQs of deprived children. More generally, a demonstration of the plasticity of IQ may be obtained whenever children experience a substantial change in their environment. In some studies, children have experienced a considerable improvement in their environment, for example, moving from a poorly equipped orphanage into foster homes, and this has been accompanied by average IQ gains of 30 points or more.[59] Hereditarians do not dispute this. Jensen, for example, writes that 'There can be no doubt that moving children from an extremely deprived environment to good average environmental circumstances can boost the IQ some 20 to 30 points and in certain extreme rare cases as much as 60 or 70 points.'[60] However, he goes on to argue that the gains achieved in compensatory education schemes have been trivially small, or attributable solely to an increase in 'test sophistication'; and that one cannot reasonably expect large IQ gains from the comparatively minor environmental changes which occur when a child participates in a compensatory education scheme. Jensen's analysis of the results of these schemes was heavily disputed at the time and subsequent studies have shown that he is wrong. Gains of the order of 20 or 30 points have been produced.[61]

These results are pleasing to environmentalists but it remains arguable whether attempts to boost IQ are of much real interest or value. It is a worthwhile endeavour only if IQ has independently been shown to be a really significant characteristic, something worth changing. In the last chapter we argued that this has not been convincingly demonstrated. Intervention schemes may certainly be a very worthwhile undertaking. Few would dispute the potential value of a literacy scheme, for example. But it is difficult to justify using IQ tests to evaluate the efficacy of intervention schemes. It is frequently said in educational circles that whoever controls the examination effectively controls the syllabus; and there is no reason why the 'syllabus' of intervention schemes should be effectively controlled by IQ test constructors.

GROUP DIFFERENCES IN AVERAGE IQ

Whenever the average IQs of different population groups are compared, considerable differences are usually found to exist; although there is also much overlap, so that group differences only account for a small proportion of the overall variability among individuals. The one exception to this rule is that both sexes have approximately the same average IQs on most tests. This is not, however, a true empirical finding but a consequence of the manner in which the tests were first constructed. Sex differences do exist for different IQ subtests, some favouring males and some favouring females, but the test constructors ensured that there would be no differences in the overall scores by a judicious selection of subtests. Thus the two sexes were *defined* to have equal intelligence rather than *discovered* to have equal intelligence. By making this decision the test constructors did a considerable disservice to those who now seek to extend hereditarian arguments to account for the scarcity of women in the most prestigious positions in society.

The test constructors did not choose to eliminate other group differences in this way, although it is difficult to find any *scientific* justification for singling out sex differences for special treatment. In his evidence in the Californian court case Kamin stated:

> I am struck by the discrepancy in the treatment of the sex differences versus the treatment of the race differences and the treatment of the social class differences for that matter. I can see no scientific ground why one should eliminate questions which appear to show that one sex is doing better than the other and not eliminate questions which appear to show that one race is doing better than the other. It seems to me that this has to reflect the preconceptions of the people who are making up these tests.[62]

Social class and black–white differences were probably built in when the tests were constructed just as sex differences were built out. The examples cited in the last chapter show that the test questions often reflect the white middle-class academic milieu of their constructors rather than any culture free conception of human cognition. Social class differences were probably also built in as a consequence of selecting test items which were predictive of educational achievement; since there are quite large class differences in educational achievement, a test which favours middle-class children would, other things being equal, correlate better with achievement than one which did not, and it would therefore stand a better chance of being included in the final test.[63]

Although social class and black–white differences are the principal focus of debate today, they are not the only population differences which have been discussed in the history of the mental testing movement. An earlier issue was the relatively better performance of urban children compared with rural children. It is instructive to consider Godfrey Thomson's 1924 summary of competing explanations for this difference, as they closely parallel those which are now put forward to account for social class and black–white differences:

> As we go out from the city into the rural districts, we find the average IQ of the children, as measured by the usual tests, becoming lower. Is this due to a real decrease in intelligence, or is it due to the fact that the country children, though intelligent enough, are less ready with verbal responses and are less familiar with the type of material used in the intelligence test? And if the decrease in intelligence is real, is it caused by the lack of book learning, lack of vocabulary, lack of stimuli to the sharpening of wits which the town child finds; or is it caused by the pull of towns taking away the more imaginative and the mentally more alert?[64]

The suggestion that the difference may be apparent rather than real would nowadays be called a 'test bias' or 'cultural difference' explanation. The suggestion that country children have a less stimulating environment would be called a

'cultural deprivation' explanation, and is the type of explanation favoured by the proponents of compensatory education schemes. The third suggestion implies that the difference is genetic: bright country people move to the towns
taking their 'bright genes' with them and leaving behind
relatively poor 'stock' in the rural areas.

As Thomson pointed out, the three explanations are not
mutually exclusive. Each could account for some part of the
observed difference. Furthermore, the cultural bias and
cultural deprivation interpretations cannot easily be disen-
tangled, and it is difficult to see how they could be in the
absence of a culturally neutral theory of cognition. Although they have profoundly different implications for
psychometrics, they can both be classed as environmental
interpretations. In the remainder of this chapter we shall be
concerned mainly with the genetic account of group
differences. Its proponents are usually prepared to concede some role to cultural influences, but they argue that
genetic differences account for the greater part of the
observed differences.

THE GENETIC INTERPRETATION OF SOCIAL CLASS
IQ DIFFERENCES

The hereditarian argument concerning social class IQ
differences, popularised recently be Herrnstein,[65] is strik-
ingly similar to Thomson's urban drift explanation for
urban–rural differences. Bright working-class children, it
is argued, are upwardly mobile, taking their 'high IQ genes'
with them into the middle-class, while a similar downward
mobility takes place for dull middle-class children. Over a
number of generations, significant genetic class differences
are likely to become established. The argument rests on IQ
having reasonably high heritability over a representative
range of environments for a number of generations, and on
IQ having a reasonably strong relation to social mobility,
again for a number of generations, during which mobility
must also have been considerable.

We have already seen that there are no good grounds for
supposing that IQ, for any particular test, does have high

heritability for any representative population sample either now or in the past; and it does not seem to be practically possible to obtain satisfactory estimates. The argument, which is therefore purely speculative, is even more unsatisfactory if we consider the relationship between IQ and social mobility. As we showed in the last chapter, the relation between IQ and subsequent occupational status is mediated entirely by way of educational achievement. We have also noted that IQ–achievement correlations, which are very far from perfect, are open to both genetic and environmental interpretations. Since 'IQ genes' can only be socially mobile in so far as they are associated with educational achievement, the argument treads a very thin speculative line.

Unlike the question of heritability, the relationship between IQ and social mobility is perfectly amenable to empirical research, but it is research which has seldom been undertaken. It should be borne in mind that Burt's fraudulent 1961 paper on the subject was intended to rebut the criticism of the hypothesis that there is a genetic basis to social class IQ differences. It should also be borne in mind that the existence of a correlation between childhood IQ and adult occupational status is irrelevant to the mobility issue; since childhood IQ is correlated with parental occupational status, the same correlation with subsequent adult occupational status would occur even if there were no social mobility at all. There does, however, exist one study which is relevant. It appeared in 1971 and it is now much quoted by hereditarians, and merits some discussion.

J. H. Waller examined data for 131 Minnesota fathers and 170 of their sons, and found a correlation of .29 between father–son IQ differences and father–son differences in socio-economic status.[66] It is not clear why hereditarians are so impressed by this rather low correlation. It indicates precisely the type of weak association which would be predicted from our examination of the relationship between IQ, educational achievement, and occupational status. IQ accounts for just under 8 per cent of the variation in social mobility in this sample, which leaves 92 per cent unaccounted for. Some of this 92 per cent may involve variation in educational achievement unrelated to IQ, and the rest to the many other factors influencing individual social mobility, such as personality and motivation, circumstance and luck. As Bane and Jencks point out after discussing the issue, '. . . when it comes to making a dollar, IQ is clearly only a small part of a big complicated picture.'[67] The 8 per cent relationship is still open to both genetic and environmental interpretations.[68] For such a phenomenon to have produced a large genetic component in social class IQ differences we would have to suppose that the relationship involves mainly genetic factors, that social mobility operates on a very large scale, and that similar large-scale social mobility has been going on for many generations. But individual social mobility based on educational achievement is a phenomenon of quite recent origin.

The genetic interpretation of social class IQ differences has also been debated in the context of adoption studies. If an ideal adoption study could be conducted, and if the genetic interpretation is correct, then adoptees who had typical working-class biological parents, for example, but were adopted into typical middle-class homes, would have the same average IQs as normally reared working-class children; under an environmental interpretation they would have average middle-class IQs. In practice, as we have seen, adoption studies are very far from perfect. Due to problems of sampling and selective placement, corrrelations between the childrens' IQs and the socio-economic status of the biological and adoptive parents are ambiguous. As we have noted, the above average IQs of adopted children appear to be consistent only with an environmental interpretation, but sampling problems make it difficult to assess whether this is sufficient to account for the whole of the social class IQ difference.

A recently published French adoption study, in which there appears to have been no selective placement, has produced results which are most embarrassing for the hereditarian cause. It was a small-scale study but it produced exceptionally clear-cut results. Thirty two adoptees who had been abandoned by their working-class parents, and adopted into middle-class homes, were found to have

above average IQs and educational achievement, corresponding almost exactly to those found for the normally-
reared biological children of similar middle-class parents. A
further twenty children were located who had been normally reared by the same mothers who had abandoned the
adoptees, and they were found to have below average
scores, again corresponding almost exactly to those found
for the children of similar working-class parents.[69] These
results correspond precisely with environmentalist predictions and are totally inconsistent with hereditarian predictions. This then is the current state of the evidence with
regard to the hereditarian claim that there is a large genetic
component to social class IQ differences, a claim which has
been a dominant theme in the mental testing movement
ever since its inception, but which hereditarians have rarely
taken the trouble to investigate empirically.

THE GENETIC INTERPRETATION OF ETHNIC GROUP IQ DIFFERENCES

The controversy about the causes of ethnic group IQ
differences has been mainly an American issue. Nowadays
the focus is on black–white differences, but differences
among the various immigrant minorities have also been a
major theme. It is a subject which does no credit to
American psychometrics, as Kamin has shown, citing the
many crude and overtly racist writings of the founders of
the American mental testing movement, writings which are
comparable with those found nowadays in the pamphlets of
neo-Nazi political groups.[70] Today's hereditarians usually
speak in more muted tones, but one can still find examples
which are reminiscent of nineteenth century racist science,
notably in the writings of the British biologist and hereditarian C. D. Darlington.[71]

The main protagonist for the genetic interpretation of
black–white IQ differences is Jensen. Although he has
succeeded in obtaining a great deal of publicity for his
views, he has not succeeded in convincing many of his
fellow psychometricians, who are nowadays much less

sympathetic to the hereditarian view on this issue than were their early forerunners in the American mental testing movement. Many who remain convinced that IQ has high heritability, and who favour a genetic interpretation of social class differences, have nevertheless argued in favour of an environmental interpretation of black–white differences, or have chosen to remain agnostic.[72]

In his *Harvard Educational Review* paper, Jensen argued that, if IQ has high heritability, then to attribute the difference in average IQs between blacks and whites to genetic differences is, as he put it, 'not an unreasonable hypothesis'.[73] The argument is fatally flawed however, as was quickly pointed out by population geneticists, and eventually half-heartedly acknowledged by Jensen.[74] It is a fundamental tenet of population genetics that there is no theoretical or empirical relation between within-groups heritability and between-groups heritability. It is theoretically possible for a characteristic to have 100 per cent heritability within each of two populations, but for a large difference to be found between the two populations which is entirely environmental in origin. When genetic differences exist between two populations, and when they are subject to different environmental conditions, and when they differ in some characteristic, it is not theoretically possible to predict the extent, *or even the direction* of any differences which might obtain if they were subjected to identical environmental conditions. Thus, if the cultural differences between American blacks and whites were somehow eliminated, and if IQ differences did not then disappear, then it is just as possible that blacks would score higher than whites than that whites would score higher than blacks.

Are there any *a priori* reasons for expecting to find genetically determined intellectual differences between different human populations? The eminent biologist G. G. Simpson thought not, when he wrote in his 1969 book, *Biology and Man*, that:

There are biological reasons why significant racial differences in intelligence, which have not been found, would not be expected. In a polytypic species races adapt to differing local conditions but the species as a whole evolves adaptations advantageous to all its races, and spreading among them all under the influence of natural selection and by means of interbreeding. When human races were evolving, it is certain that increase in mental ability was advantageous to *all* of them. It would, then, have tended over the generations to spread among all of them in approximately equal degrees. For any one race to lag definitely behind another in overall genetic adaptation, the two would have to be genetically isolated over a very large number of generations. They would, in fact, have to become distinct species; but human races are all interlocking parts of just one species.[75]

In stating that significant racial differences in intelligence have not been found, Simpson carefully avoids committing himself to the belief that IQ tests measure intelligence. It is an interesting corollary to his argument that a significant genetic component to black–white IQ differences is only likely to be present if the abilities assessed by the tests have no adaptive value. Although this may very well be true it is unlikely to appeal to hereditarians who place such importance on the hypothetical 'factor of general intelligence'.

The main residual argument deployed by Jensen and his supporters involves setting up and then refuting specific environmentalist explanations for black–white IQ differences. But the environmentalist explanations turn out to be very much men of straw. The main version involves the relationship between ethnic differences and differences in socio-economic status. Those ethnic minorities which have the lowest average IQs are usually the most economically deprived, a fact which is as unsurprising to environmentalists, as it is to the hereditarians who attribute economic deprivation to 'poor genes'. However, it is possible, to some extent, to separate the two factors and to compare the average IQs for members of different ethnic groups having the same socio-economic status. Although this always reduces the size of the ethnic group differences, it does not always eliminate them. In particular, it seems that American blacks average somewhat lower than whites with the same socio-economic status. Furthermore, some groups are more economically deprived than blacks but actually score better, at least on some of the tests. Hereditarians argue that this cannot be explained except by positing the existence of a genetic factor.[76]

The fallacy here lies in the assumption that variation in human culture can be reduced to a single numerical quantity, the socio-economic index. For anyone who believes that human intelligence can be reduced to a single quantity, labelled IQ, it is an understandable mistake, but it is still a mistake. To appreciate this, consider, as an example, a black grocer, a white grocer, a Japanese grocer, and a Mexican grocer, all living, let us say, in San Francisco. Since they all have exactly the same socio-economic status, we are supposed to assume that they all have identical cultural experiences to bring to bear when they, or their children, are given an IQ test. In fact, ethnic minorities have cultures which vary in all sorts of different ways with a variety of possible effects on the ability to answer correctly the various types of question included in IQ tests, not to mention the social ceremony of actually taking the tests. This explains why the pattern of ethnic differences varies considerably from test to test, so that one group may perform better than another group on one test, but worse on another.[77]

When the subject of black–white differences was being debated earlier in this century, the biologist J. B. S. Haldane placed the issue in perspective by pointing out that the differences were no greater than the regional differences for the white population. Blacks in some northern states had about the same average score as whites in some southern states. Hereditarians attempted to argue that this only occurred because it was the brightest blacks who migrated north, but this was then countered by showing that the scores of northern blacks increased as a function of the length of time that they had been in the north.[78]

More recent empirical studies have also supported an environmental interpretation. These studies have compared the IQs of black and white children, and children of mixed parentage, who have been brought up in circumstances where the usual cultural differences might reasonably be expected to be much reduced, if not actually eliminated. In a British study carried out at a residential nursery, no appreciable differences were found between the three groups, the differences tending, if anything, to favour the non-white groups. In a study of illegitimate German children fathered by black and white occupation soldiers, no difference was found between the two groups. After a detailed review of these and other studies, a review which is very sympathetic to the aims and methods of hereditarians, Loehlin, Lindzey and Spuhler conclude that, 'On balance, such studies can probably be assessed as offering fewer explanatory difficulties to environmentalists although they admit interpretation from a range of view-points'.[79]

The reason for this very cautious conclusion is that hereditarians can and always will argue that results such as the above are inconclusive because the children may be genetically unrepresentative of the populations from which they are drawn. Similarly, an environmentalist could always deal with an hereditarian finding by pointing out that environmental effects cannot be controlled for. In a world in which racism is rife it is difficult to imagine anyone being able to locate a group of black and white children or adults of whom it could confidently be stated that they did not have significantly different life experiences. This is why most people who have examined the issue have concluded that the hereditarian hypothesis, and consequently also the environmental hypothesis, is simply not amenable to empirical testing.

This completes our examination of scientific issues in the mental testing movement. We consider that anybody approaching this field for the first time and expecting to find a gradually accumulating body of knowledge about the role of heredity in human intellectual variation would be sadly disappointed. What is in fact to be found is a very slender quantity of empirical research distributed over a period of about fifty years, fraudulent in one important case, methodologically weak in almost all cases, and open to a wide range of possible interpretations concerning the role

6

Unnatural Science

The term 'unnatural science' was introduced by Sir Peter
Medawar in an excellent short article on the IQ controversy. Having borrowed it for the title of this chapter, we
think it appropriate to quote his own explanation of the
term:

> If a broad line of demarcation is drawn between the
> natural sciences and what can only be described as the
> *unnatural sciences*, it will at once be recognised as a
> distinguishing mark of the latter that their practitioners
> try most painstakingly to imitate what they believe – quite
> wrongly, alas for them – to be the distinctive manners
> and observances of the natural sciences. Among these
> are:
>   (a) the belief that measurement and numeration are
> intrinsically praiseworthy activities (the worship, indeed,
> of what Ernst Gombrich calls *idola quantitatis*);
>   (b) the whole discredited farrago of inductivism –
> especially the belief that *facts* are prior to ideas and that a
> sufficiently voluminous compilation of facts can be pro-
> cessed by a calculus of discovery in such a way as to yield
> general principles and natural-seeming laws;
>   (c) another distinguishing mark of unnatural scientists
> is their faith in the efficacy of statistical formulae,
> especially when processed by a computer – the use of
> which is in itself interpreted as a mark of scientific
> manhood.[1]

In Chapter 1 we outlined the methods for analysing
scientific progress which have been put forward by Popper,

Kuhn, and Lakatos. Although the differences between them are considerable, they do at least concur, and any reasonable person would also concur, in expecting to find in the history of a science major theoretical developments and changes, and concomitant developments and changes in the problem areas of interest. Judged according to this very lenient criterion alone, there is clearly something gravely amiss with psychometric science. The subject has an extra-ordinarily static quality. In the current literature, the major issues are the pros and cons of positing a g factor, the significance of IQ as a causal agent in determining educational and social inequality, and the percentage contributions of heredity and environment to individual and group IQ differences; exactly the same issues that were being debated, in essentially the same way, forty or fifty years ago. Although a considerable amount of data has been gathered and processed in the intervening period, the major sources of controversy are virtually unchanged. Thus, P. E. Vernon displays a delightful lack of guile in the preface to his new book, *Intelligence: Heredity and Environment* (1979) when he states that 'The same controversy has been going on for over fifty years, and it is doubtful that any of the protagonists have ever been persuaded to change their views.' Or, as Medawar puts it, ' . . . the more disputative IQ psychologists give the impression of being incapable of learning anything from anybody . . .'[2]

The static quality is particularly evident in the nature of the tests themselves. Although many new psychometric tests have come on to the market, none has a better theoretical foundation than the conventional IQ tests, which are still the most widely used, and which differ only to a trivial extent from the early versions of the Stanford–Binet. This has not always been fully appreciated. In his unfortunate attempt to defend hereditarian IQ psychology, discussed in Chapter 1, the philosopher of science P. Urbach[3], compares the development of IQ tests with the development of thermometers. Just as new thermometers were developed, for example to provide accurate measurements for extreme ranges of temperature, so he argues, test constructors have devised culture fair tests and tests for mentally handicapped children. A more realistic treatment of the comparison has been given by Block and Dworkin,[4] emphasising the contrast between the development of thermometers, which went hand-in-hand with the development of *theories* about heat, and the lack of significant developments in IQ testing, which reflects the *atheoretical* predisposition of the test constructors. Urbach's examples do not establish his case. Tests for individuals in the low IQ range are just tests with easy questions; similarly, tests for the 'gifted' are just tests with difficult questions. As we showed in Chapter 4, the attempts to develop culture fair tests have been a failure, precisely because psychometricians lacked any articulated theory about cognitive processes upon which to base them.

The comparison between IQ test development and thermometer development would be appropriate if the history of thermometers had been quite different from what actually took place. Suppose that it was as follows. A crude thermometer was devised. Further thermometers were then invented, and accepted as satisfactory provided that they yielded results which correlated reasonably well with those obtained from the original device. Research into the relationship between heat and other things produced roughly similar results when different thermometers were used, and when this was not the case, a variety of *ad hoc* explanations were put forward to account for this. It was not considered necessary to investigate the anomalies further because the rough similarities were considered to be much more significant than the anomalies. In this hypothetical case, we have a very good analogy with the development of IQ tests and with research into such topics as the heritability of IQ, and the relationship between IQ and educational achievement. The reason why there is such a sharp contrast between IQ psychology and what actually took place in the theory of heat and thermometer development follows from our discussion of contemporary psychobiology in Chapter 4. It proved extremely productive to conceive of heat as a unidimensional measurable quantity; it is not productive to conceive of human intelligence in this way.

To continue our search for signs of scientific healthiness in the mental testing movement, let us consider whether psychometricians have acted as good Popperians and 'stuck their necks out' by making predictions which, it could reasonably be imagined, would fail if the theories from which they were derived were wrong. As far as we can judge, there is just one example of a really strong and counter-intuitive prediction to be found, the remarkable prediction that our national intelligence is declining. As we saw in Chapter 2, this prediction proved to be a dismal failure; when the subject was investigated, national intelligence, at least as measured by IQ tests, was actually found to be rising. Hereditarians could only rescue their theory by proposing that innate national intelligence really was declining, but that the fall was masked by an even larger environmental boost. In Lakatos's terminology, the research programme had degenerated, and indeed it is now almost defunct.

Another example of a potentially falsifiable hypothesis is Spearman's original conception of g. We have examined this conception at various places in this book,[5] and perhaps it is useful to draw the issues together briefly. The origins and also the continuing influence of the concept would seem to lie in external ideological issues rather than in the internal history of psychometrics, a theme to which we shall return later. It is also tempting to speculate that in choosing the term g and identifying it with a concept of 'energy', Spearman was well aware of the connotations of these terms; G is of course the name of the gravitational constant in the great Newtonian synthesis, and the concept of 'energy' and its conservation has also been a key feature of major theoretical advances in physics.[6]

Leaving this speculation aside, if we accept Spearman's account, the concept was not arrived at in a hypothetico-deductive manner, but inductively on the basis of his examination of matrices of correlations among test scores. However the theory did go beyond merely 'predicting' that the already observed positive correlations should indeed be positive correlations. It specified a mathematical relation in the form of the 'tetrad equation'. But the Popperian nature of this prediction is in some doubt in that Spearman was obliged to select his tests judiciously if the prediction was to be successful; and he was also obliged to 'doctor up' his correlations by using the dubious 'correction for attenuation', a procedure against which even Karl Pearson found it necessary to protest.

The impressiveness of Spearman's prediction was further undermined by Thomson showing that it was also derivable from a quite different theoretical position. Spearman's theory must be unique in the annals of science in that it only made one prediction and this prediction was identical with that made by its main rival! Despite all this, the theory did retain some vestiges of potential falsifiability, and as more and more correlation matrices became available for analysis, it had eventually to be rejected; or, to be more precise, 'rescued' by the positing of an increasingly large array of more specialised 'group factors'.

As we showed in Chapter 4, the effect of this was to leave the proponent of g with the minimal prediction that the correlations among cognitive psychometric tests should always be positive to some unspecified extent, a prediction which could also be made on the basis of considering the manner in which the tests were first constructed and 'validated'. Comparatively recent findings that cognitive tests can in fact be devised which do not correlate with conventional psychometric tests would appear to refute even this minimal prediction. As a final contribution to this degenerating research programme we should like to offer factor analysts one final rescue formula; any test which does not correlate with conventional tests simply has a zero g loading. The g factor really has rather little in common with the gravitational constant as a scientific proposal; it is something which can, if one chooses, be extracted from certain sets of numerical data in much the same sense that this could be said of the retail price index.

The remainder of psychometric research is also devoid of any significant predictive achievements, and is dominated by an inductivist methodology which would be condemned by any serious natural scientist as mere stamp collecting. As we pointed out in Chapter 4, the investigation of the influence of IQ on educational achievement and occupational status has been restricted to the amassing of correlational data without any serious attempts being made to face the critical problems about the causes of these correlations. It was left to critics of IQ psychology to carry out more fine-grained analyses which, in fact, fail to support the meritocratic views of psychometricians or their belief that IQ tests measure fundamentally important cognitive abilities.

The same can be said of the research into IQ heritability discussed in the previous chapter. At worst, and this can be said of most hereditarian writing, the approach has been to sift and select from amongst a completely ambiguous body of data in order to give the unwary reader the impression that IQ differences are invariably found to be the result primarily of inherited differences. At best, and this can be said of some of the original studies, the aim has been simply to assess the percentage contribution of heredity to differences on a particular test given to a particular population, subject to a particular set of environments. No hypothesis is tested, and the practice has been condemned by geneticists as hopelessly methodologically flawed and, in any case, scientifically pointless.

Concerning the extent of hereditary and environmental influences, the only hypotheses which do appear to be falsifiable are the pure hereditarian hypothesis that environmental differences have no effect on IQ, and the pure environmentalist hypothesis that hereditary differences have no effect. Adoption studies have provided strong evidence against both of these hypotheses,[7] but their refutation hardly ranks as a notable scientific achievement. As Medawar[8] and many others (including even Galton[9]) have pointed out, both are, from a biological point of view, absurdly implausible. The only protagonist to be found on behalf of either is Kamin,[10] but his defence of the pure environmentalist hypothesis is essentially a heuristic device, adopted in order to demonstrate the methodological shortcomings of kinship investigations. There are no grounds for seriously entertaining the hypothesis that individual differences in any human skill are completely genetically determined, or completely environmentally determined; and a refutation of either is, scientifically speaking, about as exciting as a refutation of the hypothesis that the sun will fail to rise tomorrow.

So far we have argued that psychometrics possesses few of the characteristics which philosophers of science look for when analysing the growth of knowledge in mature sciences. Let us now turn to our thesis stated in Chapter 1, that psychometrics has not achieved any breakthrough to autonomous knowledge and that it remains today with all of the characteristics of a pre-paradigmatic science, as outlined by Kuhn. In particular, its concepts remain conditioned by common sense, by a one-sided dependence on the mature science of genetics, and by 'external' influences of a socio-political nature.

The concept of intelligence still lies at the heart of psychometrics and, as we argued at the beginning of Chapter 4, this concept remains very much conditioned by ordinary everyday notions of intelligence. Psychometricians argue that they have a technical definition of intelligence as that which is measured by IQ tests, or as the common factor which can be extracted from test correlation matrices, but by using terms like high/low IQ interchangeably with words like bright, dull, clever and stupid, they seek to retain all of the social importance of the 'prescientific' concept while claiming to have arrived at a new form of scientific measurement. Sometimes the efforts of psychometricians to preserve the connection and also to detach the concept from a specific socio-historical context can be ridiculous as in the case of Jensen's recent sententious pronouncement that 'I have been able to find references to what we would today call intelligence (although usually not so labelled) in the earliest literature of ancient India and ancient Greece'.[11] As we noted in Chapter 4, the concept of g has also played a useful role in maintaining the connection. Thus, in the same paper, Jensen castigates Neisser for describing IQ as an assessment of 'academic intelligence' and writes, in a manner which it would be difficult to parody:

There is ample evidence that g is involved in seemingly

quite simple and commonplace activities that are exceedingly remote from school and academic pursuits. For example, it has been shown in on-the-job work sample tests given to US cooks, equated for months of experience in the kitchen, that the various routine tasks performed by cooks are differentially g loaded. Making jellyrolls, it turns out, is much more g loaded than preparing scrambled eggs!

That psychometric science has a very one-sided dependence on the mature science of genetics should be obvious from our discussion of the concept of heritability in the last chapter. The non-specialist, upon discovering that IQ psychologists are apt to bandy about terms like dominance and epistasis, broad and narrow heritability, and to deploy some very sophisticated mathematical models, is naturally likely to form the impression that psychometrics has entered a mature phase. Even allowing that the technicalities are derived from modern genetics rather than an internal development in psychometrics, the fact that biometrical methods have been extended to measures of intellectual ability might still seem to be a notable scientific achievement. In fact, as we have seen, IQ kinship data are quite useless for fitting complex biometrical models. Furthermore, it should be emphasised once again that the estimation of heritability is considered to be of very little use in human genetics. As Feldman and Lewontin put it, 'Certainly the simple estimate of heritability, either in the broad or narrow sense, but most especially in the broad sense, is nearly equivalent to no information at all for any serious problem of human genetics.'[12]

The contrast between the histories of psychometrics and genetics is an instructive one. The origins of the study of heredity, like psychometrics, can be traced back to a pre-paradigmatic phase when Galton and his disciple Pearson were arguing for an essentially atheoretical analysis of the correlations for phenotypic characteristics. But whereas genetics entered its mature phase following the rediscovery of Mendel's laws and the gradual elaboration of genetic theory, psychometrics remained stuck in an immature state, continuing to the present day simply to analyse correlational data. Modern genetics does have something to contribute in relation to human intelligence, the Mendelian analysis of the inheritance of particular kinds of mental deficiency, such as Down's syndrome (mongolism) and phenylketonuria; but this is a far cry from psychometric science.

In describing psychometrics as pre-paradigmatic, we do not mean to imply that a paradigmatic psychometrics is, so to speak, waiting in the wings. In Chapter 4 we emphasised that modern developments in psychobiology suggest that the basic concepts and methods of psychometrics are unsound. The best prediction that can be made would probably be that the development of more powerful theories about cognitive processes will show psychometrics to have been a scientific blind alley, just as the developments of twentieth century biological science have shown that anthropometrics, the sister discipline of psychometrics, was a blind alley. The reason why psychometrics, in contrast to anthropometrics, has survived, and continued to attract adherents despite its lack of progress, may lie partly in the slow development of psychology, as compared with biology, but a more important consideration would seem to be that external ideological factors have played the main role in keeping psychometrics alive. It is to this issue that we now turn.

The centrepiece of psychometric science is unquestionably the concept of general intelligence, considered to play a major role in all forms of human excellence and to be largely inherited, so that human beings can, in principle, be ordered in a simple fashion from the most naturally able to the least. The ordering can even be carried out in practice, allowing for a certain margin of error, by using standardised IQ tests. As we have seen, it is not an idea which commends itself to anyone familiar with the biological sciences, and there is little empirical evidence to support it; but the internal history of psychometrics can reasonably be viewed as an effort to bludgeon the data into submission in order to maintain this conception, a conception which already existed fully fledged at the beginning of the discipline. What was and is its attraction?

Its attraction was initially for eugenists. A programme of racial improvement clearly required that excellence be inheritable. It was not absolutely essential that it be unidimensional, but it was obviously an enormous advantage, since, otherwise, intractable problems would have arisen as to how much any one desirable characteristic should be bred as opposed to another (problems only too familiar to plant and animal breeders who are compelled by the realities of their work to forego any commitment to unidimensionality). Thus, in the heyday of eugenics, high intelligence, or 'civic worth', was considered to encompass all forms of moral and political wisdom, and low intelligence was considered to be the cause of all forms of moral turpitude and degeneracy, which the eugenists sought to eliminate. The general factor was quite incredibly general.

Now that the eugenic doctrines of the early twentieth century have been largely and, let us hope, permanently abandoned following revulsion at their consequences in Nazi Germany, the scope of the general factor has shrunk somewhat. It is probable, although by no means certain, that today's hereditarians would accept that it is possible to be highly intelligent but wicked; or to be unintelligent but to lead a blameless life. The ideological function of the general factor is nowadays restricted to its second aspect, the rationalisation of educational and social inequality. Here the attraction of a unidimensional conception of innate ability lies in its application in hierarchical societies where occupational status, and income, are roughly unidimensional, and where assessments of educational achievement, again roughly unidimensional, form the main basis for entry into occupations, especially high status and well paid occupations. We should not forget that the mental testing movement had a progressive phase in Britain when, for a time, IQ tests may very well have increased the chances for working-class children to be upwardly socially mobile; but IQ arguments are nowadays employed solely to draw pessimistic conclusions about social mobility, and to oppose egalitarian doctrines.

In the USA at present, it is often asked why Jensen and his supporters seek evidence of lower innate intelligence among blacks, if not to promote racism. But while it is true that their writings do have the effect of promoting racism, they may be right in denying that this is their intention. Their main purpose is to argue that the elimination of discrimination, which they seem to believe has already been achieved, need not be accompanied by any large-scale upward mobility of blacks. In other words, blacks should not continue to cite their economic disadvantage as evidence of discrimination. As we saw in Chapter 1, this cause has received a serious setback in the recent Californian court decision that IQ testing, when used to place children in classes for the 'educable mentally retarded', is itself an instrument of discrimination.

In Britain the concept of innate general intelligence has been used extensively at the other end of the educational spectrum, to justify elitism in education, to defend the retention of grammar schools, and to oppose the expansion of college education on the grounds that 'more means worse'. Similarly, it is used to defend the practice of streaming, placing children from an early age into different types of classes aimed at different levels of educational achievement, and consequently at different levels of eventual occupational status. In their recent report on *Aspects of Secondary Education*,[13] HM Inspectors of Schools were effectively opposing the psychometric consensus in stating that the practice is too rigid because it prevents children from working at their best level in different subjects, and because it may serve only to reinforce teachers' earlier expectations of the pupils. Streaming and selection in education, together with the concept of innate general intelligence, can be regarded as fulfilling certain functions in a hierarchical society, rather than deriving from objective truths about the nature of human abilities.

It is instructive to compare IQ psychology with the one other branch of psychology which can rival its capacity to provoke widespread controversy, the behaviourism of B. F. Skinner. This tradition has also been criticised as scientifically unsound,[14] being based on inductivist methods, operationalism and a distaste for theory building. While IQ psychologists have derived broad generalisations from the investigation of the observed correlations among test scores, Skinnerians have derived theirs from the relationships among observed variables in a few simple animal learning situations, especially one in which rats learn to press a bar in a box to obtain food. While IQ psychologists believe that their generalisations can account for the apparently complex phenomena of educational and social inequality, Skinnerians believe that theirs can account for such theoretically daunting phenomena as the acquisition and use of language, and the occurrence of psychological disorders, now relabelled as 'behavioural disorders'. While IQ psychologists believe that the widespread use of testing can herald in a new and better meritocratic society, Skinnerians believe that the widespread use of conditioning techniques, and the careful manipulation of rewards or 'reinforcement', can eliminate all kinds of aberrant and deviant behaviour, such as schizophrenia, crime, delinquency and sexual perversion, and could lead ultimately to the creation of a conflict-free Utopia. Although the methods are quite different, the ambitions are much the same as those of the eugenists. (In his 1932 novel *Brave New World*, Aldous Huxley portrayed the consequences which might follow if behaviourists and eugenists were allowed to combine in pursuing their Utopian dreams.)

The obvious difference between the mental testers and the behaviourists is that the former stress the importance of innate differences while the latter stress that of the environment. Since the same people are apt to denounce both traditions as having objectionable ideological overtones, this contrast is sometimes used to argue that the criticisms are muddle-headed. This has been rebutted by Chomsky[15] who points out that the two traditions have been perfectly combined by Herrnstein,[16] who, like Eysenck, finds much to admire in both, and who brings them together in presenting a 'rationalisation', in both the descriptive and prescriptive senses, of social inequality. Herrnstein's argument is that the need for social efficiency requires that the most naturally able be employed in the most intellectually demanding occupations. But in order to ensure that this happens in practice, it is essential that reinforcement be

manipulated by providing the largest incomes and bestow-
ing the greatest prestige on these intellectually demanding
occupations. Otherwise, so Herrnstein seems to believe,
people of great intelligence, perhaps including himself,
would naturally drift towards intellectually undemanding
occupations such as roadsweeping.

The marriage of psychometrics and behaviourism at a
practical level has been a recent development in applied
psychology. It would only be a small exaggeration to say of
British educational and clinical psychologists, that, when
they are not administering tests, they are devising equally
controversial programmes for 'behaviour modification'.
Unfortunately, it would be beyond the scope of this book to
analyse behaviourism, although we suspect that a similar
historical/scientific analysis to that adopted here for the
mental testing movement would be of considerable interest.

In our concluding remarks, we wish to touch on the
intellectual validity of extending the historical and scientific
critiques of psychometrics into a critique of the ideological
character of science in capitalist society. Expressed very
baldly, this is to ask whether the scientific knowledge
produced within a given set of social relations can ever be
objectively detached from the everyday language, social
culture and 'world-views' with which the members of a
society 'construct' social reality and which scientists necessarily bring to their professional activities? Clearly, to
discuss the question adequately is beyond the scope of this
book; it is an issue to which philosophers devote volumes.
To ignore it altogether would be to mirror the parochialism
of the internal histories of psychology where the objectivity
and autonomy of the knowledge is taken for granted.

We have, in a sense, already broached the issue by
pointing to psychometrics as a specimen of technocratic
rationality which offers second-level treatments of political
and social symptoms, and ignores or denies their aetiology.
Furthermore, we have been at pains to emphasise psychometrics' self-identification with the calculative rationality of
the entrepreneur's market and we would claim that the
conception of 'ability' is posited on the market evaluation of
labour. But is the inability to think beyond the conceptual

categories provided by everyday meanings and everyday associations merely a characteristic of the social and behavioural sciences whose object of study is – very broadly – those meanings, or is this characteristic common to the production of all scientific knowledge?

Certain radical intellectuals would answer that it is common to all; for example, the French historian of ideas, Michel Foucault,[17] has advocated an approach to the history of science which is directed to uncovering the 'archeology' of knowledge, to exposing, that is, the epistemological ground-rules that come into play in the very existence of a scientific discourse. Although he resolutely denies this, there are inescapable affinities between Foucault's method and that tradition of 'structuralist' analysis which regards meaning and human subjectivity as produced *by* (and not simply *within*) the linguistic and other cultural systems which are given in a society. One attempt to apply Foucault's methods to the history of differential psychology has been made by Nicholas Rose,[18] which regrettably imitates many of Foucault's obscurities of style without greatly illuminating the topic.

We would argue that, while all meanings are necessarily 'social', it is quite improper to leap from this premise to the conclusion that no meanings (including scientific meanings) can be autonomous from the society and social relations within which they are produced. Part of the confusion springs from a narrow conception of 'meaning' and 'social'. Meanings cannot always be reduced to their linguistic significance and the society for whom they are fully meaningful does not always consist of a little bounded province within an overall, temporally finite, realm of meaning or a given totality of social relations.

This point may be made quite simply by considering the ancient game of chess. The modern chessboard is still populated with the symbols and landmarks of the feudal social relations which prevailed at the time when the game was first introduced into Europe (castle, knight, bishop and so on) and there was a systematic correspondence between the position of real knights and bishops in the external world of feudal relations and their symbolic representation on the chess board. But the full 'meaning' of chess cannot be reduced to a naming of the pieces and chess, as a specialised system of meaning, has clearly transcended the social relations which provided the vocabulary of the game in Europe. It is a specialised system of meaning which enables a special type of communication to go on in that international society which understands the rules. The rules enable objective decisions to be made about play, but perfect knowledge of the rules does not make for good or even competent play, whose minimum requirement is a constant and subtle adjustment of one's own intentions to those of one's opponent.

Following Kuhn, we would argue that mature sciences have developed concepts which are largely autonomous from contemporary social relations, much as this can be said of the rules of chess. Immature sciences, generally speaking, have not. To pursue the analogy, they might be compared with the popular board game of Monopoly which, as its name suggests, embeds many features of capitalist property relations, and which would be virtually meaningless, say, to a nomadic people where goods were held in common ownership.

We do not mean to imply that the distinction between mature and immature science is always hard-and-fast, or that theoretical developments in mature sciences are always perfectly autonomous and devoid of social meaning; but we think it quite wrong to cite a demonstration that psychometrics (or behaviourism, sociobiology, psychoanalysis and so on) is riddled with meanings which are, so to speak, socio-culturally local, in order to show that this is true of all science. Anyone not already committed to this belief as a matter of dogma would expect its proponents to support it by the analysis of well-established branches of the natural sciences. As far as we are aware this has not been done. It would require fine-grained historical analysis rather than the use of crude analogies where, for example, a particular theory of the structure of matter is held to 'correspond' to the structure of society at the time it was formulated. This type of analogy-mongering, which one sometimes encounters in the sociology of knowledge, is, of course, itself a feature of immature science!

The distinction between mature and immature science, or between natural and unnatural science, is quite central to much of the analysis undertaken in this book. As we have attempted to show, some of the most convincing reasons for rejecting the scientific claims of psychometricians can be derived from contemporary theories in the biological sciences, and by using methods of analysis which philosophers of science employ when examining the development of mature sciences. To seek to abolish such a productive distinction, which appears to be the current fashion in the radical science movement, seems to us to be a most misguided policy.

Appendix
Correlation and Regression

A correlation coefficient is an index of the extent to which two quantities are associated, the extent to which one is predictable from the other. If, for example, the scores of a group of individuals on two different tests were so closely associated that they appeared in exactly the same rank order for both tests, then the correlation coefficient, usually referred to as r, would be at or near its maximum value of 1.00. If they were not associated at all, so that knowing an individual's score on one would be of no help in predicting the other, then r would be close to zero, subject to a certain amount of sampling fluctuation on either side of zero. Values in between these extremes indicate the extent of association. For instance, height and weight are two measurements of individuals which are substantially, but imperfectly, positively correlated. Negative correlations, running down from zero to -1.00, are indicative of inverse relationships. An example of a negative correlation would be age and running speed for the adult population.

Statisticians recommend that correlation coefficients should be interpreted by squaring them as this indicates the level of prediction involved. Thus if r equals .70, then r squared equals .49, which means that 49 per cent of the variability on one measure is predictable from the other. A correlation of .50 indicates a 25% level of prediction, and correlations of .30 and less indicate very low levels of prediction, less than 10 per cent. Since the unsquared correlation, like the squared one, ranges from zero to 1.00

(for positive correlations), but is always higher than the squared value, there is a natural tendency to think of the unsquared correlation, which is what is normally reported, as indicating a stronger relationship than actually exists. To appreciate this, examine the scatter diagrams in Figure A.1

(i) Binet IQ×Stanford educational age (normal correlation).

(ii) Binet IQ×Stanford educational age (cross twin correlation).

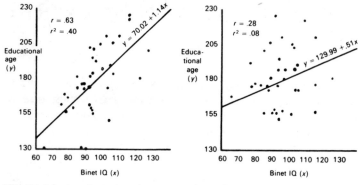

(iii) Otis IQ×Stanford educational age (normal correlation).

(iv) Otis IQ×Stanford educational age (cross twin correlation).

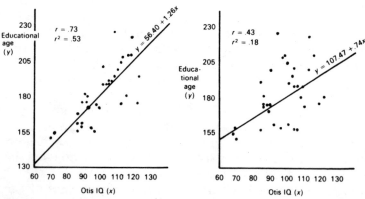

SOURCE: Recomputed from H. H. Newman *et al.*, *Twins: A Study of Heredity and Environment* (Chicago University Press, 1937). (See discussion in Chapter 5, note 4)

Figure A.1 *Scatter diagrams, correlation coefficients, and regression lines for data from separated twin study*

showing the distribution of pairs of test scores at four levels of correlation. Note that scattergrams (i) and (iii) ($r = .63$ and $r = .73$) indicate moderate relationships, while scattergrams (ii) and (iv) ($r = .28$ and $r = .43$) indicate weak relationships.

Regression lines are the 'best fitting' lines which can be used for making predictions. In Figure A.1 we have drawn in the regression lines of y (educational age) on x (IQ). This would be the line used in predicting educational age from a knowledge of IQ. (A separate regression line of x on y would have to be drawn if one wanted to reverse the procedure and predict IQ on the basis of educational age). Once again it can be seen that reasonable predictions could be made in cases (i) and (iii), but poor predictions in cases (ii) and (iv).

Notes and References

PREFACE

1. Cyril Burt, 'Individual Psychology and Social Work', *Charity Organisation Review*, no. 253, new series (January 1918) pp. 17–18, 54.

CHAPTER 1

1. W. Stern, *Über Psychologie der Individuellen Differenzen* (Leipzig, 1900).
2. Introduced by W. Stern in his *Die Differentielle Psychologie* (Leipzig, 1911).
3. J. S. Mill, *Autobiography*, 1969 edn (Oxford University Press) pp. 232–3.
4. R. J. Herrnstein, *IQ in the Meritocracy* (London: Allen Lane, 1973).
5. A. R. Jensen, 'How Much Can We Boost IQ and Scholastic Achievement?', *Harvard Educational Review*, vol. 39 (1969) pp. 1–123.
6 R. A. Fisher, 'Some Hopes of a Eugenist', *Eugenics Review*, vol. 5 (Apr 1913–Jan 1914) p. 309.
7. Ibid., p. 310.
8. A useful recent reader which includes a number of critiques is A. L. Caplan (ed.), *The Sociobiology Debate* (London: Harper and Row, 1978).
9. C. D. Darlington, 'Intelligence, Psychology, and the Process of History', *British Journal of Psychology*, vol. 54 (1963) p. 295.
10. Darlington does not cite specific empirical studies; but see our comments in Chapter 5, pp. 153–6, 172–3.
11. Darlington, 'Intelligence, Psychology', p. 297.
12. Jensen, 'How Much Can We Boost IQ?'.
13. W. Shockley, 'Dysgenics – A Social-Problem Reality Evaded by the Illusion of Infinite Plasticity of Human Intelligence?', in C. Karier (ed.), *Shaping the American Educational State* (New York: Macmillan, 1975).
14. Herrnstein, *IQ in the Meritocracy*.
15. H. J. Eysenck, *Race, Intelligence, and Education* (London: Temple Smith, 1971) and *The Inequality of Man* (London: Temple Smith, 1973).

16. See, for example, the replies to Jensen in *Harvard Educational Review*, Spring and Summer 1969.
17. This criticism is described at length in Chapters 4 and 5. Many of the major American critiques have been reprinted in N. Block and G. Dworkin (eds), *The IQ Controversy* (London: Quartet, 1977). A number of important critiques were also provided in Britain. See the articles by Bodmer, Rose and Ryan in K. Richardson, D. Spears and M. Richards (eds), *Race, Culture and Intelligence* (London: Penguin, 1972). See also H. Rose and S. Rose 'The IQ Myth', *Race and Class*, vol. 20 (1978) pp. 63–74.
18. Leon Kamin, *The Science and Polictics of IQ* (Hillsdale, New Jersey: Erlbaum, 1974).
19. Gillie's findings were first reported in *The Sunday Times*, 24 Oct 1976. He has provided further accounts in the *New Statesman*, 24 Nov 1978, and *Science*, vol. 204 (1979) pp. 1035–7.
20. For further discussion and references, see Chapter 5, pp. 159–63.
21. *Larry P* et al. v. *Wilson Riles* et al., US District Court (Northern California) Judge's Opinion (filed 16 Oct 1979) p. 3.
22. Ibid., p. 8.
23. Ibid., p. 41.
24. Ibid., p. 43.
25. A. R. Jensen, 'The Current Status of the IQ Controversy', *Australian Psychologist*, vol. 3 (1978) p. 8.
26. P. Urbach, 'Progress and Degeneration in the "IQ Debate" ', *British Journal for the Philosophy of Science*, vol. 25 (1974) pp. 99–135 and 235–59. Quote is from p. 100. See also the replies in the same journal by J. Tizard, vol. 27 (1976) pp. 251–7 and M. A. B. Deakin, vol. 27 (1976) pp. 60–5.
27. C. B. Cox and A. E. Dyson (eds), *Black Paper Two, The Crisis in Education*. Undated but approximately 1970 published by the Critical Quarterly Society.
28. See Noam Chomsky's article and exchange with Herrnstein in Block and Dworkin, (eds) *The IQ Controversy*.
29. J. Habermas, *Toward a Rational Society* (London: Heinemann, 1971). Chapters 4–6. See especially pp. 82ff.
30. J. M. Blum, *Pseudoscience and Mental Ability* (London: Monthly Review Press, 1978).
31. For a brief résumé of Popper's work on the philosophy of science, see his intellectual autobiography, *Unended Quest* (London: Open Court, 1976).
32. T. Kuhn, *The Structure of Scientific Revolutions* (University of Chicago Press, 1970).
33. Ibid., pp. 10–12.
34. The remarks in this paragraph are based on T. Kuhn, 'The History of Science', in D. Sills (ed.), *International Encyclopedia of the Social Sciences* (New York: Macmillan, 1968).
35. I. Lakatos, 'Falsification and the Methodology of Scientific Research Programmes', in I. Lakatos and A. Musgrave (eds), *Criticism and the*

Growth of Knowledge (Cambridge University Press, 1970). This is a most useful collection which also has contributions from Popper, Kuhn, Feyerabend, and others.

36. P. Feyerabend, *Against Method* (London: New Left Books, 1975) and *Science in a Free Society* (London: New Left Books, 1978).

37. For example, E. B. Brody and N. Brody, *Intelligence: Nature, Determinants, and Consequences* (London: Academic Press, 1977).

38. J. P. White, 'Intelligence and the Logic of the Nature–Nurture Issue', *Proceedings of the Philosophy of Education Society of Great Britain*, vol. 8 (1974) pp. 30–51.

39. See note 17.

CHAPTER 2

1. Concrete abilities were taken to be those specific to the manipulation of concrete objects. In the 1920s and 1930s, there was some support in the British psychological community for the maintenance of a distinction between a general intelligence concerned with abstract thought and symbols and a general concrete intelligence. For a contemporary discussion, see W. P. Alexander, 'Intelligence, Concrete and Abstract', *British Journal of Psychology Monograph Supplement*, (1935) No. 19.

2. A. G. Hughes and E. H. Hughes, *Learning and Teaching: an Introduction to the Psychology of Education* (London: Longman, 1937) p. 57. Brian Simon draws attention to the influence of this manual in *The Politics of Educational Reform* (London: Lawrence and Wishart, 1974) p. 243.

3. Robert Thouless, *General and Social Psychology*, 2nd ed. (London: University Tutorial Press, 1937) p. 441.

4. Ibid., p. 444.

5. G. Sutherland and S. Sharp estimate that 70 out of 146 local authorities in England and Wales were using intelligence tests in their eleven plus exams by 1940. See 'The fust official psychologist in the wurrld: aspects of the professionalization of psychology in early twentieth century Britain', Fn. 36 (In *History of Science*, forthcoming.)

6. P. E. Vernon (ed.), *Secondary School Selection: A British Psychological Society Inquiry* (London: Methuen, 1957) p. 88.

7. Lewis Terman, *The Measurement of Intelligence*, 1919 ed. (London: Harrap) p. 11.

8. Ibid., p. 17. For a discussion of the socio-political views of the early American mental tests see Leon Kamin, *The Science and Politics of IQ* (New Jersey: Lawrence Erlbaum, 1974; Harmondsworth: Penguin, 1977) chs 1 and 2.

9. B. Hart and C. Spearman, 'General Ability, its Existence and Nature', *British Journal of Psychology*, vol. 5 (Mar 1912) p. 78.

10. C. Spearman, The Abilities of Man: their Nature and Measurement (London: Macmillan, 1927) p. 8.

11. Max Weber, *The Theory of Economic and Social Organization* (Part 1 of *Economy and Society*), edited by Talcott Parsons (New York: Free Press, 1947) p. 261.
12. F. W. Taylor, the American engineer, rather ruefully acknowledged as their father-figure by industrial psychologists, evolved the modern strategy of scientific management based on the breaking-down of skilled work into its simplest operations, the concentration of craft knowledge in management, payment by output and the 'scientific' selection of labour. For the best discussion of Taylor's system and its relations with industrial psychology see Harry Braverman, *Labor and Monopoly Capital* (New York: Monthly Review Press, 1974) *passim*. Burt, in the historical chapter he wrote for the Board of Education, *Report of the Consultative Committee on Psychological Tests of Educable Capacity* (and their possible use in the public system of education) (London: HMSO, 1924) traced the beginnings of psychological selection to Taylor's experiments, p. 49.
13. G. Lukács, *History and Class Consciousness* (London: Merlin Press, 1971) p. 88.
14. Ibid., p. 104.
15. H. Spencer, 'The Principles of Psychology' given in C. Spearman, *Psychology Down the Ages* (London: Macmillan, 1937) vol. 1, p. 120.
16. Cited in Th. Ribot, *English Psychology* (London, 1873) translated from the French, p. 210.
17. From H. Spencer, *The Study of Sociology* (London, 1873) cited in Philip Abrams, *The Origins of British Sociology* (University of Chicago Press, 1968) p. 201.
18. C. Spearman, *The Nature of Intelligence and the Principles of Cognition*, 1923 ed. (London: Macmillan) p. 2.
19. L. S. Hearnshaw, *Cyril Burt: Psychologist* (London: Hodder & Stoughton, 1979) p. 48.
20. C. Spearman, *Autobiography* in C. Murchison (ed.), *A History of Psychology in Autobiography*, vol. 1 (1930) p. 301. C. Burt, *Autobiography* in E. G. Boring *et al.* (eds), *A History of Psychology in Autobiography* (Worcester, Mass: International University Series in Psychology, 1952) vol. 4, p. 59.
21. Hearnshaw, *Cyril Burt*, p. 46.
22. J. McK. Cattell, 'Mental Tests and Measurements', *Mind*, vol. xv (1890).
23. F. Galton, *Hereditary Genius* (London, 1869, Fontana reprint, 1962) p. 126.
24. Ibid., p. 415.
25. Ibid., p. 56.
26. F. Galton, 'The Possible Improvement of the Human Breed under the Existing Conditions of Law and Sentiment', originally 1901, an expanded version appeared in *Essays in Eugenics* (London 1909). For a discussion of the concepts of correlation coefficient and regression see the appendix in this volume pp. 195–7.

27. The four volume biography by Karl Pearson, *The Life, Letters and Labours of Francis Galton* (Cambridge University Press, 1914–30) remains the richest source for Galton.

28. F. Galton, 'Hereditary Talent and Character', *Macmillan's Magazine* (1865) given in R. S. Cowan, 'Francis Galton's Statistical Ideas: the Influence of Eugenics', *Isis*, vol. 63 (1972).

29. Pearson, *Francis Galton*, vol. 2, p. 211.

30. Cowan, 'Francis Galton's Statistical Ideas'.

31. Pearson, *Francis Galton*, vol. 2, p. 231.

32. Ibid., p. 243.

33. F. Galton, *Inquiries into Human Faculty and its Development* (1883) given in Pearson, *Francis Galton*, vol. 2, p. 251.

34. See Pearson, *Francis Galton*, vol. 3a, p. 218.

35. Pearson, *Francis Galton*, vol. 2, p. 261.

36. A comment made by Dr. Eliot Slater, quoted in Burt, 'Francis Galton and his contributions to Psychology', *The British Journal of Statistical Psychology*, vol. xv (May 1962).

37. F. Galton, 'Psychometric Experiments', *Brain* (1879) given in Pearson, *Francis Galton*, vol. 2, p. 233.

38. Given in Pearson, *Francis Galton*, vol. 2, p. 268.

39. Given in Burt, 'Francis Galton', p. 38.

40. See, for example, E. G. Boring, *History, Psychology and Science* (New York and London: John Wiley, 1963) p. 155.

41. See Pearson, *Francis Galton*, vol. II p. 256.

42. For this, and the rest of this paragraph, see Burt, 'General Ability and Special Aptitudes', *Educational Research*, vol. I, no. 2 (Feb 1959). There is a striking parallel between this conception of cognition and the recent developments in cognitive psychology which make extensive use of computer analogies and which view the mind as a hierarchy of information processing systems culminating in an 'Executive System'. See, for example, U. Neisser's seminal *Cognitive Psychology* (New York: Appleton-Century-Croft, 1967).

43. On the Eugenics movement, see G. R. Searle, *Eugenics and Politics in Britain* (Leiden: Noordhof International, 1976).

44. Udny Yule, 'Mendel's laws and their probable relations to inter-racial heredity', *New Phytologist* (1902). See also Hearnshaw, *Cyril Burt*, p. 21.

45. R. A. Fisher, 'The correlation between relatives on the supposition of Mendelian inheritance', *Trans. Roy. Soc. of Edinburgh*, vol. 52 (1918). For an interesting analysis of the origins of Fisher's paper and the extent to which his ideas were shaped by his own eugenic sympathies see B. Norton, 'Metaphysics and Population Genetics: Karl Pearson and background to Fisher's Multi-factorial theory of Inheritance', *Annals of Science*, vol. 32 (1975).

46. C. Spearman, 'The Proof and Measurement of Association between two things', *American Journal of Psychology*, vol. 15 (1904) p. 96.

47. C. Burt, 'Intelligence and Fertility', *Occasional Papers in Eugenics*, no. 2, 1946. See also Hearnshaw, *Burt*, p. 29.

48. See Searle, *Eugenics and Politics*, p. 106.
49. Given in Abrams, *Origins*, p. 124.
50. For the general background see Bernard Semmel, *Imperialism and Social Reform* (London: Allen & Unwin, 1960).
51. S. Webb, 'Lord Roseberry's Escape from Houndsditch', in E. J. T. Brennan (ed.), *Education for National Efficiency* (London: Athlone Press, 1975) p. 80.
52. Given in A. Fried and R. Elman (eds), *Charles Booth's London*. (Harmondsworth: Penguin, 1969) pp. 55, 60.
53. See, for example, the prominence given to Spearman's theory in Jensen's article, 'The current status of the IQ controversy', *The Australian Psychologist*, vol. 13, no, 1 (1978).
54. H. J. Eysenck (ed.), *The Measurement of Intelligence* (Lancaster: Medical and Technical Publishing, 1973) p. 480.
55. Spearman, *Autobiography* p. 322.
56. Ibid., p. 323.
57. See C. Spearman, ' "General Intelligence": Objectively Determined and Measured', *American Journal of Psychology*, vol. XV (1904) p. 204. 'Psychic' was commonly used to mean simply mental, and 'psychoses' meant mental processes; neither term had the current associations with para and abnormal psychology.
58. C. Spearman, *Autobiography*, vol. 1, p. 319.
59. Spearman states this quite explicitly in *Psychology down the Ages*, vol. 2, p. 219.
60. C. Spearman, *Autobiography*, vol. 1, p. 322.
61. C. Spearman, 'General Intelligence', p. 259. Spearman's correction for attenuation embroiled him in a controversy with Pearson who, at a meeting of the British Association in 1910, attacked it as an illicit procedure for 'cleaning up' intrinsically dirty data. For further discussion of the invalidity of this procedure see Chapter 4, pp. 141–2.
62. Ibid., p. 272.
63. Ibid., p. 273.
64. C. Spearman, 'The Heredity of Abilities', *Eugenics Review*, vol. 6 (Apr 1914–Jan 1915) p. 220.
65. C. Spearman, 'General Intelligence', p. 271. Spearman was particularly enamoured of the discovery that the g theory 'rationalised' the predominantly classical education of the British ruling class. He reiterated the point in other articles, for example, 'The Heredity of Abilities'.
66. C. Spearman, *The Abilities of Man* (London: Macmillan, 1927) p. 60. His characterisation of Binet's concept of intelligence scarcely does justice to Binet who, over a long period, moved towards the idea of intelligence as a shifting complex of interrelated functions. See Theta Wolf, *Alfred Binet* (University of Chicago Press, 1973) p. 208.
67. C. Burt, 'Experimental Tests of General Intelligence', *British Journal of Psychology*, vol. 3 (Dec 1909) p. 169.
68. Ibid., p. 176. See also Hearnshaw, *Burt*, p. 57.

69. See C. Spearman, 'The Theory of 2 Factors' in *The Psychological Review*, vol. 21 (Mar 1914) p. 105 and 'The Heredity of Abilities' where the work of C. S. Sherrington and F. W. Mott in neurology and physiology is invoked in defence of *g* as mental energy. The question of the physiological evidence for a central factor is discussed in Chapter 4, pp. 119–23.

70. Spearman and Hart, 'General Ability', p. 77.

71. C. Spearman, *The Nature of Intelligence and the Principles of Cognition*, (London: Macmillan, 1923) p. 5.

72. Ibid., *passim*.

73. C. Spearman, *Psychology down the Ages*, vol. 2, p. 132.

74. Ibid., p. 233.

75. C. Spearman, *The Nature of Intelligence and the Principles of Cognition*, p. 353. Spearman made similar claims for *g*. In *Psychology down the Ages* he mentioned 'the prospects held out by *g* for the not distant future. An outstanding example is its suggested property of being innate. Such a property, if ever proven, might enable it almost to re-create important spheres of sociology and anthropology', vol. 2, p. 241. How, exactly, such social sciences were to be re-constructed is unclear.

76. See Spearman, *The Abilities of Man* (1927) p. 84.

77. See Godfrey Thomson, 'A Hierarchy without a General Factor', *British Journal of Psychology*, vol. 8, pt 3 (Sept 1916). (Thomson's paper was actually prepared in 1914 but he postponed publication, because of the intervention of the First World War.) See also, G. Thomson, 'The Hierarchy of Abilities', *British Journal of Psychology*, vol. 9 (May 1919) and G. Thomson, *The Factorial Analysis of Human Ability* (University of London Press, 1939) ch. 3.

78. C. Spearman, 'Correspondence note', *Eugenics Review*, vol. 6, Apr 1914–Jan 1915.

79. Spearman, *Psychology down the Ages*, vol. 2, p. 221. For further discussion of the concept of a central factor see Chapter 4, pp. 119–30.

80. Spearman, 'The Heredity of Abilities', p. 223.

81. See E. G. Boring, *A History of Experimental Psychology* (New York: Century, 1950) p. 465.

82. C. Burt, 'The Historical Development of the Guidance Movement in Education in England', *Year Book of Education 1955*, pp. 83–8. This interesting account is marred by Burt's habit of minimising Spearman's priority in intelligence theory.

83. See Searle, *Eugenics and Politics*, p. 88.

84. W. McDougall, 'Psychology in the Service of Eugenics', *Eugenics Review*, vol. 5 (Apr 1913–Jan 1914) pp. 295–308 (and for the following citations.)

85. G. Thomson, 'The Trend of National Intelligence' (The Galton Lecture for 1946, published as *Occasional Papers in Eugenics*, no. 3.)

86. Dean Inge, 'The Future of the English Race', reprinted in D. Inge *Outspoken Essays* (London: Longman, 1921) p. 99.

87. D. Inge, 'Eugenics', *Edinburgh Review* (July 1922).

88. Fisher, 'Eugenics: can it solve the problem of the decay of civilisations?', *Eugenics Review*, vol. 18 (1926) p. 131.

89. Birmingham Education Committee, *Report of an Investigation upon Backward Children in Birmingham* (by Cyril Burt) (1921) pp. 5, 9.

90. Board of Education and Board of Control, *Report of the Mental Deficiency Committee*, pt 2, The Mentally Defective Child, p. 76.

91. This was later established by Lionel Penrose. See J. I. Cohen, 'Intelligence and the Birth-Rate', *Nature*, vol. 32, no. 3620 (Mar 1939).

92. G. Thomson and H. E. G. Sutherland, 'The Correlation of Intelligence with size of family', *British Journal of Psychology*, vol. 17 (1926) pp. 81–92; H. E. G. Sutherland, 'The Relationship between IQ and size of family', *Journal of Educational Psychology*, vol. 20 (1929) pp. 81–90; J. L. Gray, *The Nation's Intelligence* (London: Watts, 1936) p. 143.

93. See E. J. G. Bradford, 'Can Present Scholastic Standards be maintained', *The Forum of Education*, vol. 3 (1925) and T. Lentz, 'The relation of IQ to size of family', *Journal of Educational Psychology*, vol. 18 (1927) pp. 486–492, two pieces influential in raising the alarm.

94. An error made by Lentz.

95. D. Caradog Jones, 'Eugenic aspects of the Merseyside Survey', *Eugenics Review*, vol. 26 (Mar 1936). See also A. M. Carr-Saunders, 'Eugenics in the light of population trends', *Eugenics Review*, vol. 27 (April 1935).

96. R. B. Cattell, *The Fight for our National Intelligence* (London: P. S. King, 1937) p. xvii.

97. Ibid., pp. 42–3.

98. Ibid., p. 2.

99. Ibid., p. 52.

100. Ibid., p. 60.

101. Ibid., p. 88.

102. J. B. S. Haldane, *Heredity and Politics* (London: Allen & Unwin, 1938) p. 117.

103. J. L. Gray, *The Nation's Intelligence* (London: Watts, 1936) p. 22.

104. C. Burt, 'Intelligence and Fertility', p. 22. (This paper summarised his evidence to the Royal Commission on Population.)

105. See the record of the discussion appended to Thomson's 'The Trend of National Intelligence'.

106. Penrose put forward this theory in the *American Journal of Mental Deficiency*, July 1948. For a brief discussion see *The Trend of Scottish Intelligence* (University of London Press, 1949) (Scottish Council for Research in Education) pp. x–xii.

107. *The Intelligence of Scottish Children* (University of London Press, 1933) p. 4. (Scottish Council for Research in Education).

108. *The Trend of Scottish Intelligence*, p. viii.

109. R. B. Cattell, 'The Fate of National Intelligence: Test of a Thirteen

Year Prediction', *Eugenics Review*, vol. 42, No. 3. (1949).

110. See I. Lakatos, *The Methodology of Scientific Research Programmes*, vol. I (Cambridge University Press, 1978) pp. 16–19 where the point is amusingly made by reference to a fictional Newtonian astronomer.

CHAPTER 3

1. C. S. Myers, *Industrial Psychology in Britain* (London: Jonathan Cape, 1926) pp. 114–115.
2. F. W. Lawe, 'The Economic Aspects of Industrial Psychology', in C. S. Myers (ed.), *Industrial Psychology* (London: Thorton Butterworth, 1929) p. 219.
3. Lawe, for example, wrote 'If further psychological study results in a better understanding of those industrial mental disorders known as strikes and lock-outs, it may serve well the economic life of the nation.' Ibid., p. 227.
4. This is based on 'The early history of the National Institute of Industrial Psychology' in *Journal of the NIIP*, vol. 1, pt 1 (Jan 1922).
5. T. H. Pear, 'C. S. Myers', *British Journal of Educational Psychology*, vol. 17, pt 1 (Feb 1947).
6. See Myers, *Industrial Psychology in Britain*, p. 18–19.
7. See E. P. Allen Hunt and Percival Smith, *The Teachers' Guide to Intelligence and other psychological testing* (London: Evans, 1935) pp. 1–9.
8. See Birmingham Education Committee, *The Value of Vocational Tests as aids to choice of employment* (1932) (First Report), (1940) (Second Report); *Selection of Skilled Apprentices for the Engineering Trade* (1931) (First Report), (1939) (Third Report).
9. From an article in the *Glasgow Herald* 15 Sept 1936 on the work of the NIIP, filed in PRO Lab. 19/9.
10. See the script of Myers's broadcast in *Journal of the NIIP*, vol. 1, no. 8 (Oct 1923); also a broadcast by Sir Robert Witt, *Journal of the NIIP*, vol. 2, pt 2 (April 1924) and Winifred C. Cullis, *Journal of the NIIP*, vol. 2, pt 3 (July 1924).
11. See Spearman, *The Nature of Intelligence* (London: Macmillan, 1923) p. 2 and also the Board of Education, *Report of the Consultative Committee on Psychological Tests of Educable Capacity* (London: HMSO, 1924) p. 39.
12. Boring, *History of Experimental Psychology* (1950 ed.) p. 488.
13. 'The Principles of Vocational Guidance', *Proceedings* of the VIIth International Congress of Psychology (1923) pp. 314ff.
14. A. G. Hughes and E. H. Hughes, *Learning and Teaching* (London: Longman, 1937) pp. 64, 71.
15. C. Burt, 'The Mental Differences between Individuals', Presidential Address to Section J of the British Association for the Advancement of Science, (1923).
16. They were raised by G. Thomson at the VIIth International

Congress of Psychology in a paper 'The Nature of General Intelligence and Ability', *Proceedings*.

17. C. Burt, Presidential Address, (1923), p. 215.

18. Ibid.,

19. See Tyrrell Burgess, *A Guide to English Schools* (Harmondsworth: Penguin, 1964) p. 120.

20. Scottish Records Office Ed. 48/886/1. It is clear that some of these ten were using them only in exceptional cases.

21. At least, this was asserted by P. B. Ballard, 'The Free Place Exam', *The 1938 Year Book of Education* (London: Evans, 1938) pp. 284–294. For a conclusive assessment, historians await the publication of Dr. Sutherland's researches.

22. PRO Ed. 136/648. Memo. of 12 May 43.

23. J. L. Gray and P. Moshinsky, 'Ability and Opportunity in English Education', in Lancelot Hogben (ed.), *Political Arithmetic* (London: Allen & Unwin, 1938); J. W. B. Douglas, *The Home and the School* (London: MacGibbon & Kee, 1964).

24. Alfred Yates and D. A. Pidgeon argued that 'The logical error that occurs most frequently consists in levelling criticisms against procedures of selection that are in fact based on objections to the ends that these procedures are designed to serve.' 'Transfer at Eleven Plus', *Educational Research,* vol. 1 (Nov 1958) no. 1. Whether the NFER's exclusive preoccupation, over a very lengthy period, with the *technology* of selection was the most intellectually fruitful use of its energies is a question which came to trouble Ben Morris, its long-time secretary. By the mid-1960s, he felt it imperative for educational psychology to undertake 'a constant scrutiny of its presuppositions' and the country's leading educational research institution had patently failed to do that. See B. Morris, 'The contribution of Psychology to Education' in J. W. Tibble (ed.) *The Study of Education* (London: Routledge & Kegan Paul, 1966); See also Brian Simon, *Intelligence, Psychology and Education* (London: Lawrence & Wishart, 1978) p. 234.

25. For what follows we are greatly indebted to G. Sutherland, 'The Magic of Measurement: Mental Testing and English Education 1900–1940', *Transactions of the Royal Historical Society,* 5th Series, vol. 27 (1977) pp. 135–153.

26 C. Burt, 'The Historical Development of the Guidance Movement in England', *The 1955 Year Book of Education*, (London: Evans), p. 88.

27. *Annual Report for 1912 of the Chief Medical Officer of the Board of Education*, Cd. 7184 (London: HMSO, 1912) pp. 1913, Appendix E.

28. E. P. Allen Hunt and P. Smith, *The Teachers' Guide to Intelligence and other psychological testing* (London: Evans, 1935) p. 9.

29. Board of Education, *Supplementary Memorandum on Examinations for Scholarships and Special Places in Secondary Schools* (London: HMSO, 1936).

30. On streaming in schools generally see 'Classification and Streaming:

A Study of Grouping in English Schools 1860–1960', in Simon, *Intelligence, Psychology and Education*, pp. 200–236.

31. Board of Education, *Report of the Consultative Committee on the Primary School* (London: HMSO, 1931) p. 131.

32. Hunt and Smith, *Teachers' Guide*, p. 21.

33. Percy Nunn, 'Psychology and Education', *British Journal of Psychology*, vol. 10 (Mar 1920).

34. See J. Floud, A. H. Halsey and F. M. Martin, *Social Class and Educational Opportunity* (London: Heinemann, 1957) p. 131.

35. Figures from *Annual Reports* of the Board of Education. See also Statistical Tables 1, 2, and 3 in Brian Simon, *The Politics of Educational Reform* (London: Lawrence & Wishart, 1974) pp. 362–5.

36. PRO Ed. 12/328 S654/5 Memorandum on Intellectual Tests 25 April 22.

37. Board of Education, *Report of the Departmental Committee on Scholarships and Free Places*, Cmd. 968 (London: HMSO, 1920) p. 21, para. 67.

38. C. Burt, *Report on Psychological Tests* . . . (London: HMSO, 1924) p. 37. (Dr. Sutherland has apparently been unable to confirm this, but it seems a little odd that Burt should, in 1924, have distorted the record in a quasi-official document which was bound to attract attention in local authority offices.)

39. See G. Thomson, *Instinct, Intelligence and Character* (London: Allen & Unwin, 1924) pp. 220–1.

40. C. Burt, *Report on Psychological Tests*, pp. 64–6.

41. Ibid., pp. 117–18, 141.

42. See, for example, the review of the *Report on Psychological Tests* by Myers in the *Journal of the NIIP*, vol. 2, pt 5 (Jan 1925).

43. See, for example, Cattell, *The Fight for our National Intelligence* (London: King, 1937) p. 47.

44. Board of Education, *Report on the Primary School*, p. 258.

45. Given in M. Hyndman, 'Multilateralism and the Spens Report: Evidence from the Archives', *British Journal of Educational Studies*, vol. 24, no. 3 (Oct 1976).

46. *Report on the Consultative Committee on Secondary Education* (Spens) (London: HMSO, 1938) p. 123.

47. Ibid., p. 291.

48. P. B. Ballard, 'The Free Place Exam'.

49. Hughes and Hughes, *Learning and Teaching*, p. 370. R. S. Wood, Deputy Secretary of the Board of Education, put the point even more strongly in 1941: ' . . . the exam at eleven plus bids fair to prove the curse of the junior school'. Given in P. H. J. Gosden, *Education in the Second World War* (London: Methuen, 1976) p. 248.

50. Only 37 of the 109 authorities who responded to the NUT 1946 enquiry appeared to be using an essay in their eleven plus examination (these authorities dealt with 85 per cent of the English and Welsh school population). See NUT, *Transfer from Primary to Secondary Schools* (London: Evans, 1949) appx. 1. See also P. E.

Vernon (ed.), *Secondary School Selection* (London: Methuen, 1957) p. 123.

51. Cattell, *Fight for National Intelligence*, p. 47.
52. *White Paper on Educational Reconstruction*, Cmd. 6458 (London: HMSO, 1943) p. 6, para. 17.
53. NUT, *Transfer from Primary to Secondary Schools* (London: Evans, 1949) pp. 57–9.
54. Central Advisory Council for Education, *Children and their Primary Schools* (London: HMSO, 1967) vol. 1, p. 153.
55. Wm. McClelland, *Selection for Secondary Education* (University of London Press, 1942) p. 77.
56. In this decade, 43 of the authorities replying to the NUT adopted intelligence tests for their eleven plus exam, NUT, *Transfer from Primary to Secondary Schools*, p. 111.
57. Given in Gosden, *Education*, p. 248.
58. *White Paper on Educational Reconstruction*, p. 9, para. 27.
59. Norwood Committee, *Report of the Secondary Schools Examinations Council on Curriculum and Examinations in Secondary Schools* (London: HMSO, 1943) p. 17.
60. PRO Ed. 12/479 Norwood Committee papers.
61. PRO Ed. 12/480 Norwood Committee papers.
62. See G. Sutherland and S. Sharp, 'The fust official psychologist in the wurrld': aspects of the professionalization of psychology in early twentieth century Britain'. Forthcoming in *History of Science*.
63. C. Burt, 'Ability and Income', *British Journal of Educational Psychology*, vol. 13 (June 1943) p. 83.
64. L. Kamin, *The Science and Politics of IQ* (New Jersey: Lawrence Erlbaum, 1974; Harmondsworth: Penguin, 1977) pp. 55–6; L. S. Hearnshaw, *Cyril Burt: Psychologist* London: Hodder & Stoughton, 1979 p. 141.
65. See C. Burt, 'Ability and Income', pp. 93–4. At a number of points in his biography, Hearnshaw mentions Burt's indifference to sociological theory and it seems, therefore, of some interest that on one of the few occasions Burt did turn to sociology for guidance he chose classical elite theory.
66. C. Burt, 'Ability and Income', p. 97.
67. Ibid., p. 92.
68. C. Burt, 'An Inquiry into Public Opinion Regarding Educational Reforms', in two parts, see *Occupational Psychology*, vol. 17, no. 4 (Oct 1943) and vol. 18, no. 1 (Jan 1944).
69. C. Burt, 'The Education of the Young Adolescent: the Psychological Implications of the Norwood Report', *British Journal of Educational Psychology*, vol. 13 (1943) p. 131.
70. Ibid., p. 135.
71. Comments by Burt for a Symposium on the selection of pupils for different types of secondary schools, *British Journal of Educational Psychology*, vol. 17, pt. 2 (1947) p. 63.
72. Ibid., p. 67.

73. W. J. Campbell, 'The Influence of Home Environment on Educational Progress', *British Journal of Educational Psychology*, vol. 22 (1952) p. 101. (This piece of research was clearly inspired by Burt's remarks.)

74. Robin Pedley, *The Comprehensive School* (Harmondsworth: Penguin, 1963) p. 43.

75. Ibid.

76. See J. Floud and A. H. Halsey's 'Intelligence Tests, Social Class and Selection for Secondary Schools', *British Journal of Sociology*, vol. 8 (1957) pp. 33–9 and, for a more general statement A. Yates and D. A. Pidgeon (for the NFEREW) *Admission to Grammar Schools* (1957) p. 189.

77. Vernon (ed.) *Selection*, p. 17.

78. From the Conservative party programme for education at the time of the 1955 election, quoted in *The Times Educational Supplement*, 13 May 1955.

79. Yates and Pidgeon, *Admission*, p. 26.

80. See *Children and their Primary Schools* (Plowden Report) (London: HMSO, 1967) vol. 2, appx. 11, p. 551.

81. Douglas summed it up in these words: 'streaming by ability reinforces the process of social selection . . . . Children who come from well-kept homes and who are themselves clean, well-clothed and shod, stand a greater chance of being put in the upper streams than their measured ability would seem to justify. Once there they are likely to stay and improve in performance in succeeding years. This is in striking contrast to the deterioration noticed in those children of similar measured ability who were placed in the lower streams . . . ', *The Home and the School* (London: MacGibbon & Kee, 1964) p. 150.

82. See Julian Blackburn, *Psychology and the Social Pattern* (London: Kegan Paul, 1945) ch. 5 and Alice Heim, *The Appraisal of Intelligence* (London: Methuen, 1954) *passim*.

83. Vernon (ed.), *Selection*, p. 111.

84. Ibid., p. 77.

85. Cited in Willem van der Eyken (ed.), *Education, the Child and Society* (Harmondsworth: Penguin, 1973) pp. 454, 459.

86. C. Burt, 'The Mental Differences between Children', C. B. Cox and A. E. Dyson (eds), *Black Paper Two: The Crisis in Education* (1969) p. 16.

87. A. R. Jensen, 'The Current status of the IQ controversy', *The Australian Psychologist*, vol. 13, no. 1 (1978).

88. C. Burt, 'Is Intelligence Distributed Normally?', *British Journal of Statistical Psychology*, vol. 16 (1963) pp. 175–190.

89. A. R. Jensen, 'The Nature of Intelligence and its Relations with Learning', *Melbourne Studies on Education* (Melbourne University Press, 1978).

90. P. Vernon, *Intelligence and Cultural Environment* (London: Methuen, 1969) given in H. Butcher and D. Lomax (eds), *Readings in Human*

Intelligence (London: Methuen, 1972) pp. 354, 359.
91. Evelyn Lawrence, *An Investigation into the Relation between Intelligence and Inheritance* (British Journal of Psychology Monograph Supplement, 1931).
92. Ibid., p. 32.
93. Ibid., p. 68.

CHAPTER 4

1. A. R. Jensen, 'The Nature of Intelligence and its Relation to Learning', in S. Murray-Smith (ed.), *Melbourne Studies in Education* (University of Melbourne, 1978).
2. A. R. Jensen, 'How Much Can We Boost IQ and Scholastic Achievement?', *Harvard Educational Review*, vol. 39 (1969) p. 8.
3. U. Neisser, 'General, Academic, and Artificial Intelligence', in L. B. Resnick (ed.), *The Nature of Intelligence* (Hillsdale, New Jersey: Erlbaum, 1976).
4. N. Block and G. Dworkin, 'IQ, Heritability, and Inequality', in N. Block and G. Dworkin (eds), *The IQ Controversy* (London: Quartet, 1977) p. 429.
5. For a thorough analysis of the shortcomings of this operationalist doctrine, see Block and Dworkin, ibid., pp. 414–29.
6. The concept of 'test reliability' is discussed later in this chapter (pp. 141–2). The point here is simply that IQs for different versions of the same IQ test are much better correlated than IQs for different IQ tests, and this is inconsistent with the view that different tests measure the same thing but with varying 'reliability'.
7. See, for example, E. Gibson and H. Levin, *The Psychology of Reading* (Massachusetts Institute of Technology Press, 1975).
8. D. Layzer, 'Science or Superstition? A Physical Scientist Looks at the IQ Controversy', in Block and Dworkin (eds), *IQ Controversy*.
9. The best textbook account by a psychometrician of factor analysis and factor models of intelligence is still G. Thomson, *The Factorial Analysis of Human Ability*, 5th ed. (University of London Press, 1951).
10. This roughly characterises Jensen's current position, see 'The Nature of Intelligence'. For an interesting discussion of the development of thermometers compared with the development of IQ tests, see Block and Dworkin (eds), *IQ Controversy*, pp. 419–23.
11. The standard introductory textbook of cognitive psychology is P. H. Lindsay and D. A. Norman, *Human Information Processing, An Introduction to Psychology*, 2nd ed. (New York: Harcourt Brace Jovanovich, 1977).
12. The best current textbook of neuropsychology is H. Hecaen and M. L. Albert, *Human Neuropsychology* (London: Wiley, 1978).
13. This is the highest figure currently cited by Jensen. See 'The Nature of Intelligence'. It should be borne in mind that weak, but statistically significant, associations have also been found between IQ and

seemingly irrelevant characteristics, such as eye colour.
14. Otherwise it would not correspond to the 'g loadings' obtained for conventional IQ tests.
15. H. J. Eysenck, *The Inequality of Man* (London: Temple Smith, 1973) p. 78.
16. Jensen's recent paper 'The Nature of Intelligence' is a masterpiece of obscurantism with regard to the concept of *g*. After emphasising its importance on the basis of factor analytic studies, he then proposes that factor analytic data is probably best explained in terms of Thomson's sampling model with a variety of distinct hypothetical neural characteristics corresponding to Thomson's 'mental bonds'. But Thomson's model was put forward as an *alternative* explanation to the *g* theory! (see the next section of this chapter).
17. For a detailed account of the Spearman and Thomson models see Thomson, *Human Ability*.
18. L. Wittgenstein, *Philosophical Investigations* (Oxford: Blackwell, 1968) pp. 31–2.
19. For twelve siblings the probablity that one or the other will occur is .022; for sixteen it is .001.
20. Jensen, 'How Much Can We Boost IQ?', pp. 9–11.
21. R. C. Lewontin, 'Race and Intelligence' in Block and Dworkin (eds), *IQ Controversy*, pp. 81–2.
22. H. J. Butcher, *Human Intelligence, Its Nature and Assessment* (London: Methuen, 1968) pp. 43–4.
23. For a detailed account see Thomson, *Human Ability*.
24. See, for example, P. Urbach, 'Progress and Degeneration in the "IQ Debate"', *British Journal for the Philosophy of Science*, vol. 25 (1974) pp. 111–3.
25. See Thomson's contribution to E. G. Boring *et al.*, *History of Psychology in Autobiography*, vol. IV (New York: Russell and Russell, 1952) p. 288.
26. Contemporary factor analysts have arrived at a somewhat arbitrary compromise between the Thurstone and Spearman models, and have subdivided g into g_x and g_c using Cattell's concept of 'fluid' and 'crystallised' intelligence. For a practitioner's survey of the current confused state of the subject, see J. L. Horn, 'Human Abilities: A Review of Research and Theories in the Early 1970s', *Annual Review of Psychology*, vol. 27 (1976) 437–87. See also J. M. Blum, *Pseudoscience and Mental Ability* (London: Monthly Review Press, 1978) pp. 109–12.
27. This may do Thomson an injustice. In Boring's *History of Psychology in Autobiography*, after briefly describing his model, he gives the following intuitively appealing interpretation: 'The psychological meaning of all this is that if, when we attack some task, some test, our ability to solve it depends upon a large number of things – genes we have inherited, pieces of information we have acquired, skills we have practised, little habits of thought we have formed, all and sundry influences from past and present – then the correlation coefficients between performances in tests will show exactly the same

relationships with one another as they would have done had our ability depended on our possession of a small number of common "factors" (plus specifics).' p. 253.

28. H. W. Stevenson *et al.*, 'Longitudinal Study of Individual Differences in Cognitive Development and Scholastic Achievement,' *Journal of Educational Psychology*, vol. 68 (1976) 377–400. The psychometric literature also contains examples of tests which appear to involve complex cognitive processes, but which yield scores uncorrelated with IQ. The first successful demonstration of this was by M. A. Wallach and N. Kogan, *Modes of Thinking in Young Children* (New York: Rinehart and Winston, 1965). Other examples are cited in Horn's review of factor analytic studies, 'Human Abilities'. The proponent of *g* is of course free to argue that such tests have a zero *g* loading, but this is *post hoc*. Since the choice of items to include in a factor analysis is arbitrary and subjective, what more reasonable refutation could we ask for than that a test be devised which appears (subjectively) to involve complex cognitive processes, but which yields scores uncorrelated with IQ?

29. Quoted by Block and Dworkin (eds), *IQ Controversy*, who provide a useful critique of the concept of general intelligence (pp. 462–73).

30. Blum, *Pseudoscience*, pp. 105–9. Blum mainly cites reviews of the tests which appeared in O. Buros (ed.), *Mental Measurement Yearbook*, 6th ed. (Highland Park, New Jersey: Gryphon Press, 1965).

31. See, for example, J. E. Hunter and F. L. Schmidt, 'Critical Analysis of the Statistical and Ethical Implications of Various Definitions of Test Bias', *Psychological Bulletin*, vol. 83 (1976) pp. 1053–71.

32. R. Lynn, 'Ethnic and Racial Differences in Intelligence', in R. T. Osborne, C. E. Noble and N. Wehl (eds), *Human Variation, The Biopsychology of Age, Race and Sex* (New York: Academic Press, 1978).

33. Jensen, 'How Much Can We Boost IQ?', p. 100.

34. W. Labov, 'The Logic of Nonstandard English', in N. Keddie (ed.), *Tinker, Tailor . . . The Myth of Cultural Deprivation* (Harmondsworth: Penguin, 1973).

35. See, for example, the articles by M. Cole and S. Scribner in P. N. Johnson-Laird and P. C. Wason (eds), *Thinking: Readings in Cognitive Science* (Cambridge University Press, 1977).

36. This was conceded by the leading psychometricians who unsuccessfully defended the tests in *Larry P.* et al. v. *Wilson Riles* et al., US District Court (Northern California) 1977–9. Extracts from the ruling have already been given in Chapter 1 pp. 10–11.

37. Stevenson, 'Individual Differences'.

38. For much more detailed developments of the arguments given in the remainder of this section, see Block and Dworkin, (eds), *IQ Controversy*, pp. 432–62 and Blum, *Pseudoscience*, ch. 6.

39. A key study is that of S. Bowles and V. Nelson, 'The "Inheritance of IQ" and the Intergenerational Reproduction of Economic Inequality', *Review of Economics and Statistics*, vol. 56 (1974) pp. 39–51. The results of this study are discussed at length in S. Bowles and

H. Gintis, *Schooling in Capitalist America* (London: Routledge, 1976) ch. 4. See also the discussions cited in the previous note.

40. See, for example, J. Lumsden, 'Test Theory', *Annual Review of Psychology*, vol. 27 (1976) pp. 251–80, and 'Tests are Perfectly Reliable', *British Journal of Mathematical and Statistical Psychology*, vol. 31 (1978) 19–26.

41. Ibid., p. 276.

42. See Ch. 1, pp. 10–11.

43. G. S. Coles, 'The Learning Disabilities Test Battery: Empirical and Social Issues', *Harvard Educational Review*, vol. 48 (1978) p. 335.

44. See, for example, E. Goodacre, 'What is Reading: Which Model?' in M. St. J. Raggett *et al.*, *Assessment and Testing of Reading: Problems and Practices* (London: Ward Lock, 1979).

45. S. Feshbach, 'Early Identification of Children with High Risk of Reading Failure', *Journal of Learning Disabilities*, vol. 7 (1974) p. 54.

CHAPTER 5

1. J. L. Jinks and D. W. Fulker, 'Comparison of the Biometrical, Genetical, MAVA, and Classical Approaches to the Analysis of Human Behaviour', *Psychological Bulletin*, vol. 73 (1970) pp. 311–49.

2. A. R. Jensen, 'How Much Can We Boost IQ and Scholastic Achievement?', *Harvard Educational Review*, vol. 39 (1969) p. 58.

3. This is a particularly important question when applied to the correlation matrices from which a *g* factor is extracted. A number of animal behaviour geneticists have pointed out that the lesson to be learned from their own field of research is that genetic mechanisms are highly specific rather than general. Thus, animals bred for learning ability in a given experimental set up are usually found to learn no better than control group animals when the experimental set up is changed appreciably. On the basis of this and other findings they have argued that an inherited *g* factor is an implausible conception. See T. R. McGuire and J. Hirsch, 'General Intelligence and Heritability', in I. C. Uzgiris and F. Weizmann (eds), *The Structure of Experience* (New York: Plenum, 1977). See also two much earlier papers by R. C. Tryon in the *Psychological Review*, vol. 39 (1932) pp. 324–51, 403–39.

4. A method for resolving this question which has not, to our knowledge, hitherto been employed, involves re-analysing data for separated identical twins who have been given IQ and scholastic achievement tests. The method is to compare the normal IQ – achievement correlations with 'cross twin correlations' between each twin's IQ and the co-twin's achievement score. Since the twins have identical genes, a genetic interpretation of the normal IQ – achievement correlations leads to the prediction that the cross twin correlations should remain as high as the normal ones; any drop in size of the cross twin correlations would be attributable only to environmental effects. Unfortunately, the only available data is for a

1937 American study of 19 pairs of separated twins marred by the presence of correlated environments (H. H. Newman, F. N. Freeman and K. J. Holzinger, *Twins: A Study of Heredity and Environment* (Chicago University Press, 1937). See our discussion of separated twin studies later in this chapter, pp. 156–7). The results, however, are of some interest and are as follows:

	Normal correlation	Cross twin correlation
Binet IQ × Stanford educational age	.63	.28
Otis IQ × Stanford educational age	.73	.43

Squaring the correlations, we find that, for the normal correlations, Binet IQ and Otis IQ can predict respectively 40 per cent and 53 per cent of the variation in achievement, figures which are quite typical of those found for large samples of the general population. On the other hand, for the cross twin correlations, the figures drop to 8 per cent and 18 per cent respectively. Owing to the presence of correlated environments, these latter figures probably also have an environmental component, but the sharp drop in size is sufficient to show that there is a large environmental contribution to normal IQ –achievement correlations. (Scatter diagrams displaying the data for these correlations are given in the Appendix: fig A. 1, p. 196).

5. L. Hogben, 'Correlation Technique in Human Genetics', *Journal of Genetics*, vol. 27 (1933) pp. 379–406.
6. R. C. Lewontin, 'Race and Intelligence', together with an interchange with A. R. Jensen, in N. Block and G. Dworkin (eds), *The IQ Controversy* (London: Quartet, 1977); R. C. Lewontin, 'The Analysis of Variance and the Analysis of Causes', *American Journal of Human Genetics*, vol. 26 (1974) pp. 400–11; R. C. Lewontin, 'Genetic Aspects of Intelligence', *Annual Review of Genetics*, vol. 9 (1975) 387–405; M. W. Feldman and R. C. Lewontin, 'The Heritability Hang-up', *Science*, vol. 190 (1975) pp. 1163–8 (see also correspondence and reply in *Science*, vol. 194 (1976) pp. 7–14). For a further recent account, see D. Layzer, 'Heritability of IQ Scores, Science or Numerology?', *Science*, vol. 183 (1974) 1259–66.
7. P. B. Medawar, 'Unnatural Science', *New York Review of Books*, 3 Feb 1977.
8. J. B. S. Haldane, *Heredity and Politics* (London: Allen & Unwin, 1938) p. 37.
9. J. A. H. Waterhouse, 'Heredity and Environment in Relation to Education', *The 1950 Yearbook of Education* (London: Evans, 1950) p. 103.
10. See Medawar, 'Unnatural Science'.
11. R. A. Fisher, 'The Correlation Between Relatives on the Supposition of Mendelian Inheritance', *Transactions of the Royal Society of Edinburgh*, vol. 52 (1918) pp. 399–433.
12. See Feldman and Lewontin, 'Heritability Hang-up', p. 1164.

13. Ibid., p. 1163.
14. Hogben, 'Correlation Technique', p. 399.
15. In a recent article directed at non-specialists, A. R. Jensen states quite blandly, 'But the question of IQ heritability in the broad sense, is no longer a serious topic of controversy among workers in this field. Most would agree that the lower probable limit of the broad heritability of IQ is about .50 (i.e. >50% of the IQ variance is attributable to variance in genotypes), and most estimates fall in the range from about .65 to .80. (Heritability is not a universal constant, but a population statistic, and so no one is concerned with trying to determine the "true" or "exact" heritability of IQ in general; that is an inappropriate aim)'. 'The Current Status of the IQ Controversy', *Australian Psychologist*, vol. 13 (1978) p. 14.
16. Of the analyses which are now considered to be acceptable by hereditarians, the first is Jinks and Fulker's 1970 paper ('Analysis of Human Behaviour'). This included the highest of all recent estimates (86 per cent) and this estimate was based on Burt's fraudulent data. Reviewing estimates based on large sets of kinship data, A. Goldberger ('Heritability', *Workshop Paper No. 7826* (1978) Social Systems Research Institute, University of Wisconsin, Madison), found that they varied from 21 per cent to 85 per cent. Excluding estimates which used Burt data leaves a range from 21 per cent to 68 per cent. Low estimates have included a value of 15 per cent (M. Schwartz and J. Schwartz, 'Evidence Against a Genetical Component to Performance on IQ Tests', *Nature*, vol. 248 (1974) pp. 84–5) and one of 34 per cent (B. Adams, M. Ghodsian, and K. Richardson, 'Evidence for a Low Upper Limit of Heritability of Mental Test Performance in a National Sample of Twins', *Nature*, vol. 263, (1976) pp. 314–6). Using different features of the data from their adoption study, S. Scarr and R. A. Weinberg ('Intellectual Similarities within Families of Both Adopted and Biological Children', *Intelligence*, vol. 1 (1977) pp. 170–91) obtained estimates ranging from 11 per cent to 76 per cent.
17. However, methodological differences alone can be shown to produce an enormous amount of variation in the estimates, as Goldberger shows in various papers, (see below, note 37).
18. L. Kamin, *The Science and Politics of IQ* (Hillsdale, New Jersey: Erlbaum, 1974). Page references here are to the 1977 Penguin edition.
19. Ibid., ch. 5.
20. The hereditarian H. Munsinger has in fact proposed that the effect may be due to sampling anomalies ('The Adopted Child's IQ: A Critical Review', *Psychological Bulletin*, vol. 82 (1975) pp. 623–59), but he presents very little evidence in support of this view. See the subsequent exchange between Kamin and Munsinger, in *Psychological Bulletin*, vol. 85 (1978) pp. 194–206. To appreciate fully the degree of confusion which surrounds the interpretation of adoption studies, it is advisable to read the above articles together with

Kamin's own review of the subject in his book, *The Science and Politics of IQ*, and also the original research reports upon which Kamin and Munsinger base their reviews.

21. Kamin, *Politics of IQ*, pp. 149–50.
22. See, for example, Munsinger, 'The Adopted Child's IQ'.
23. In addition to Kamin's book, *Politics of IQ* and his comments on Munsinger's review (in *Psychological Bulletin*, vol. 85), see also his comments on Munsinger's own adoption study, *Behaviour Genetics*, vol. 7 (1977) pp. 403–6 and his review of two books by Jensen, *Contemporary Psychology*, vol. 20 (1975) pp. 545–7. See also A. Goldberger, 'Jensen on Burks', *Educational Psychologist*, vol. 12 (1976) pp. 64–78 and 'Mysteries of the Meritocracy', in Block and Dworkin, (eds) *IQ Controversy*.
24. Kamin's view that parent–child IQ correlations do not lend support to the hereditarian position is confirmed by a detailed analysis of all parent–child IQ correlations (including normally reared as well as adopted children) by M. McAskie and A. M. Clarke, 'Parent–Offspring Resemblances in Intelligence: Theories and Evidence', *British Journal of Psychology*, vol. 67 (1976) pp. 243–73.
25. Scarr and Weinberg, 'Intellectual Similarities'. J. M. Horn, J. C. Loehlin, and L. Willerman, 'Intellectual Resemblances Among Adoptive and Biological Relatives: The Texas Adoption Project', *Behaviour Genetics*, vol. 9 (1979) pp. 177–208.
26. They probably do contain sufficient information to demonstrate the *presence*, but not the *extent*, of genetic and environmental influences. Following criticism of Kamin (see especially N. J. Mackintosh's review of Kamin's book in *Quarterly Journal of Experimental Psychology*, vol. 27 (1975) pp. 672–86), and following the development of improved correlational comparisons in the new adoption studies (ibid.), it is probably fair to say that a reasonable man would consider that there is enough evidence to reject Kamin's zero heritability hypothesis, and to conclude that inherited differences have *some* effect on IQ. Similarly, a reasonable man would reject the hypothesis of 100 per cent heritability and conclude that environmental differences have *some* effect on IQ. But these are utterly trivial conclusions. As Hogben pointed out in his article on 'Correlation Techniques' in 1933, 'So long as the use of correlation methods is confined to the recognition that gene differences or differences due to nurture exist, there is little room for disagreement. The difficulties of interpretation begin when we attempt to clarify what is meant by calculating the "numerical influence . . . of the total genetic and non-genetic causes of variability".'
27. J. Shields, *Monozygotic Twins Brought up Apart and Brought up Together* (Oxford University Press, 1962).
28. See the biographical sketches in the appendix to Shield's book, *Monozygotic Twins*.
29. For example, A. R. Jensen, 'IQs of Identical Twins Reared Apart', *Behaviour Genetics*, vol. 1 (1970) pp. 133–48.

30. Jinks and Fulker, 'Analysis of Human Behaviour'.
31. See Kamin, *Politics of IQ*, ch. 3, for references and detailed critical analysis.
32. As with adoption studies, separated twin correlations can probably be used to demonstrate the presence of *some* hereditary effects despite Kamin's attempted refutation of this (see Mackintosh, in the *Quarterly Journal of Experimental Psychology*, vol. 27). Similarly they can be used to demonstrate the presence of *some* environmental effects (differences between the twins' IQs are correlated with environmental differences, see Kamin, *Politics of IQ*, ch. 3). But they cannot be used to assess the relative importance of each (again, see the comment of Hogben quoted in note 26). For further comments on the difficulty of estimating heritability from separated twin data see Layzer, 'Heritability of IQ scores'.
33. Kamin, *Politics of IQ*, pp. 132–46. A. Goldberger, 'On Jensen's Method for Twins', *Educational Psychologist*, vol. 12 (1976) pp. 79–82.
34. Hogben, 'Correlation Technique', p. 381.
35. Kamin, *Politics of IQ*, p. 135.
36. In the studies reviewed by Kamin the estimates vary from minus 7 per cent to 153 per cent. The sensitivity of heritability estimates, based upon this type of data, to arbitrary assumptions about parameters has also been emphasised by R. M. Hogarth, 'Monozygotic and Dizygotic Twins Raised Together and Apart: Sensitivity of Heritability Estimates', *British Journal of Mathematical and Statistical Psychology*, vol. 27 (1974) pp. 1–13.
37. See especially A. Goldberger, 'Heritability', *Workshop Paper No. 7826* and 'Models and Methods in the IQ Debate, Part 1 (Revised)' *Workshop Paper No. 7801*, both 1978, Social Systems Research Institute, University of Wisconsin, Madison. See also the following papers by Goldberger: 'Twin Methods: A Sceptical View', in P. Taubman (ed.), *Kinometrics* (Amsterdam: North-Holland, 1977); 'The Non-Resolution of IQ Inheritance by Path Analysis', *American Journal of Human Genetics*, vol. 30 (1978) pp. 441–5; 'Pitfalls in the Resolution of IQ Inheritance', in N. E. Morton and C. S. Chung (eds), *Genetic Epidemiology* (New York: Academic Press, 1978).
38. Goldberger, 'Models and Methods', p. 8.
39. For full details see Kamin, *Politics of IQ*, pp. 55–71.
40. Jensen acknowledges his intellectual debt to Burt in his *Genetics and Education* (London: Methuen, 1972) pp. 8–9.
41. Hereditarians, at least when writing for non-specialists, have claimed that Burt's data do not yield unusually high heritability estimates (see, for example, Jensen's letter to *The Times*, 9 Dec 1976). But this is quite untrue. Burt's data do lead to the highest estimates as Goldberger shows ('Heritability', pp. 2–15). See also note 16 above.
42. C. Burt, 'Ability and Income', *British Journal of Educational Psychology*, vol. 13 (1943) pp. 83–98. The results cited are given on pp. 90–91. For a fuller discussion of this paper see Chapter 3, pp. 100ff.
43. Kamin, *Politics of IQ*, pp. 55–71.

44. L. S. Hearnshaw, *Cyril Burt, Psychologist* (London: Hodder & Stoughton, 1979) pp. 240ff.
45. See, for example, B. Rimland and H. Munsinger, letter to *Science*, vol. 195 (1977) p. 248, and also P. E. Vernon, 'Invited Address: Scottish Council for Research in Education. Intelligence Testing and the Nature/Nurture Debate 1928–78; What Next?', *British Journal of Educational Psychology*, vol. 49 (1979) p. 6.
46. A. R. Jensen, 'Kinship Correlations Reported by Sir Cyril Burt', *Behaviour Genetics*, vol. 4 (1974) pp. 1–28. This paper actually appeared shortly before the publication of Kamin's book and it is sometimes suggested that Jensen's critical analysis was unconnected with Kamin's and is testimony to the high critical standards of hereditarians. But in fact Kamin had been lecturing on the subject since 1972, mimeographed copies had been circulating very widely as a kind of *samizdat*, and indeed Jensen acknowledges Kamin's primacy in a footnote. The remarkably rapid publication of Jensen's article by the editors of *Behaviour Genetics* and a number of other unusual features of this particular chapter in the history of psychometrics have been the subject of some caustic comments by J. Hirsch, 'Jensenism, the Bankruptcy of "Science" without Scholarship', *Educational Theory*, vol. 25 (1975) pp. 3–27. See especially Hirsch's footnote 22.
47. Ibid., p. 25.
48. D. D. Dorfman, 'The Cyril Burt Question: New Findings', *Science* vol. 201 (1978) pp. 1177–86. See also the subsequent correspondence in *Science*, vol. 204 (1979) pp. 242–54; vol. 205 (1979) p. 1204; vol. 206 (1979) pp. 142–4.
49. For example, P. E. Vernon recently stated that 'I cannot myself regard Burt's work as fraudulent; almost all the discovered inconsistencies are so stupid that he would surely have made his results much more plausible if he had been intentionally faking', 'Invited Address', p. 6. In an addendum to this paper Vernon concedes, following Hearnshaw, *Cyril Burt*, that Burt did fake his data. In a letter to *The Times*, 9 Dec 1976, Jensen wrote, 'Even the most statistically stupid undergraduate could do a neater job of faking his quantitative results, if that were his aim.'
50. H. J. Eysenck, *British Journal of Mathematical and Statistical Psychology*, vol. 25 (1972) p. iv.
51. A. R. Jensen, *Psychometrika*, vol. 37 (1972) p. 117.
52. Scarr and Weinberg, 'Intellectual Similarities'; Horn, Loehlin, and Willerman, 'The Texas Adoption Project'.
53. See note 6.
54. This is something of an oversimplification since reported kinship correlations for height and weight vary almost as much as for IQ. See P. Mittler, *The Study of Twins* (Harmondsworth: Penguin, 1971) pp. 62–4. Excluding the ubiquitous Burt 'data' the remaining studies reviewed by Mittler yield estimates varying from 48 per cent to an impossible 104 per cent for height; and from 48 per cent to 76 per cent for weight.

55. For some details and further references, see J. Blum, *Pseudoscience and Mental Ability* (London: Monthly Review Press, 1978) p. 49 and his note 18.
56. Block and Dworkin (eds), *IQ Controversy*, pp. 101–2.
57. Jensen, 'Current Status of IQ Controversy', p. 25.
58. Block and Dworkin (eds), *IQ Controversy*, pp. 236–8.
59. See P. E. Vernon, *Intelligence: Heredity and Environment* (San Francisco: W. H. Freeman, 1979) ch. 9.
60. Jensen, 'How Much Can We Boost IQ?', p. 100.
61. See Vernon, *Intelligence*.
62. *Larry P* et al. v. *Wilson Riles* et al. US District Court (Northern California) 1977–9. Transcript p. 875.
63. See Block and Dworkin (eds), *IQ Controversy*, pp. 444–7.
64. G. Thomson, *Instinct, Intelligence and Character: An Educational Psychology* (London: Allen & Unwin, 1924) pp. 218–9.
65. R. J. Herrnstein, *IQ in the Meritocracy* (London: Allen Lane, 1973).
66. J. H. Waller, 'Achievement and Social Mobility. Relationship Among IQ Score, Education, and Occupation in Two Generations', *Social Biology*, vol. 18 (1971) pp. 252–9.
67. Block and Dworkin (eds), *IQ Controversy*, p. 330.
68. An environmental interpretation would be based upon within-families environmental variation, generally acknowledged to contribute something to IQ differences even by hereditarians estimating heritability. It seems reasonable to suppose that an environmental effect which is likely to make one son score better than another on an IQ test is also likely to favour upward social mobility.
69. M. Schiff *et al.*, 'Intellectual Status of Working Class Children Adopted Early Into Upper-Middle Class Families', *Science*, vol. 200 (1978) pp. 1503–4.
70. See Kamin, *Politics of IQ*, chs 1 and 2.
71. We have already quoted some of Darlington's extraordinary views on genetics and social class (pp. 6–7). For his views on race see his contribution to R. T. Osborne, C. E. Noble and N. Wehl (eds), *Human Variation, The Biopsychology of Age, Race and Sex* (New York: Academic Press, 1978).
72. See for example the replies to Jensen in the *Harvard Educational Review*, Spring and Summer 1969.
73. Jensen, 'How Much Can We Boost IQ?', p. 82.
74. See for example the exchange between Lewontin and Jensen in Block and Dworkin (eds), *IQ Controversy*. See also the correspondence in *Science* following Feldman and Lewontin's paper, 'The Heritability Hang-Up'.
75. G. G. Simpson, *Biology and Man* (New York: Harcourt, Brace and World, 1969) p. 104.
76. See A. R. Jensen, 'How Much Can We Boost IQ?' and *Educability and Group Differences* (London: Methuen, 1973). Also H. J. Eysenck, *Race, Intelligence, and Education* (London: Temple Smith, 1971).

77. An hereditarian interpretation for this result can also be given by proposing that there are genetic differences between groups in patterns of specific abilities. See J. C. Loehlin, G. Lindzey, and J. N. Spuhler, *Race Differences in Intelligence* (San Francisco: Freeman, 1975) ch. 7. Since there is no obvious way to derive predictions about group differences in average IQ or patterns of ability on the basis either of hereditarian or environmentalist interpretations, the issue is an empty one.
78. See H. J. Butcher, *Human Intelligence: Its Nature and Assessment* (London: Methuen, 1968) pp. 250–8 for further details.
79. Loehlin *et al.*, *Race Differences*, p. 133.

CHAPTER 6

1. P. B. Medawar, 'Unnatural Science', *New York Review of Books*, 3 Feb 1977.
2. Ibid.
3. P. Urbach, 'Progress and Degeneration in the "IQ Debate" ', *British Journal for the Philosophy of Science*, vol. 25 (1974) pp. 99–135, 235–259.
4. N. Block and G. Dworkin (eds), *The IQ Controversy* (London: Quartet, 1977) pp. 419–424.
5. See Ch. 2 pp. 50–61, Ch. 4 pp. 119–29, Ch. 5, note 3.
6. It is perhaps worth noting that there were several attempts to obtain more accurate estimates of the gravitational constant between 1895 and 1901, the time of Spearman's first investigation of *g*. See *Encyclopaedia Britannica*, 1910–11 edn, 'Gravitation constant and mean density of the earth'.
7. See Chapter 5, notes 25, 26, 32.
8. P. B. Medawar, 'Unnatural Science'.
9. F. Galton, *Inquiries into Human Faculty and its Development* (London: Macmillan, 1892 edn) p. 131.
10. L. Kamin, *The Science and Politics of IQ*, (Hillsdale, New Jersey: Erlbaum, 1974).
11. A. R. Jensen, 'The Nature of Intelligence and its Relation to Learning' in S. Murray-Smith (ed.), *Melbourne Studies in Education* (University of Melbourne, 1978).
12. M. W. Feldman and R. C. Lewontin, 'The Heritability Hang-Up', *Science*, vol. 190 (1975) p. 1168.
13. H. M. Inspectors of Schools, 'Aspects of Secondary Education in England' (London: HMSO, 1979).
14. A notable criticism is N. Chomsky's review of *Verbal Behaviour* by B. F. Skinner in *Language*, vol. 35 (1959) pp. 26–58. See also B. D. Mackenzie, *Behaviourism and the Limits of Scientific Method* (London: Routledge, 1977).
15. N. Chomsky, *For Reasons of State* (London: Fontana, 1973) ch. 5.
16. R. J. Herrnstein, *IQ in the Meritocracy* (London: Allen Lane, 1973).

Index